The Search for a Common Language

The Search for a Common Language
Environmental Writing and Education

Edited and with an Introduction

by

Melody Graulich and Paul Crumbley

Utah State University Press
Logan, Utah

Utah State University Press
Logan, Utah 84322-7800
www.usu.edu/usupress

Poems from "Bestiary" copyright © 2002 by Ken Brewer are printed here with the author's
permission.
An earlier version of "What Is the L. A. River?" by Jennifer Price was published in the *L. A.
Weekly*.
"The Natural West" by Dan Flores is distilled from *The Natural West* (Norman: University
of Oklahoma Press, 2001).
"Separation Anxiety" copyright © 2002 and "Brain Damage" copyright © 2001 by Ellen
Meloy are reprinted with the author's permission.
"The Pleiades," excerpted from *Navigating by the Stars*, copyright © 2002 by Susan J. Tweit,
is reprinted with the author's permission.
Poems from *Bosque Redondo: The Encircled Grove* copyright © 1998 by Keith Wilson are
reprinted with the author's permission.

Manufactured in the United States of America
Printed on acid-free paper

Library of Congress Cataloging-in-Publication Data

Graulich, Melody, 1951–
        The search for a common language : environmental writing and education/ ed-
ited and with an introduction by Melody Graulich and Paul Crumbley.
                p. cm.
        Includes bibliographical references.
        ISBN 0-87421-612-5 (pbk. : alk. paper)
1. Communication in the environmental sciences. 2. Environmental education. 3. Environmental sciences—Poetry. I. Crumbley, Paul, 1952– II. Title.
GE25.G73 2005
333.72—dc22
                                                                    2005011921

Contents

Acknowledgments

Our foremost thanks go to the Obert C. and Grace A. Tanner Foundation for providing major funding for the 2002 Tanner Symposium which led to this book. We also particularly thank Bishop Carolyn Tanner Irish for representing her family at the symposium and for her dedication to the environment.

We benefitted from the support of two deans of the College of Humanities, Arts, and Social Sciences at Utah State University, Stan L. Albrecht and Elizabeth Grobsmith. We also received considerable help in planning, organizing, and running the symposium from Angie Hoffman and Monica Stapley in the HASS office. Patrick Hunter, computer guru for HASS, created a Web site and provided much appreciated technical support.

Jeffrey Smitten, head of the English Department, supported our activities from their inception, as did our colleagues in American studies. Marina Hall, director of media and outside relations, provided expert advice and publicity assistance.

We thank the Tanner Symposium Advisory Board members at Utah State University for their ideas, guidance, help, and participation in the events: Thad Box, Chris Conte, Richard Krannich, Pat Lambert, Barbara Middleton, Jennifer Peeples, Michael Sweeney, and Tom Wilkerson. Robert Michael Pyle, certainly among the most generous colleagues any of us has ever known, deserves special thanks. In the one semester he spent at USU as a visiting professor of creative writing, he energized us all and contributed immeasurably to the symposium and this book.

Many of our colleagues from the College of Natural Resources offered suggestions and counsel, met with symposium participants, and introduced speakers.

Matt Burkhart, Thomas J. Lyon editorial fellow at *Western American Literature,* served as contact person for the symposium, keeping track of registration, answering questions, helping with publicity, and handling difficulties and organization at the actual event. He was aided by numerous other American studies graduate students, most notably Matthew Stiffler, Brandon Schrand, and Michaela Koenig. Matt Lavin, 2004–2006 Thomas J. Lyon editorial fellow, contributed computer expertise and suggestions for the final manuscript preparation. As always, *Western American Literature* managing editor Sabine Barcatta provided superlative supervisory skills.

Chapter Two Books, a local independent bookstore now driven out of business by corporate booksellers, underwrote a reception and book signing.

The Utah Humanities Council provided a grant to help fund the readings and discussions by Bill Kittredge and Annick Smith, which were, like all events, free and open to the pulic.

Introduction

Paul Crumbley and Melody Graulich

> *Because scientists and poets are curious, they ask questions. Early in his work, Einstein asked himself, "What would the world look like if I were riding on the beam of light coming from that clock tower?" That's a child's question, but an immensely intriguing one that led to Einstein's theory of relativity. An entomologist asks: How does a bumble bee manage to lift its heavy weight and fly? Poet Pablo Neruda asks whimsically: How many bees are there in a day? The work of both scientist and poet begins with curiosity and a question. . . . And like children, poets and scientists possess a flexibility of thought, a willingness to modify their approach or stance toward a subject or object. Like children, they have an openness to surprise, to what experience of the physical world may be telling them that they didn't expect.*

> —Pattiann Rogers, "Wonder in Science and Poetry"

In *A Sand County Almanac,* first published in 1949, Aldo Leopold defined the importance of an "ecological" education. "One of the requisites for an ecological comprehension of land," he wrote, "is an understanding of ecology." This understanding, he added, "does not necessarily originate in courses bearing ecological labels; it is quite as likely to be labeled geography, botany, agronomy, history, or economics."[1] His conclusion that "this is as it should be" certainly follows from his exhortation earlier in the book that we must think at "right angles" from accepted knowledge, a process that "calls for a reversal of specialization; instead of learning more and more about less and less, we must learn more and more about the whole biotic landscape."[2] Like the natural processes on which it is based, Leopold's ecological education is systemic, asking us to stand back from our own disciplines and look at the interrelationships among various modes of inquiry. When he complains that "whatever the label, ecological training is scarce," he speaks about individual courses but also about the scarcity of fruitful cross-pollination among disciplines.[3]

As ecological awareness has grown, thanks to Leopold and many others, over the past fifty-some years, the specialization he decried has only increased in colleges and universities, fields becoming narrower and narrower and language more technical. While established disciplines have added courses based on new approaches, such as environmental history, environmental education, and ecocriticism, the departmental structure of universities and the specialized nature of academic conferences too often do not encourage sustained conversation among scholars and researchers in different fields—perhaps particularly between humanists and scientists, usually housed in different colleges. And while writing about science and the environment for a general audience has become progressively more popular, very often the technical language of the specialist hampers sharing that knowledge with a deeply concerned public.

As a land-grant university with strong programs in natural resources in a state with magnificent national parks and monuments, Utah State University has a long tradition of nature writing, environmental research, and outreach programming uniting trained academics with members of the regional community to ensure an informed and sensitive approach to environmental appreciation and management. Notably, in 1989, students from the English Department and from the College of Natural Resources united to found *Petroglyph: A Journal of Creative Nature Writing*. Entirely student run, *Petroglyph* published poetry, fiction, and natural-history essays together as varied approaches to represent the natural world and included works by both students and celebrated writers such as Rick Bass, William Stafford, and Terry Tempest Williams. The journal was funded only through grants and sales until 1994, when the English Department became its institutional home, which gradually weakened the partnership with the College of Natural Resources. To reinforce that link and bring together writers from various disciplines, the editorial staff, led by Brooke Bigelow, initiated a field writing workshop to be held at the Forestry Experimental Station in Logan Canyon. This event became the first of the "*Petroglyph* Up the Canyon" weekend writing workshops.

In the late 1990s, faculty in the humanities and environmental sciences once again began to form partnerships to encourage dialogue across the disciplines, responding, in part, to the desires of students in both areas to do crossover work. Increasing numbers of students well trained in fields of environmental science wanted to take courses in nature writing and environmental literature, to find a way to write for the general public. As one put it, he wanted not only to count buffalo while doing his fieldwork but also to write about his work in ways that counted. During a visit to USU in 1999 to discuss environmental writing with a variety of groups, Barry Lopez responded to a student's question about how best to prepare for a career in nature writing with this succinct answer: "Major in one of the sciences."

In fact, students at USU were already following Lopez's directions, students such as Ben Quick, who described his desire to unite his undergraduate degree in forestry with a graduate program in American studies. Initially fearful of the sciences, Quick found that after he

> waded through college algebra, statistics, and biology, as an unexpected result, [I] came to see value in these fields and to find pleasure in the completion of equations and the internalizing of guiding concepts. Parts of my brain that had long atrophied came to life. But it wasn't until I took a forest ecology course in my junior year that I truly became excited about the processes that drive the natural world. To witness the hot print of fire on the shapes and sizes of forests, to see with my own eyes the influences of slope aspect and elevation on a forest's character, how the age and density of forests can tell us what kinds of animals are able to live in and under forest canopies, awoke in me a new sense of just how ornate and dramatic the details of our living planet really are—and how much they matter. As the semester progressed, I felt welling in me—even stronger than the predictable desire to dive deeper into the natural sciences—the urge to record what I was seeing and feeling in words accessible to everyone.

In his graduate program in the English Department, Quick finds himself "feeling a little lost sometimes without a mess of Carhartts and Wranglers to keep me company, still getting used to the notion that terms like *mitigation* and *collaboration* are not unique to the field of natural resource management, but knowing in my core that I'm where I'm supposed to be. I am—after all—a writer, and I hope to be a good one by the time I'm through [italics added]." His intellectual journey leads him to conclude that

> the distinction between the arts and the sciences is largely cosmetic; the best scientists are always artists, pushing the boundaries of reason in ways that can only be described as efforts of supreme creativity, tapping into the mysterious powers of the right brain seemingly at will. And the best artists, by necessity, are scientists, perfecting techniques, memorizing the laws and technical principles of their respective trades before they can even dream their greatest works. But if the wall between art and science is merely a façade, if they are linked and bound in the synapses of the mind, dependent on each other like twins, why then does society choose to go about the teaching of the two siblings in such conflicting ways?

Attempting to respond to the questions and needs of students like Ben Quick and aware that training in the methodologies and practices of *both* the sciences and the humanities would benefit students and faculty as well, members of the American Studies Advisory Committee began to look around for a way to initiate new and fruitful conversations and further the strong tradition of environmental education that is a distinctive feature of Utah State. The former dean of the college of Natural Resources, Thad Box, provided the first opportunity by approaching the English Department to administer a scholarship for natural-history writing. The Thad and Jenny Box Creative Writing Award, chosen by a committee of faculty members in both English and natural resources, is now awarded during an annual event where a celebrated environmental writer reads from his or her work.

One of our most generous local groups, the Marie Eccles Caine Foundation, provided funds to continue our initiative. It first funded Barry Lopez's weeklong visit in spring 1999, when he met not only with students but also with faculty, deans, and the provost to discuss curriculum innovations, most notably providing more coherence in undergraduate education by designing an interdisciplinary major made up of courses in a variety of fields, all focused on the study of the environment.

Lopez's recommendation that anyone who wants to write about nature should have training in the sciences led to a plan to bring a visiting writer to USU who combined the sciences and humanities in his or her work and background. With the help of a significant grant from the Caine Foundation, we were lucky enough to hire Robert Michael Pyle to spend a semester teaching environmental nonfiction writing to both undergraduates and graduates from numerous fields. Although Bob Pyle would be housed in the English Department, he was chosen particularly for his ability to attract students and faculty in natural resources. Pyle has a Ph.D. in ecology from Yale, and he has received many awards from scientific organizations, such as a Distinguished Service Award from the Society for Conservation Biology in 1997. Along with hundreds of essays, poems, and stories, he has written many books, popular with both academics and the general audience. They include *Where Bigfoot Walks: Crossing the Dark Divide, Wintergreen* (winner of the 1986 John Burroughs Medal for distinguished nature writing), *Chasing Monarchs: Migrating with the Butterflies of Passage, Nabokov's Butterflies, The Thunder Tree,* and *Walking the High Ridge: Life as Field Trip.* During his semester at USU, Pyle gave presentations for groups in natural resources, the local Aububon Society, and many others.

Robert Pyle became a keystone in our plans to sponsor a large event to highlight the intersection between the sciences and the humanities at USU. The Obert C. and Grace Tanner Foundation offered the opportunity. The Tanner Foundation has provided the College of Humanities, Arts, and Social Sciences at Utah State University with funds every two years to sponsor symposia intended to engage the university community with the public in exploring topics of general concern. Through a grant process, faculty in the interdisciplinary program American studies, which includes coursework in many departments in the humanities, the social sciences, and natural resources, were awarded funds to organize a symposium entitled "The Search for a Common Language: Environmental Writing and Education."

The symposium would publicly explore the particular ways environmental writing educates the public through a fusion of science and literary expression. The premises behind the grant were that reading and writing about the environment can stimulate the humanities curriculum, encourage interdisciplinary links, and highlight the too-often-overlooked connections between both the social sciences and the humanities and the humanities and the sciences. The first half of the title suggested one key goal: to learn to share specialized knowledge across disciplinary boundaries in language accessible to those not trained in particular fields as well as to an interested lay audience. The second half of the title reflected the belief that environmental writing, broadly defined, could and should be central to a student's education, whether in an elementary school or a university. By making the focus of the symposium the interrelationship of environmental writing and *education*, we planned to raise questions about new ways to conceptualize a core university curriculum, and we created a bridge to primary- and secondary-school curriculums. Echoing Leopold, Barry Lopez has pointed out the importance of taking children into the woods, literally and metaphorically:

> In speaking with children who might one day take a permanent interest in natural history—as writers, as scientists, as filmmakers, and anthropologists—I have sensed that an extrapolation from a single fragment of the whole is the most invigorating experience I can share with them. I think children know that nearly anyone can learn the names of things; the impression made on them at this level is fleeting. What takes a lifetime to learn, they comprehend, is the existence and substance of myriad relationships: it is these relationships, not the things themselves, that ultimately hold the human imagination.[4]

The 2002 Tanner Symposium would, we hoped, explore the myriad relationships Lopez believes all of us are perpetually engaged in learning.

The Tanner Symposium Advisory Board, composed of representatives from English, history, sociology, anthropology, communication, language and philosophy, landscape and environmental planning, journalism, the College of Natural Resources, and the Space Dynamics Lab, determined that an important focus for the conference should be the illumination of critical links connecting local and global environments. To that end, each of the three days of the conference was given a global, regional, or local focus. The program thereby revealed the extent to which even the most immediate and seemingly isolated encounters with the environment reflect changes taking place on a global scale. Each day included presentations by prominent representatives of the sciences and humanities, whose work was associated with global, regional, or local environments. This allowed presenters to think about the challenges posed by writing for an audience composed of specialists in other disciplines, as well as the larger issue of communicating technical scientific knowledge to the broader public.

We were extremely fortunate in attracting to the conference a remarkably accomplished and diverse group of scholars and writers whose work spans the humanities and the sciences (biographies precede each essay in this volume). We asked speakers to think about the role "the search for a common language" plays as they seek to share their creative insights or scholarship in words accessible to the general public. We also gave them a series of questions formulated by our advisory board to stimulate discussion. They included

- In what ways do you see science influencing human engagement with the landscape?
- What are the most important environmental issues in your field, and how does science shape cultural responses to these issues in local, regional, or global settings?
- What specific projects are you currently engaged with that clarify the importance of language in communicating specialized knowledge to a broad public audience?
- How can reading and writing about the environment function in various educational settings? What are the different effects of disparate genres of writing about nature and the environment—creative nonfiction, poetry, polemical essays, history, anthropology, scientific writing?
- How do stories, folklore, and material culture help us to understand the environment? What can American popular culture reveal to us about our assumptions about "nature"?
- How is human history written in the natural world? How can we use representations of nature to understand the past?
- What are the current debates about definitions of *nature, wilderness, place, environment, region,* and *natural resources?* Are these socially constructed designations, changing over time? What determines their meaning?
- What is the relationship among nature, culture, race, and class? How do cultural differences impact the representation and uses of nature?

How has the environmental-justice movement affected understanding of the relationships among cultures and between humans and the
environment?

- "Are you an environmentalist, or do you work for a living?" What is
the relationship between attitudes about work and leisure and the
ethical treatment of the environment and human cultures? What
assumptions are at play in this dichotomy? How is this relationship
portrayed, over time, in various historical discourses?

- How can we evaluate environmental change?

Each day of the conference included four major presentations, discussion sessions, and evening readings. Field biologist Susan Tweit offered
concurrent field writing workshops. We include in this volume the major
presentations, as well as selected poems from the two poets in residence,
Ken Brewer and Keith Wilson.

The first day of the symposium focused on global environmental issues
and opened with remarks by Bishop Carolyn Tanner Irish. Her talk, "Preliminary Reflections on Matters Environmental," effectively set the tone
for much of what ensued during the next three days. Irish proposed that
in our deliberations we give the "search" part of "the search for a common
language" precedence over any effort to codify a language all parties could
agree upon. Identifying "the environment, the natural world, creation, or
whatever we choose to call it" as the shared referent, Irish suggested that
sustaining a "conversation among a whole variety of languages and disciplines" was more productive than determining a transcendent common
language. She eloquently urged the community to sustain productive polarities, such as those that persist between the sciences and the humanities,
as well as between culture and wilderness, as a means of generating creativity and resisting complacency. She also made the case that in an under-
taking like this symposium that so clearly combines science with politics
and the emotions humans have so long invested in the environment, we
move forward with the understanding that hope is always more productive
than fear. Irish's contemplative, reasoned approach to the central themes of
"search" and "language" provided a clear sense of shared purpose and possibility that many speakers drew on in subsequent presentations.

Ken Brewer, Utah poet laureate, wrote five poems in honor of the symposium, dedicating one to each of the featured speakers. Ken then selected eight poems from his previous work that complemented the remaining presentations during the symposium. For this reason, we decided to
distribute his poems throughout the collection, positioning each before
the essay it addresses, even though he read all the poems at once on the
third day of the symposium. "Painted Lady," for instance, a poem about a

butterfly, precedes Robert Michael Pyle's opening essay because it was written in recognition of Pyle's expertise on butterflies; similarly, "The Silliest Debate," a poem about humans and gorillas, comes before Craig Stanford's essay, identifying his primary research interest and the subject of his discussion. On the other hand, "Why Dogs Stopped Flying" was not written with Hartmut Grassl in mind but appears before his essay because it conveys with supreme irony the arrogant self-absorption that Grassl associates with political reluctance to address global change.

Even more important, perhaps, than the topical links that unite these poems with particular essays is the way each poem is itself a meditation on the many intimate connections that bind the human spirit to the nonhuman universe. Brewer repeatedly demonstrates that we could not be human without the nonhuman and that we delight, often unconsciously, in discovering the animal, the river, the firmament in our own bodies. The humor that lightens almost every poem frequently balances an almost painful desire for deeper forms of communion. As he states in "Scarlet Penstemon," "shimmering, / the scarlet penstemon pouts, / and, oh sweet Jesus, to be / a broad-tailed hummingbird then."

Robert Michael Pyle's "Who Lost the Limberlost? Education and Language in a Mis-Placed Age" examined the diminished importance of nature in the education of average Americans as symptomatic of a growing indifference to the environment occurring on a worldwide scale. Citing Gene Stratton Porter's 1909 novel, *A Girl of the Limberlost,* as a model of environmental literacy once so central to the American citizen's sense of self, Pyle pointed to the departure of naturalists from institutions of higher learning and the advisory boards of political leaders as an important index of the change that separates our present age from the era of Porter, Theodore Roosevelt, and John Muir. Now, Pyle observed, "the term *naturalist* has come to be confused with *naturist,* so the idle spectator, hearing that naturalists are about, goes on the lookout for nudie cuties instead of net wielders. Or the practitioner is seen as a nature nazi, dweeb, ecoterrorist, or irrelevant stumblebum." Such disregard for environmental knowledge on a worldwide scale has contributed to the acceleration of global warming and the increasing scarcity of water. Pyle proposed that the knowledge most useful in negotiating these looming environmental challenges comes from reestablishing personal intimacy with nature. "To get back," Pyle noted, "or forward (for surely we have never really been there), we will need every facility and sensibility of both science and art, every clever trick of both education and literature, every good impulse of every rich discipline until we find the right combination of head, bone, and hormone." "Maybe then," he concluded, "we can rename, and reclaim, our places."

Craig Stanford's "Cousins: What the Great Apes Tell Us about Human Origins," built on his extensive research into the behavior of East African primates, made the case that human attitudes toward the environment may be traceable to species adaptation in the prehistorical past. Stanford argued that the "hunting ecology of wild chimpanzees" sheds important "new light on the current debate about the origins of human behavior." This debate is concerned with questions about "when meat became an important part of the diet of our ancestors" and "what are the likely similarities in meat-eating patterns between chimpanzees and early hominids?" Focusing specifically on Gombe chimpanzee hunting binges, when chimpanzees hunt and kill large numbers of colobus monkeys, Stanford identified significant social influences that must be considered along with nutritional needs when assessing ecological motives. In a startling firsthand account of a chimpanzee hunt and the ensuing distribution of meat, Stanford described the sexual rewards clearly dispensed to dominant males. Without drawing any definitive conclusions, Stanford speculated that it is "quite probable" that early humans did "hunt and eat meat in a pattern similar to the one described for wild chimpanzees." As a consequence, early human attitudes toward the environment may have been the result of social competition rather than nutritional needs or species sensitivity to ecological balances.

To help symposium participants understand global approaches, we invited two members of the Max-Planck-Institute für Meteorologie in Hamburg. The presentation by Jen Bösenberg, who helps coordinate a large European lidar network to study the spatial and temporal distribution of aerosols on a continental scale, was informative and thoughtful, but he chose not to write an essay. We are able to include Hartmut Grassl's talk, "How Science and the Public can Lead to Better Decision Making in Earth Science Management," in which he directly addressed the need for members of the scientific community to engage policy makers through mainstream media. "Environmentalists are already on board," he declared; now is the time for governments to begin supporting global research into climate change. The way to achieve this, Grassl argued, is by communicating sound information in a manner that will attract the attention of politicians. Leaders like George W. Bush and Gerhard Schroder are so preoccupied with crisis management "partly caused by neglect of global change" that they have little interest in long-term research and are too often swayed by the "disinformation campaigns" of lobbyists. "Politicians," Grassl pointed out, "make decisions when they see that there is sufficient minority public opinion to override the pressure mounted by lobbyists."

Central to winning the sort of public support essential to influencing the direction of political decisions is overcoming the misguided belief among politicians and the general public that effective environmental action demands acceptance of a reduced standard of living. Grassl passionately affirmed that the reverse is actually the case: "We have seen instead that technical innovation plays the key role for environmentally less-damaging lifestyles while supporting a rising standard of living." To make his point, Grassl cited numerous examples, such as the growing popularity of wind power, the replacement of coal with natural gas, the rapid appearance of CFC-free refrigerators, and the development of fuel-cell cars. Grassl advocated "earth system management" as a means to establish coordinated global responses to pressing environmental concerns. He presented the international response to depletion of the ozone layer as one example of the way a unified sense of scientific knowledge can produce effective change worldwide.

In "What Is the L.A. River?" Jennifer Price issued a call to "nature writers to come to the cities where most Americans live, to see nature in these places, and to write nature newly into the American urban imagination." Price situated her discussion in the global context by citing the Seine in Paris as a precedent for the multiple environmental and cultural benefits that can derive from a river that runs through a city in "a concrete channel." As a writer seeking to address urgent environmental problems specific to the experiences of Angelenos, Price linked her own efforts to a broad coalition of other writers, artists, politicians and community activists who have transformed the public perception of the L.A. River. Their collective efforts over the last seventeen years have made the greening of the river a unifying force drawing together organizations as diverse as the Chinatown Yard Alliance, the Sierra Club, and the Latino Urban Forum. Where in 1985 the river was viewed as a joke and citizens of Los Angeles regularly asked, "What river?" Angelenos now collectively contemplate the best means to resurrect a universally valued environmental asset.

One of the most astonishing facts Price introduced to demonstrate the potential benefit of resurrecting the river focused on the concrete channel's efficient removal of half the annual rainfall by shooting it directly into the ocean. The prospect of recovering this valuable water without risking floods from torrential winter storms that by "one estimate" can "pelt L.A. with a year's water supply" in a single "truly heavy" downpour has spurred significant community action. But, as Price pointed out, such action was only possible after writers, artists, and scientists came up with a language that made clear to Angelenos not only that they had a river but that they could take pride in it.

Ted Kerasote introduced the symposium's focus on regional environments with his keynote address titled, "The Unexpected Environmentalist: Building a Centrist Coalition." Kerasote proposed that significant environmental objectives, such as the preservation and management of wilderness lands, constitute a substantial middle ground that can potentially unite regional political interests that currently waste limited resources by competing with each other. Citing the long-standing division between "forever-wild preservationists" and "multiple-use conservationists," Kerasote made the case that hard-core environmentalists had much to gain by forming alliances with the fishing and hunting community. Identifying Aldo Leopold, Olaus Murie, Stewart Udall, and Jimmy Carter as hunters who significantly advanced environmental legislation, Kerasote suggested that traditional aims of hunters, like the preservation of "ruffed grouse habitat," may also serve the preservationists' interest by "simultaneously protect[ing] a home for golden-winged warblers, common yellowthroats, and towhees." For a potentially powerful centrist coalition to exist, Kerasote argued, "protectionists" must come to see "that they haven't cornered the market on caring about nature," and "hunters and anglers" must understand "that they have made a contribution to preserving and restoring ecosystems as well as to growing more targets for their guns and rods." Kerasote closed his keynote with the provocative suggestion that preservationists might gain significant political ground if they were to "soft-pedal" gun control and join forces with the National Rifle Association.

Louis Owens's essay, "At Cloudy Pass: The Need of Being Versed in Human Things," tracked the way changing perceptions of "wilderness" can devalue human engagements with it and inadvertently erase important cultural connections to the natural world. With a distinctly ironic twist, Owens recalled the summer of 1976 when he "was dispatched from the Darrington District Ranger Station in the Mount Baker Snoqualmie National Forest to a place called White Pass." His job at White Pass was to burn an old shelter that had finally collapsed under the weight of repeated snows. Owens wrote of taking particular pride in the thoroughness with which he dismantled and burned the old shelter, so that after five days "it was impossible to tell that a human construction had ever been there." Pleased with his success at implementing the Forest Service policy "dictating that man-made objects be removed from wilderness areas," Owens proceeded down the mountain with a light heart, only to encounter "two Native Upper Skagit sisters who looked to be in their seventies" determined to hike the "eleven miles of river trail and switchbacks to camp in the log shelter their father had built at White Pass before they were born." Trading on Robert Frost's poem, "Being Versed in Country Things," Owens concluded that in learning the common language of nature, we must all become versed in "human things," remembering that "the shelters we build, the footprints we leave, the very thoughts that form within and around us are natural and acceptable and even, at times, beautiful strands woven into the natural fabric."

Kent Ryden's "Tuttle Road: Landscape as Environmental Text" proposed that landscapes can function as texts communicating important information about the human things that Owens draws attention to in his essay. Ryden began by challenging the traditional notion that written language stands in sharp opposition to the materiality of nature. Having stated that he prefers "to see continua between spaces and between linguistic and material texts, not frontiers," Ryden proceeded to describe landscapes as "complexly authored texts, rich blends of natural and cultural process, deeply suggestive artifacts, material culture carrying within it the evidence of the many hands and minds that have shaped it over time."

To demonstrate the practical applicability of this approach to landscapes, Ryden dedicated the bulk of his presentation to "reading" the landscape he encountered on a random summer walk down Tuttle Road in rural Maine. After noting cultural stories imbedded in the landscape that told of a failed agricultural economy and overgrown farmland transformed into a state park and a network of trails to support outdoor recreation, Ryden reflected on the triumph of nature: "regardless of our best intentions, we'd be best off doing what we can to conform our actions to the limits inherent in the environment, not making the environment conform to the dreams of our unlimited imaginations." Ryden closed by recommending that Phoenix and Freeport also be read as ongoing stories not so different from Tuttle Road as they may appear at first glance. For Ryden, the environmental degradation represented by urban sprawl and strip-mall homogenization is only part of the story these landscapes have to tell. In the end, nature's limits will emerge, cultural history will change, and the story Tuttle Road tells will find expression in these landscapes as well.

Annick Smith also addressed the way regional landscapes convey stories, only for her these stories are rooted in rivers. In "Begin with a River," Smith asked that we consider the extent that "river talk is our common language as riversheds are our common homes." After reminding us of the centrality of rivers in the writing of Mark Twain, Ann Zwinger, Annie Dillard, Norman Maclean, and Jennifer Price, Smith turned her attention to the river most important to her: the Blackfoot River that flows beside her Montana home. Motivated by the fear that her "beloved river . . . was in danger of being killed off at its headwaters by a huge, cyanide heap-leach gold mine," Smith decided to place her talent in the service of environmental preservation by uniting with other writers to produce a collection of stories celebrating the Blackfoot River. The eventual outcome was *Headwaters,* an anthology of contributions from forty-seven Montana writers that was distributed free of charge to the Montana legislature. Smith mentioned that the book became a cause célèbre when it was confiscated by the sergeant at arms for containing "dirty words." The resulting media coverage increased the value of the book and drew much-desired public attention to the environmental cause.

Acknowledging that writers "aren't that great, often, as organizers," Smith recommended that books like *Headwaters* represent one important means for writers to participate in environmental politics. As a way of making her point, Smith listed works like *Testimony*, by Terry Tempest Williams and Steve Trimble; *Arctic Refuge*, by Carolyn Servid and Hank Lentfer; Mary Clearman Blew's *Written on Water: Essays on Idaho Rivers*, and the Clark Fork Coalition's *The River We Carry with Us* as examples of the way environmental writers have supported similar political projects by doing what they do best: writing about the landscapes they love.

Dan Flores dedicated his "The Natural West" to an analysis of the way stories now unfolding about the American West convey important information about the course of environmental history. Flores began by focusing on a paradigmatic western moment—sunrise following the first heavy autumn snowfall in Montana's Bitterroot Valley—and immediately linked his delight in that highly particularized time and place to the entire span of human history. He achieved this by pointing out that the way we imagine the West reflects a familiar pattern of distorting history by glorifying those narratives of the past most conducive to present cultural values. In the case of the American West, the contemporary "touchstone" is "Lewis and Clark's upper Missouri River paradise of 1806." According to Flores, this account supports "our deeply internalized impression of a pristine West" while denying vast swaths of the human past that include the strategic use of fire and tribal warfare, both influences that shaped the environment Lewis and Clark encountered.

Flores then encouraged us to consider "the Great Plains and the Rocky Mountain West" as "a kind of 'dream landscape' in American history" that justifies close scrutiny at the present moment precisely because each region embodies a very different ecological ethos and therefore presents a potential turning point in American environmental history. "The Great Plains," Flores explained, "is western America's great experiment with privatization, the Rockies our historic communal-land experiment." Flores speculated that "the communal Rockies strategy" would "serve as a model for the future of the West" because historically "we have done better by nature when we've emphasized communal effort . . . than when we've allowed pure self-interest to dominate." He concluded by stating that the ultimate outcome will be most useful in terms of what it tells us about our "true" environmental history; that is, "*Who we actually are*" rather than who we imagine we are.

In "Separation Anxiety: The Perilous Alienation of Humans from the Wild," Ellen Meloy introduced the symposium's third-day emphasis on local environments by joining Annick Smith in acknowledging both the resistance to political action often felt by writers and their need to discover effective ways to enter public discourse. "So here we are," Meloy observed, "we poor nature writers. You want us to write like Melville *and* save the Arctic National Wildlife Refuge." In response to this dilemma, Meloy recommended that nature writers run the risk of writing "out of place," by which she means being willing to assume the role of "misfit" while continuing to offer a "voice that speaks *from* a place, a certain geography." Citing "passion" as the motivating force that ultimately unites "science, art, and activism," Meloy inserted into "the symposium's discussion of 'common language' . . . a plea for raw instinct, the uncooked act of creativity." To illustrate the form such writing might take, Meloy produced a lyrical overview of her own struggle to reach beyond the familiarity of memory and the comfort of private life. "When we writers wake up," she concluded, "and stop working in our pajamas all day, . . . we will be free to go out and do kind, practical things." The time has come "to put the brain fevers to good use" by going out and committing "acts of aggressive beneficence."

In "Going South," William Kittredge joined Meloy in stressing the importance of telling stories that matter, stories that are useful because they break familiar patterns of behavior and "remind us of who and what we are." Kittredge described the self illuminated in these stories as "an evolving creature who's profoundly dependent on the goodwill of others"; for that reason, the stories remind us to "stay alert because our relationships, even if only with ourselves, must be constantly, all and every day, reinvented." Taking the title of his keynote from the custom of "going south" to flee the harsh winter of the northern Rockies, Kittredge urged that such flight be viewed as "a technique for staying in touch, a wake-up call, not a diversion but a responsibility." Valuable as the virtues of rooted life are, variation is essential to ensuring that the stories we tell about ourselves and the place we live continue to yield productive futures. "We all know a lot of stories," Kittredge stated, "and we're in trouble when we don't know which one is ours, or when the one we inhabit doesn't work anymore and we stick with it anyway."

One of the old stories most in need of revision is "the one about radical independence." Kittredge illustrated this point by telling of his grandfather's weekly slaughter of magpies, a ritual act he justified by simply stating, "Because they're mine." Similar stories of independence and absolute ownership persist in much of the West, despite the fact that today we find it "hard to imagine that a man will ever again think he owns the birds." To register the ongoing need for new stories that accurately reflect the ceaseless change that characterizes all locales, Kittredge recommended that we make a regular practice of traveling beyond our familiar interior and exterior landscapes, whether by car or the transporting power of language that inverts the norms we think immutable. "We need and yearn to believe," Kittredge concluded, "yet to survive, we need to be deflated and driven to start over continually by reexamining what we believe."

Susan Tweit's essay, "The Pleiades," belongs among the presentations from the third day because she links language to that most intimate of all local environments: the human body. Beginning with the childhood story her mother told about the Pleiades based on the seven sisters of Greek mythology, Tweit explored the way her own sense of place within the universe grew out of a personal search for similar stories. Crucially, her search proved most productive when she contracted a rare autoimmune disease and discovered that her body's new demand for silence enabled her to hear more clearly the "quiet rhythm" and "pulse of nature" she could then incorporate into her own writer's voice. This reinvigorated sense of her own voice then enabled Tweit to position herself within the vast community of writers that stretches from her own extended family to writers from other cultural traditions and finally back to the Pleiades. "The voice I heard most clearly," Tweit recalls, "was that of my mother's grandfather, Dr. William Austin Cannon," who "had been one of the early practitioners in my specialty of ecology." As she absorbed the sounds of her own specific environment—the "soft chatter of a black-chinned hummingbird . . . the buzzing of digger bees . . . the mutter of distant thunder"— Tweit came to understand that her responsiveness to a particular place united her with writers similarly bonded to their localities. In this way, she came to see her own impulse to tell stories reflected in the Nisqually tribal leader who told her, "I speak for the salmon" because the salmon "is out there swimming around and cannot come in here and talk to you." In her own writing, Tweit uses the science of ecology to tell the stories of earth's ecosystems, all the while remembering her grandmother Chris's story of the Pleiades, itself but one of the stories each culture tells to link its particular world to the heavenly constellations.

Keith Wilson is a native of New Mexico whose poems continuously celebrate the rejuvenating power of language that arises through humanity's historical entanglement with place. As he states in the opening lines of "The Encircled Grove," "written here is the ceremony of the land / itself, without commentary." Like Owens and Ryden, Wilson proclaims that the power of place does not stand apart from the history of human habitation. "I am not the desert," the speaker of "Desert Cenote" confesses, "but its name is not so far from mine." We placed Wilson's poems after Tweit's essay because their work shares a deep attachment to the same region, as well as the conviction that nonhuman nature makes demands on those who would know its splendors. Wilson's speaker in "Night" stands in moonlight on the

Llano, alone, while old men sleep with curtains drawn, "the Llano moon locked / outside," where he is. For Wilson, difficult as doing so may prove to be, you must sing the ceremony of the land to know it fully. A far cry from the antimodernist wish to preserve an idealized nature unsullied by civilization, Wilson's poems illuminate the wild beauty of nature humans help to create. This is a point he makes in "Valley of the Rio Chama" when he describes a group of artists "caught embarrassed before this magnificence, / these glories of canyons." When the speaker's new friend, a painter, says, "I'm old enough to know / better than to try painting all that!" the speaker responds in terms that capture Wilson's philosophy of writing: "But colors are words the voices of rock and canyon speak. / How can they not be spoken? How can we not listen?"

The indispensable Bob Pyle was given the Herculean task of providing a summary comment on the symposium as a whole, with only forty-five minutes between the final session and his concluding remarks. He dashed into the auditorium looking rather like Alice's white rabbit and then, ecologist that he is, delivered insightful comments on each presentation and the connections between them. As his presentation, "Common Cause in Common Voice," concluded the event, so it ends this volume.

The audience for this nationally advertised symposium was as diverse as the speakers, and their comments and questions contributed greatly to the conversation. Some participants came for the whole symposium from as far away as Connecticut, New York, and Texas. Others came from throughout Utah. Each session included a large number of USU students and faculty. The evening readings in particular attracted a large local audience. Responses on evaluation forms and e-mail after the conference were uniformly enthusiastic. "Weeks later, I'm still thinking about the ideas discussed," responded a man who writes for a nonprofit agency. A retired journalist wrote,

> Even trying to be hypercritical, I cannot find flaws. I assume those were honorarium checks you were distributing Saturday evening; all of the speakers earned them. When I go out to dinner, I expect to be cooked for. Each of the presenters brought a blend of energy, thoughtfulness, stage presence, personality, relevance, and approachability that one seldom finds in one stable of high-energy, high-strung folks.

Since the 2002 Tanner Symposium, participants have continued to develop programs at USU based on interdisciplinary conversations. In an address titled "Defining an Environmental University," USU President Kermit Hall called for the university to take a leading role in the field. The English Department hired an environmental-science writer, Christopher

Cokinos, the author of *Hope Is the Thing with Feathers,* an award-winning book exploring the natural and cultural history of extinct birds, to direct its creative writing curriculum. As the new editor of *Petroglyph,* Cokinos provided the journal with a new direction to reflect the growing interest in scientific nature writing, renaming it *Isotope: A Journal of Literary Nature and Science Writing.* The journal's new mission incorporates its former one: *"Isotope* seeks to embrace the tradition of nature writing—and move beyond it (even challenge it) by including a wide range of work that engages such fields as astronomy, artificial intelligence, genetic engineering, sexuality, urban ecosystems, restoration ecology, physics and math."[5] The title, of course, suggests the journal's attempts to emphasize a link between the literary and the scientific: an isotope is two or more forms of an element having the same or very closely related chemical properties.

The English Department is also developing an environmental-writing minor, including courses not only on nature writing but also grant and technical writing. The College of Natural Resources has developed a new major, Environment and Society, and an advisory committee now meets regularly to develop a new initiative in environmental education uniting the humanities, the sciences, the social sciences, and public-policy programs.

These are just the kind of conversations and compacts advocated by renowned scientist E. O. Wilson in his influential 1998 book, *Consilience: The Unity of Knowledge.* Remembering the moment he "was captured by the dream of unified learning," he argues that an "alliance" between the arts and sciences to promote creative thinking is "long overdue." "Neither science nor the arts can be complete without combining their separate strengths. Science needs the intuition and metaphorical power of the arts, and the arts needs the fresh blood of science."[6] "The key to the exchange between them," he adds, "is not hybridization, not some unpleasantly self-conscious form of scientific art or artistic science."[7] Instead, he offers this solution: "As the century closes, the focus of the natural sciences has begun to shift away from the search for new fundamental laws and toward new forms of synthesis—'holism,' if you prefer—in order to understand complex systems. . . . No compelling reason has ever been offered why the same strategy should not work to unite the natural sciences with the social sciences and humanities."[8] We hope the Tanner Symposium's search for a common language moved us toward this goal.

Preliminary Reflections on Matters Environmental

Carolyn Tanner Irish

Carolyn Tanner Irish returned to her native state in 1996, having been elected as bishop of the Episcopal Diocese of Utah. She was the fourth woman in the United States, and sixth in the worldwide Anglican Communion to lead a diocese. She thinks of her return in the terms described by the poet T. S. Eliot:

We shall not cease from exploration
and the end of all our exploring will be to arrive
where we started
and know the place for the first time.

"Utah has been both fulcrum and culmination in my spiritual journey," she said. "There is a special sense of belonging for me here—both historically, as my ancestors were part of settling this territory, and in terms of landscape or place."

Bishop Irish studied philosophy at Stanford University, the University of Michigan, and Oxford University. After teaching some years in Washington D.C., she received her master of divinity degree from the Virginia Theological Seminary, the largest Anglican seminary in the world. Ordained first as deacon and then as priest, she served congregations in Washington, Virginia, and Michigan and was the first woman to serve as an archdeacon in the United States. Bishop Irish has spoken and written extensively on the theology of creation, and the moral implications of its care.

I.

I am delighted to be here and honored to be asked, once again, to participate in a Tanner Symposium. I do so not only as the daughter of one of its principal benefactors but also because of my own deep concern for and commitment to matters environmental. That is my own catchall phrase: *matters environmental.* It includes just about everything, doesn't it?

I wondered how I might introduce our theme, given that it has no clear boundaries. I begin, as so often, with the title: "The Search for a Common Language: Environmental Writing and Education." Titles are important because they give us the governing theme or the rubric around which we gather. In this case, I am not altogether clear about the *search* part of the title—the search for a common language. As broad and pervasive as our subject is, I'm not sure quite what a common language would look like, actually, if we found it. What the title does suggest is that we *already* share a common interest and concern about the environment, arising from our thoughts and feelings, experience and disciplines, and from an aesthetic appreciation and other spiritual feelings such as thanksgiving, too. So the convivial discussion in this symposium invites us to bring together richly diverse ways of encountering and considering this world.

We may be seeking a more inclusive appreciation of the many ways we may address our interests and concerns through the disciplines of literature, science, economics, sociology, geopolitics, ethics, and religion, to name just a few. Whether that counts as a common language remains to be seen. But the common referent of our work—the environment, the natural world, creation, or whatever we choose to call it—that is the crucial thing. I tend to think that it is this conversation among a whole variety of languages and disciplines that is the most valuable to us rather than a common language transcending them all.

One of my dad's favorite phrases was "walking around something." If he had something on his mind, he'd often say, "Come and walk around this with me for a little while." So I had that image of us here, gathered to *walk around* this wonderful theme—to let it give us its own methodology—its own surprises and ways of connecting. For besides our common interests and concerns, we also share the fact and the experience of being an integral *part of* the environment, the natural world, creation; we are not simply independent or objective observers, but we are subjects, objects, and agents *within* this world.

II.

Let me now invite your attention to two general and prelinguistic kinds of human experience, which I think have a bearing on how we encounter the world and are learning to encounter it in new ways. This approach may even be a bit simplistic, but it gets us started, and I like starting with experience, even raw experience, rather than verbal assumptions or premises. The first kind I'm going to call the experience of *wonder.*

Wonder happens in a vast range of times and places: lying under the stars at night; giving birth to a fully formed and living baby; or, as a gardener, say, noticing the connection between light and the growth of plants, or the connection between the death of plants and good soil. Often our wonder is a kind of awe, simply that something is the case, even *that* we exist. This perception may form the basis of what we later call a religious or spiritual experience.

I recall once hiking across a mountain meadow in England—actually it was a moor; it was untilled ground, but it was a meadow because amazing little flowers were all about. There were no roads, no telephone poles, no signs of people or civilization anywhere. I would expect that in the American West, but it surprised me to find it in England! And as I thought about that, I was suddenly overcome with amazement and delight—that I was there and alive, part of that setting for even an hour or two. I actually sat down and cried for a while, and then (much to my surprise) I thanked God. Even though I was in a period of rabid atheism in my life, I felt a need to give thanks, and it didn't seem quite right to thank anyone else. Such an experience of wonder and appreciation often creates a sense of peace or at-one-ment with the divine.

It may also give rise to aesthetic expression: to the desire to capture, record, or even witness the experience of a giftlike encounter with the world. We do that through writing and painting, through poetry and storytelling, music and photography. All of us have been beneficiaries of such aesthetic responses, and I believe we'll hear some examples later in this symposium.

Finally, though, the experience of wonder may produce a desire to figure things out, to understand natural processes, even to control them or use them, which is sometimes good. Surely much of science and applied science must have begun in wonder, in curiosity about the *how* of things or the *why* (in the sense of cause and effect). Thus, wonder is a seminal human experience as well as the basis of many, varied responses to the mystery of our existence on this earth.

Another such elemental experience is what I'm going to call, for want of a better word, the experience of *judgment.* This is a feeling—perhaps equally as powerful as wonder at times—that we are responsible for much of the damage, degradation, and, yes, desecration of our environment, the natural world, God's creation—its waters, atmosphere, soil, forests, and other creatures. And again, I offer an example of this experience from my own life, cautious, as I do so, that judgment is a word nobody likes to hear.

About fifteen years ago, I was on my way to church one ordinary Sunday morning. I had the sermon all prepared, the liturgy and program in hand. As I left home I glanced at the front page of the *Detroit News,* which pictured a large number of dead dolphins washed up on a beach somewhere. I felt devastated, absolutely devastated. I had no specific knowledge about how they had died—no one did at that time. But I nonetheless sensed that we human beings had had something to do with it. I didn't want to preach good news that morning at church; I didn't want to celebrate. Rather, I felt pain, and anger, grief, guilt, sorrow, repentance, lamentation—all of those ways the sense of judgment comes to us. I was impassioned and a bit garbled in the pulpit that day. But the congregation knew exactly what I was talking about, and they understood why I felt as I did.

This experience of judgment seems to be relatively common to many in our generation; at least in this country, many of us have had a dead dolphin or "silent spring" kind of experience, even if we don't necessarily think of it as judgment. Again, a variety of responses may follow: thinking that it is a result of our ignorance, we want to master the problem and fix it; thinking that it's an effect of the greed and overconsumption in our culture, we want to withdraw from it, to "live simply and lightly on the earth," as the Quakers and Native Americans say; thinking it a consequence of unregulated individualism in our society, we may press for changes in public policy.

But no matter how we think of it or act on it, it is our *moral sensibilities* that have come to life here. And this is a part of this whole conference as well, and why I use the word *judgment.* The sense of environmental responsibility has been most painfully poignant in our generation. It is not that moral sensibilities were absent earlier in the twentieth century, but they were focused on wars, economic depressions, various ideological battles, and other social issues. When it comes to matters environmental, it seems to me that both science and religion were "asleep on their watch" during the first two-thirds of the twentieth century. Individual thinkers and writers woke us up and got us engaged in all this. I'm thinking now of people like Rachel Carson, Barry Commoner, Wendell Berry—you can name others—and you know what that feeling of waking up is like. Indeed, it has only been in these last few years that the words *environment* and *ecology* have come to signify what they do to us today.

So learning to live more responsibly on this planet; the theologian Sally McFague offers three "house rules": "take only your share, clean up after yourself, and leave the place in good repair for others." Easily said. How do we get there? And how do we get other people there?

I'm aware that fear is a very powerful incentive, and it is rapidly becoming a part of this whole issue in our lives. Tragedy and disaster are also powerful, as we all know. But to me the energies that fear and pain unleash are often passing. We forget them. Also they sometimes lead us to just hunker down and take care of ourselves. I'm not sure they leave us wiser—and that really is what we're seeking at this conference, a kind of wisdom that is beyond just information or data. So I look to positive motivations, the spirit of thanksgiving, dedication, hope. I find myself thinking often of this earth and my life on it as a gift. And, for me, that evokes more lasting motivations and responses.

We are not apart from this world. We are not masters of it, as we so often think of ourselves. And guess what: we're not exactly stewards, either. That is the religious term for much of what this care and responsibility are about, but I remember Russell Train saying one time to a group of us who were on a committee in Washington, "I don't know why you keep wanting to talk about stewardship. It seems to me that creation was doing really well until the stewards came along." So I always have to think about that when I use the word. In any case, we are not apart from this world, nor are we simply masters or stewards—but we *are* response-*able* creatures. We have a capacity for response and maybe for care, for foresight, for planning. And so, being response-*able*, we can also be accountable, responsible.

III.

Let me now point out just one or two cautions about our search for a common language. I don't think there's much danger of them in this program, but I mention them because sometimes when we seek commonality in something, we ignore certain diversities or polarities or tensions that we actually need. These exist between what is particular and what is general, what is personal and what is communal, what is wild and what is cultural. Trying to rid ourselves of the tensions, paradoxes, or conflicts that these opposing realities present is not actually a great help because it (a) encourages denial and pretense, and (b) discourages creativity and imagination of the kind that such tensions often lead us to discover if we're patient. The fact is that we share a living world—a *living* world—where parts and places and processes change constantly, generation after generation. So I hope we will always be open to the surprise and mystery in that, even as we also value our common knowledge and expertise.

Also I think we should maintain a little modesty and humility in our endeavors. Annie Dillard recalls the comment of an old black farm woman, who said to her, "Seem like we just set down here. Don't any of us know why." I find a certain truth and goodness in the humility of that remark. It comes back to me frequently because I often get the big "why" questions on my doorstep, as in "Why is there suffering? What is the purpose of my life?" *Don't any of us know why.* Humility can abide, even with all the sophistication of our various disciplines. Wendell Berry commented to the effect that, "we act on the basis of our knowledge but must also learn to act on the basis of our ignorance, that is, what we don't know." It may be that only environmentalists understand what he meant, but that only highlights the wisdom of the remark.

Thank you. Let the conversation begin!

The Poets

Ken Brewer is professor emeritus at Utah State University, where he won several teaching awards. He is the current poet laureate for the state of Utah. Among his many books of poetry are The Place in Between, Lake's Edge, Hoping for All, Dreading Nothing, To Remember What Is Lost, The Collected Poems of Mongrel, Round Again, Sum of Accidents, *and* Places, Shadows, Dancing People. *His poems are interspersed throughout this book between other contributions.*

Keith Wilson, a native New Mexico writer, is professor emeritus at the University of New Mexico. His books include Graves Registry, Homestead, Bosque Redondo: The Encircled Grove, Desert Cenote, While Dancing Feet Shatter the Earth, *and* Stone Roses. *Forthcoming are* To the Cause of Rite: A Compendium and Collected Poems of Keith Wilson. *His poems begin on page* 164.

Painted Lady

Ken Brewer

—for Robert Michael Pyle

She unfolds on a yellow zinnia
as if posing for camera shots:
the orange midriff, the black and white tips.

She cannot live here through winter.
Cold, snow, and Rocky Mountain wind
will shred her diaphanous wings.

Before flight, having crawled among thistles,
the Painted Lady has only this dream:
live sweet or die.

Who Lost the Limberlost?
Education and Language in a Mis-Placed Age

Robert Michael Pyle

Robert Michael Pyle has a Ph.D. in ecology and environmental studies from Yale University. Along with hundreds of essays, poems, and stories, he has published many books, among them Where Bigfoot Walks: Crossing the Dark Divide *(subject of a Guggenheim fellowship);* Wintergreen: Rambles in a Ravaged Land *(winner of the 1986 John Burroughs Medal for distinguished nature writing);* Chasing Monarchs: Migrating with the Butterflies of Passage; Nabokov's Butterflies; The Thunder Tree: Lessons from an Urban Wildland; *and* Walking the High Ridge: Life as Field Trip. *In 1997 he received a Distinguished Service Award from the Society for Conservation Biology. He lives near the mouth of the Columbia River, and his column, "The Tangled Bank," appears in each issue of* Orion Magazine.

Once upon a time, we knew where we lived, and it was *some* place. Some *where*. Somewhere *was* someplace. Each and every *where* was a *place*. And each of us had a nice legible label safety-pinned to our jacket just like Paddington Bear. "Hello!" it said. "I'm Bobby Pyle. I live at 5040 Tejon Street, Denver, Colorado, east of the Front Range, where the paved road meets the dusty road, by the marshes of Clear Creek just above the Platte River. Please see me home safely." No one blessed with a home was ever lost.

Gene Stratton Porter's home lay by the great hardwood forest and swamp known as the Limberlost in northeastern Indiana. For a time, Porter's 1909 novel, *A Girl of the Limberlost,* may have been the most widely read and beloved book in America. I don't know a book between that and Barbara Kingsolver's *Prodigal Summer* that so richly apprehends a woman's sensibility all wrapped up in the particularities of the eastern deciduous forest, including especially her neighbors, counted among the moths, birds, mammals, and humans. That woman in Porter's novel, note, is named Mrs. Comstock. *Prodigal Summer* is also extremely popular with readers. One difference between the two books is steamy versus implied romance; another is that the modern protagonist's attachment to her animal neighbors seems quaint or eccentric to many modern readers. In Porter's time, it was the main point: she lived to see her great Limberlost drained and cut in 1916, well before her popular novels went to Hollywood.

A contemporary of Porter's, also widely read—and this is probably not a coincidence—was Anna Botsford Comstock. In 1903 she took over the Nature-Study program at Cornell from Liberty Hyde Bailey, a student of Louis Agassiz. The program arose following an agricultural depression with a view toward interesting rural children in better farming. Agassiz liked to say, "If you study nature in books, when you go out-of-doors, you cannot find her."[1] Comstock organized Junior Naturalist Clubs all over New York State and elsewhere, wrote pamphlets, and conducted correspondence courses, all aimed at kindling real understanding of nature through study and direct contact, out-of-doors. She came to believe that "the reason why nature-study has not yet accomplished her mission, as thought core for much of the required work in our public schools, is that the teachers are as a whole untrained in the subject."[2] To remedy this lack, in 1911 she published her massive *Handbook of Nature Study*, replete with hundreds of lessons, poems, photographs, and vignettes—not to replace, but to stimulate, outdoor learning.

Comstock's book tapped a vein thirsty for blood knowledge of the land and its occupants. Many imitators followed. My collection of contemporary nature-study texts is a bookshelf broad, and I still come across new titles, published between the 1890s and the 1940s. While they take different approaches, what they all have in common is a devotion to firsthand experience with the animals and plants being studied. Clifton Hodge, in *Nature-Study and Life,* called this kind of direct contact "the sheet anchor of elementary education, all the more necessary as modern life tends to drift away from nature into artificialities of every sort."[3] And that was in 1902! What would he think a hundred years later, when children are more likely to recognize a Palm Pilot than a palm tree?

The implicit goal of all these books and the movement that inspired them, along with Audubon Nature Clubs that followed, the novels of Gene Stratton Porter, the philosophy and writings of Theodore Roosevelt, the essays of Joseph Wood Krutch and Edwin Way Teale, and an entire culture of nature study, is just this: *essential nature literacy.* In a shocking line that seems hyperbolic today but may have been quite true in 1911, Comstock claimed that her weighty work "does not contain more than any intelligent country child of twelve should know of his environment, things he should know naturally and without effort, although it might take him half his lifetime to learn so much if he should not begin before the age of twenty."[4]

My grandmother, Grace Phelps Miller, grew up in Denver, frequently visiting uncles on ranches in western Colorado. One, Amos, made better bricks than beef and left to build a brick plant on Whidbey Island in Washington. His daughter Leila was Grace's favorite cousin, so she and her sister Helen, after graduating from the University of Denver in the first decade of the twentieth century, followed Amos and Leila to Washington. After receiving their MAs at the University of Washington, they became pioneer teachers. Gram's first job offer came from Chelan, a fruit and mining (now tourist) town at the foot of a spectacular glacial fjord deep in the Cascades. To get there, she took the streetcar to Everett, the Northern Pacific railroad up to Stevens Pass and through its tunnel, a riverboat on the undammed Columbia River north from Wenatchee, and a stagecoach up the canyon around Chelan Falls. Once in Chelan, she found the school board—all three of them—awaiting her arrival. She stepped from the stage onto the hem of her long traveling skirt and went right down onto her knees, skinning them. The superintendent, helping her up, said, "There is no need to show such a degree of obeisance at this point, Miss Phelps!"

Gram would get into trouble one more time in Chelan, and not because it was discovered that she was actually Mrs. Miller. It was for leading botany walks on Sundays. Nor were the walks the issue; the Sabbath was simply no proper time for teaching anything but Sunday School. As for the flower walks, they were absolutely de rigueur. Anna B. Comstock was in almost every classroom, and botany forays were frequent. The presence of nature study in the schools was no more questioned than other basics.

Back in Seattle, U. W. Professor Orson Bennett Johnson had lately presided over a Young Naturalists' Society that included the most prominent citizens as members. That was a time when a fundamental acquaintance with flora and fauna was widely considered a desirable thing for children, and the naturalists were still highly respected in the universities. It's a long way from the campus of "Bug" Johnson to the University of Washington today, where half the students have cell-phone implants, and the other half wouldn't know a Douglas-fir from a dogwood.

In the first half of the nineteen hundreds, Illinois and other states sustained natural history surveys. The University of California tenured a cadre of professors of natural history, of which only one remains, emeritus. He is emblematic of what occurred: a purging of the naturalists from the academies. More and more, their science of direct experience was seen as anecdotal, romantic, fuddy duddy, and beside the point. The biochemical-molecular-mathematics-computer revolutions hastened the process. Most of the old-time naturalists were retired without replacement, and the younger ones were often denied tenure.

Not that there are no good naturalists in the universities today: Bernd Heinrich, E. O. Wilson, and many others—notably at this institution— prove otherwise. However, their employment is often in spite of the fact rather than because of it. They keep their field hats down and don't speak the term *natural history* too loudly. Stock in the title and the term have dropped both in academia and among people at large. Where once John Burroughs and John Muir were among the most respected men in the land—preparing the soil for Anna and Gene—the term *naturalist* has come to be confused with *naturist,* so the idle spectator, hearing that naturalists are about, goes on the lookout for nudie cuties instead of net wielders. Or the practitioner is seen as a nature nazi, dweeb, ecoterrorist, or irrelevant stumblebum. Here, for example, is a direct quote from a granola package I recently purchased: "American Mills Granola was created for one very simple reason: The world needs good granola. Not that cheap kind that conjures up memories of the time you ate wood chips as a kid, and not that overpriced kind of granola made for pretentious 'naturalists' who enjoy it in the woods while scaring every last trace of wildlife away with the sound of their portable cappuccino maker." So this is now the home of the naturalist in popular discourse. Marginal doesn't begin to say it. Whereas the first, third, and twenty-sixth presidents of this country were accomplished naturalists, and respected for it, and the thirty-ninth wasn't half bad and a decent poet to boot, the very idea of president as poet or naturalist seems about as consistent at the moment as climate change in Camelot or passenger pigeons in the Bronx.

And why should this matter? Surely the concerns of the naturalist are peripheral to the central preoccupations of the day? Maybe not. Precisely because climate change is the reality, not Camelot; because passenger pigeons are less likely to darken the skies than dust from the desiccating Gobi Desert. Even if our antipoet laureate gave the go-ahead for the U.S. to sign the Kyoto Accord tomorrow, the Northwest Passage will be ice free before the greenhouse notices the flick of the thermostat. A coleopterist friend of mine, now at the Smithsonian, studying the flower beetles at oases in the Palestinian region, predicted decades ago that water would soon become the limiting factor in the Middle East for beetles and people alike—a fact about which neither the PLO nor the Knesset can be unaware. Let the talk be of homelands, religion, and oil; water will call the shots. In short, natural history is simply the operating manual for the whole works. A deep (or at least passing) familiarity with water, beetles, and all the rest of our nonhuman neighbors and their needs would seem to be the very least sign of respect for the neighborhood as a whole. Yet the prevailing indifference says the opposite. When you don't give a drowned rat's ass for the rest of creation, is it any wonder that you are willing to mar the Arctic to gas up your Arctic Cat?

So how came all this to pass? We got here partly by "hovering like angels in order to mate like rabbits,"[5] as David James Duncan described mayflies in a lecture at Utah State University, and partly through our schools, our language, and our lack of care for them. Our hearts, what is left of them, followed. For as the academy went, so went the public schools. As natural history came to be seen as "soft" and intellectually flaccid, anecdotal, lacking in experimental rigor and robustness—all charges with a seed of truth to them—it also began to lose adherents and supporters on the school boards. Anna and Gene were dead and gone. Habitats were retreating from easy access by the schools. Between the world wars, emphasis shifted from agriculture to armaments, from the countryside to the city. And then came Sputnik, the coup de grâce for old-time nature study in the public schools.

Let me tell you about Mrs. Frandsen, for she was on the cutting edge of that extinction event. As I described her in *Walking the High Ridge*: "In her brown suits, sheer blouses over mysterious layers of lingerie, still reddish hair, and stern but affectionate demeanor, she inspired a blend of loyalty and terror. . . . She loved the language, and her diction would be rare in the classroom today. . . . Mrs. Frandsen cared about nature. She taught us about conservation, and what it meant to her."[6] Maude Frandsen is long gone, and while there still may be teachers with her inclinations and sensibilities, rare is the classroom where they have full rein. Instead, we have environmental education, thank the gods, the heroic bulwark of the resistance to those who would sack the nature-school connection altogether— and those forces are strong.

But one week at E.E. camp in the sixth grade, or the occasional field trip if they even exist, is not the same as doing nature study on a daily basis. E.E. is an uphill battle in a time when people knowing more about how living systems work is seen as a bad thing in the seats of corporate and government leadership, if that's not a redundancy. And in my opinion, a lot of E.E. tends to concentrate on systems, processes, and relationships while neglecting the names and lifeways of the participant species—which can be a lot like watching a Russian play without a cast list.

Even some of the institutions that have traditionally spoken up for nature study now question that role. The National Wildlife Federation for many years offered splendid family natural-history camps called Conservation Summits, at which I taught, as did Barbara Middleton and Leila Schultz, highly respected E.E. and botany teachers in this university. But the powerful federation has now largely forsaken its longtime dedication to such programs, and thereby its understood commitment to nature literacy. In contrast, the National Audubon Society, under the suitably named president John Flicker, has restated its vows, announcing plans for a thousand neighborhood nature centers in ten years—though many Audubon chapters, already doing this work, see this program as an imperial adventure by the national body that will drain off their fund-raising base and members' energies. Meanwhile, birding, butterflying, and wildflower watching have all undergone booms. But we must ask: is it enough, and is it in time?

Along with natural history in academia went systematics and taxonomy: the science and practice of classifying and sorting out the relationships among life forms. This is vital work: you cannot save what you don't even know. At a time in history when the screaming need to catalogue and understand biodiversity has never been greater, the training and employment of systematists in universities and museums have shrunken perilously. Species are passing even without formal recognition, let alone understanding, and all organismal biologists know this to be true. I recently returned from the worldwide Biology of Butterflies Conference in Leiden, Holland, and I can report that systematics is back in a way: molecular phylogeny and cladistics, relying on DNA analyses and giving new insights into evolutionary histories, are going strong. But most of the practitioners ("cooks," as they jokingly call themselves) have little acquaintance with their subjects in the field. Nor are they actively curating collections, which are the bureaus of standards for biodiversity, against which the losses should be measured. The recent closure of the Entomology Department at Oregon State University, the most important insect repository in the Northwest, is typical. As cost-cutting measures, such elisions are first-class false economies. Biologists Tom Eisner and David Wilcove consider the institutional turning away from natural history to be one of the biggest mistakes of our time. The new biology is good, but how sad to lose a healthy collegiality between the young turks on the cutting edge and the old farts with all the facts.

Anna Comstock said, "It is absolutely necessary to have a wide knowledge of other plants and animals"[7] to understand our relationship to any one kind. As one kind of animal ourselves, in deep need of righting our relationship with the rest, the names and addresses of our local flora and fauna should be common knowledge. But when the people we delegate to study, manage, and interpret the natural world are unversed in its parts and ways, how is the ordinary citizen supposed to achieve ecological literacy?

By getting out, that's how, with eyes and minds wide open. In my view, all the noble nature centers notwithstanding, we live in an era of immense ignorance of our world. There was a time when every member of the society was a competent naturalist or died. But when we gave up what the writer Sally Tisdale calls "our mammalian vigilance,"[8] we traded our wits, experience, ecological adeptness, and knowledge for predictability and security, such as it ever was. And we gave up more. I feel that the loss of ordinary experience and know-how leaves us up a creek without a clue. As common species and textures drop out of our immediate environs, people become increasingly isolated and inured to monotony. This "extinction of experience," [9] as I call it, leads to alienation, apathy, and ultimately and inevitably, still greater losses: a particularly vicious cycle of loss without redemption. The only antidote is intimacy.

Recently in the Netherlands, I noticed a lad on my train with a net on his back. I assumed that he must be heading to our butterfly conference. But no, he was on his way to study early spring hoverflies in the countryside. No one batted an eye; here, carry a net on a train, if you can find one, and get ready for guffaws, winks, and general hilarity. But then, Holland has millions and millions of bicycles, and thousands and thousands of miles of bicycle paths. Great-crested grebes nest and display all along the canals and in a moat around Schipol Airport, and people actually know what they are. Not that the Low Countries are a natural nirvana. Their undisturbed habitats are few and small, but the natives guard them zealously.

For all their loss of wilderness, the Dutch strike me as maintaining an intimacy with their surroundings that few Americans approach. We, in contrast, do our darnedest to alienate ourselves from nature and then act surprised when a dirty rain, from dust storms over the Gobi, muddies every window in town. As Native Alaskan villages slip off soggy not-so-permafrost into rivers, Senator Stevens rails against climate change even as he rants in favor of drilling oil in the Arctic National Wildlife Refuge.

If the extinction of experience weren't doing quite well enough on its own, now Enter the Virtual. Maybe the tube and the net make it possible to learn more, faster; maybe. But maybe not better. Teachers agree that no Web site can substitute for a spiderweb, while the scintillating pixels on a glowing screen will never replace the scintillant scales on a butterfly's wing. Nor will CD ROMs and virtual field trips make up for canceled trips to the field.

Of course television has long diverted attention from the actual. In *The Desert Smells Like Rain,* Gary Nabhan described an encounter between a slick city TV reporter and a Tohona O'odham Indian elder in southern Arizona for a program about traditional agriculture and its decline. "Tell me," asked Jan, the anchorwoman, "why do you think the younger generation is not keeping up these traditions?"

"Laura listened," writes Nabhan, "stopped dead in her tracks, unloosened her arm from that of Jan's, and pointed straight at the camera, frowning: 'It's *that TV!* They're all watching *that TV!* They just sit around in front of it, they hardly go outside anymore, so how can they plow or plant or gather the fruit? That's the problem, *right there!*'"[10]

Anna Botsford Comstock's lessons were designed to get kids out-of-doors. Nowadays secondhand connection is the rule. Even butterfly metamorphosis, that greatest of classroom experiences, which traditionally involved going out with a teacher to gather larvae or pupae, now involves bugs in a box that come in the mail, feed on an artificial diet, then fly free (if not suffering from inbreeding depression) in a location far from their point of nascence. At least they are alive, a rarity in classrooms today. That old kid-and-creature chemistry largely went out with the slate board. Yet, as Calvin said to Hobbes one trying day, "The world's not so bad, when you can get out in it!"

So who lost the Limberlost? It was, of course, the local farmers who drained it, seeking to make "wild and useless" land into something productive. And it was Gene; her alter ego, Mrs. Comstock; and her many readers who also lost it, along with a big chunk of their hearts. But who lost the Limberlost inside each of us? We all have—by going along with the mis-placing of America. Sad to say, this process has been spearheaded, and enabled, by language. Our rhetoric, as much as our complacency, has lost the land inside of us. Lawrence Buell of Harvard, speaking in Salt Lake City this spring, called rhetoric "the art of words in the interests of persuading." A beautiful thing; but how it can be perverted, how the words can go ugly in the service of anything-but-gentle persuasion!

Hear these examples from recent news stories: In a *Salt Lake Tribune* piece entitled, "Fond or Otherwise, Worldwide Images of Utah May Be Fleeting," Christopher Smith quoted Utah Travel Council head David Reeder: "How does all the media coverage translate into residual benefits? I hate to say it, but people saying, 'Let's change our plans and go to Utah!'—that's not going to happen automatically," Reeder said. "We have to recall the Olympic memories for them and attach the emotion for the Games to what we call the Utah brand."[11] So the land becomes a brand.

Or hearken to William Arkin, in a *Los Angeles Times* story under the title, "Pentagon Revamps Nuke Use." The story quotes the Bush administration's review of post-9/11 nuclear options thus: "In addition to the new weapons systems, the review calls for incorporation of 'nuclear capability' into many of the conventional systems now under development. For example, it calls for research to begin next month on fitting an existing nuclear warhead into a new 5,000-pound 'earth-penetrating munition.'"[12] It is not enough simply to devastate the Earth's surface; now we will be able to penetrate its very integument. Anyone who misses the subtext needs to read more Barbara Kingsolver and less Gene Stratton Porter. But just as education and rhetoric can undergird and even encourage the most philistine, mercantile, and dunderheaded behavior toward the living world, so can they counter, assuage, and, I believe, ultimately reduce the rascals to irrelevant rubble—which will happen eventually anyway, with or without us. How much better if it takes place in time for us and ours to enjoy what's left, and to build on it for evolutionary and redemptive opportunities to come?

Next week I will be visiting a second-grade class engaged in a study unit on butterflies. Perhaps Brooke, my former student and teacher/host for the visit, will become these students' Mrs. Frandsen? And I think of a midwestern Forgotten Language Tour by the Orion Society, a pack of unruly writers on a road trip. We were driving between Oberlin and Grinnell via Muncie, and we each had our agenda. Kim Stafford wanted to stop at a famous pie shop. Scott Sanders wanted to bypass his home campus in Bloomington by as many miles as possible. I wanted to stop and look for butterflies in the autumn weave of goldenrod and purple asters. And Pattiann Rogers mostly wanted to get to our destination, where Ann Zwinger would join us and the gender ratio would improve. But when we saw the sign, we unanimously hit the brakes, for we were right smack in the ancient Limberlost. If you can make a pilgrimage by serendipity, we did, visiting Gene's old home, now a museum, with her moths fading on the wall. It was a thrill to see her books and writing desk but a deep sadness to view the fields where the stories, the moths, the great swamp once lived. So what a balm, the next day at Ball State University, to meet Ken Brunswick—a farmer-turned-founder of Limberlost Remembered!, a band of restoration rabble-rousers. They have acquired land, restored the flow of water, and planted the nub of a native forest: they have re-found the Limberlost!

And as for language, who has the tools if not us? Who has the means, the opportunity, and most certainly the obligation to bring the language to the people, language with which to whack the un-placed alongside the head? To give courage to all who read, listen, or at least think now and then, to re-place themselves? We do have that language. It is what Thoreau meant in his essay "Walking" when he equated the ability to be "equally at home everywhere" with "the secret of successful sauntering."[13] It is exactly what Pattiann Rogers had in mind in her poem "The Family Is All There Is" when she evoked "the grasp of the self on place."[14] And the same remedy is implicit in essayist Kim Stafford's prescription for "weaving a rooted companionship with home ground."[15]

To get back, or forward (for surely we have never really been there), we will need every facility and sensibility of both science and art, every clever trick of both education and literature, every good impulse of every rich discipline until we find the right combination of head bone and hormone—that high ridge, as Vladimir Nabokov called it, "where the mountainside of scientific knowledge meets the opposite slope of artistic imagination."[16] Maybe then we can rename, and reclaim, our places. To Nabokov, it was no mystery. It was simply "all that I love."[17]

Oh! *There's* the word. That, and Hope. Surely what we're trying to do is nothing more than what Bill Kittredge, in that classic of the misplaced land, *Hole in the Sky*, told us we must. We must, he said, go "out, away, to the world, with hope"[18]

The Silliest Debate

Ken Brewer

—for Craig Stanford

The mountain gorillas of Bwindi
need their legs, their arms, their hands.
Unlike humans, they do not need syntax.

Syntax is like the grid of a city—
we need it to find our way
to work, to home, to school,
to the Super Wal-Mart with its own grid
laid out like a Melville sentence.

Some humans claim syntax
makes us smarter than gorillas.
We have Maalox, Tylenol, Anusol, Viagra,
and we can compose compound-complex
sentences that have multiple nouns and verbs.

We are the Adamic species.
We name everything, even "ecotourists,"
humans who pay to watch
the mountain gorillas of Bwindi
sleep, eat, nurture, have a little sex.

Imagine mountain gorillas
paying to watch humans
run through the maze of Detroit.

Cousins
What the Great Apes Tell Us about Human Origins

Craig B. Stanford

Craig B. Stanford, professor of anthropology and biological sciences and co-director of the Jane Goodall Research Center at USC, is best known for his groundbreaking work on chimpanzees, conducted in collaboration with Jane Goodall. He currently directs the Bwindi Impenetrable Great Ape Project, a study of mountain gorillas and chimpanzees in Uganda. He is the author of many technical and popular scientific papers and essays and seven books, including Chimpanzee and Red Colobus, The Hunting Apes, *and* Significant Others: The Ape-Human Continuum and the Quest for Human Nature.

Cousins

On a sun-dappled East African morning four million years ago, several dozen small apelike hominids are foraging for plant foods in scattered forest along a river course when they come upon a large group of monkeys in an isolated tree. Some of the male hominids climb the tree, and although their upright posture and adaptation to ground living make them more at home there, through cooperative action some pursue the monkeys in the branches while others wait below. The monkeys scatter and try to flee, but several are caught in the tree crown while others fall to the ground; the hominids kill their prey by flailing them against tree limbs, and the carcass meat immediately becomes the focus of excited competition and begging. Males dole out chunks of meat to their allies and sexually receptive females while withholding meat from their political rivals. Females that have large estrous swellings beg for meat and, in exchange for it, copulate with the males who control it. Although the monkey prey are individually small, the combined weight of several is more than thirty kilograms; this small group of hominids may catch and eat more than a thousand kilos of meat per year, much of it in the dry season when plant foods are scarce. Because every scrap of meat, bone, and skin is eaten, no remains are left for a future archeologist to discover.

While this portrait of hunting behavior in our earliest human ancestors may sound fanciful, it is precisely the pattern of predatory behavior that occurs routinely in our closest living relative, the chimpanzee, whose ancestors had recently split from our common evolutionary line when this scenario occurred. When Jane Goodall first observed wild chimpanzees hunting and eating meat thirty years ago, skeptics suggested that their behavior was aberrant and that the amount of meat eaten was trivial. Today we know that chimpanzees everywhere eat mainly fruit but are also predators in their forest ecosystems. In some sites, the quantity of meat eaten by a chimpanzee community may approach one ton annually. Recently revealed aspects of predation by chimpanzees, such as its frequency and the use of meat as a political and reproductive tool, have important implications for research on the origins of human behavior. These findings come at a time when many anthropologists argue for scavenging rather than hunting as a way of life for early human ancestors. Research into the hunting ecology of wild chimpanzees may therefore shed new light on the current debate about the origins of human behavior.

Meat Eating in Human Evolution

One of the most important and intriguing questions in human evolution is when meat became an important part of the diet of our ancestors. Physical anthropologists and archaeologists have explored a number of techniques to try to answer this question. The presence of primitive stone tools in the fossil record tells us that 2.5 million years ago early hominids were using stone implements to cut the flesh off the bones of large animals that either they had hunted or whose carcasses they had scavenged. The pattern of obtaining and processing meat by more recent people has been studied by examining archaeological sites in Europe and elsewhere, as well as by studying the hunting and meat-eating behavior of modern foraging people, the so-called hunter-gatherers. Before 2.5 million years ago, however, we know very little about the foods that hominids ate, or the role that meat may have played in their diet. We know that the earliest upright-walking (bipedal) hominids, the australopithecines, evolved in Africa about five million years ago and that they shared a common ancestor with modern chimpanzees shortly before that time. Modern people and chimpanzees share an estimated 98.5 percent of their DNA sequence, making them more closely related to each other than to any other animal species.

Therefore, understanding chimpanzee hunting behavior and ecology may tell us a great deal about the behavior and ecology of those very-earliest hominids. This is the approach I have taken in my field study of the hunting behavior of wild chimpanzees, and especially their relationship with the animal that is their major prey, the red colobus monkey. What are the social and ecological factors that predict when chimpanzees will hunt and whether they will be successful? What is the effect of chimpanzee predation on the populations of their prey animals, such as the red colobus? What are the likely similarities in meat-eating patterns between chimpanzees and the earliest hominids?

In the early 1960s, when Dr. Jane Goodall began her now-famous study of the chimpanzees of Gombe National Park, Tanzania, it was thought that chimpanzees were strictly vegetarian. In fact, when Goodall first reported this behavior, many people were skeptical and claimed that meat was not a natural part of the chimpanzee diet. Today hunting by chimpanzees at Gombe has been well documented,[1] and hunting has also been observed at most other sites in Africa where chimpanzees have been studied, including Mahale Mountains National Park[2] (also in Tanzania) and Taï National Park in the Ivory Coast in West Africa.[3] At Gombe, we now know that chimpanzees may kill and eat more than 150 small and medium-sized animals such as monkeys, wild pigs, and small antelopes each year. Chimpanzee society is called fission fusion to indicate that there is little cohesive group structure apart from mothers and their infants; instead, temporary subgroupings called *parties* come together and separate throughout the day. These parties vary in size in relation to the abundance and distribution of the food supply[4] and the presence of estrous females (who serve as a magnet for males),[5] so the size and membership of hunting parties vary greatly, from a single chimpanzee to as many as thirty-five. The hunting abilities of the party members along with the number of hunters present thus influences when a party hunts as well as whether it will succeed in catching a colobus.

Chimpanzee Predatory Behavior

After three decades of research on the hunting behavior of chimpanzees at Gombe, we already know a great deal about their predatory patterns. We know that although chimpanzees have been recorded to eat more than twenty-five types of vertebrate animals,[6] the most important vertebrate prey species in their diet is the red colobus monkey. At Gombe, red colobus account for more than 80 percent of the prey eaten. But Gombe chimpanzees do not select the colobus they kill randomly; infant and juvenile colobus are caught in greater proportion than their availability; 75 percent of all colobus killed are immature.[7] Chimpanzees are largely fruit eaters, and meat comprises only about 3 percent of the time they spend eating overall, less than in nearly all human societies. Adult and adolescent

males do most of the hunting, making about 90 percent of the kills recorded at Gombe over the past decade. Females also hunt, though more often
they receive a share of meat from the male who either captured the meat
or stole it from the captor. Although lone chimpanzees, both male and
female, sometimes hunt by themselves, most hunts are social. In other species of hunting animals, cooperation among hunters may lead to greater
success rates, thus promoting the evolution of cooperative behavior. Such
cooperation has also been posited as important in our own evolution.[8] In
both Gombe[9] and the Taï forest in the Ivory Coast, there is a strong positive
relationship between the number of hunters and the odds of a successful hunt.[10] Christophe Boesch has documented highly cooperative hunting
behavior by the chimpanzees at Taï along with meat-sharing behavior after
a kill that rewards those chimps that participated in the hunt.[11]

One of the main recent findings about hunting by chimpanzees is its seasonality.[12] At Gombe, nearly 40 percent of the kills of colobus monkeys occur in the dry-season months of August and September. This is apparently
a time of food shortage in the forest since the chimpanzees' body weights
do decline.[13] Hunting at Gombe is actually less strongly seasonal than in the
Mahale Mountains, where 60 percent of kills occur in a two-month period
during the early wet season. Why do chimpanzees hunt more often in some
months than in others? This is an important question because studies of
early hominid diets have shown that meat eating occurred most often in
the dry season, the same time that meat eating peaks among Gombe chimpanzees.[14] And the amount of meat eaten, even though it composes a small
percentage of the chimpanzee diet, is substantial. I estimate that in some
years, the forty-five chimpanzees of the main study community at Gombe
kill and consume more than fifteen hundred pounds of prey animals of
all species. This is far more than most previous estimates of the weight of
live animals eaten by chimpanzees. A large proportion of this amount is
eaten in August and September. In fact, during the peak dry season, the
estimated per-capita meat intake is about sixty-five grams per day for each
adult chimpanzee. This approaches the meat intake by the members of
some human foraging societies in the lean months of the year. Chimpanzee
dietary strategies may thus approximate those of human hunter-gatherers
to a greater degree than we imagined.

Several other aspects of hunting by Gombe chimpanzees are notewor-
thy. First, although most successful hunts result in a kill of a single colobus
monkey, two to seven colobus may be killed in some hunts. The likelihood of such a multiple kill is tied directly to the number of hunters in the
party. Interestingly, the percentage of multiple kills rose markedly in the
late 1980s and early 1990s, which in turn meant that many more colobus

overall were being eaten in the late 1980s compared to five years earlier.[15] This fact is most likely due to changes in the age and sex of the chimpanzee community. The number of adult and adolescent male chimpanzees in the study community rose from five to twelve during the 1980s due to a large number of young males who were maturing and taking their places in hunting parties. One could therefore say that the fate of the Gombe red colobus monkeys is in the hands of the chimpanzee population; this is reflected in the colobus mortality rate in relation to the number of hunters available during a given era.

Throughout her years of research, Jane Goodall has noted that the Gombe chimpanzees tend to go on "hunting crazes," during which they hunt almost daily and kill large numbers of monkeys and other prey.[16] The explanation for such binges has always been unclear. My own research has focused on the causes for such spurts in hunting frequency, with unexpected results. The explanation for sudden changes in frequency seems to be related to whatever factors promote hunting itself; when such factors are present to a high degree or for an extended period of time, frequent hunting occurs. For example, the most intense hunting binge we have seen occurred during the dry season of 1990. From late June through early September, a period of sixty-eight days, the chimpanzees were observed to kill seventy-one colobus monkeys in forty-seven hunts. It is important to note that this is the observed total, but the actual total of kills that includes hunts where no human observer was present may be one-third greater. During this time, the chimpanzees may have killed more than 10 percent of the entire colobus population within their hunting range.[17]

To try to solve the binge question, my colleagues and I examined the database of hunts recorded over the past decade to see what social or environmental factors coincided with hunting binges. Knowing that hunting is seasonal helped: I expected binges to occur mainly in the dry season, and this proved to be the case. But other interesting correlations leapt out as well. Periods of intense hunting tended to be times when the size of chimpanzee foraging parties was very large; this corresponded to the direct relationship between party size and both hunting frequency and success rate. Additionally, hunting binges occurred especially when there were female chimpanzees with sexual swellings (the large pink anogenital swellings that females exhibit during their periods of sexual receptivity, or estrus) traveling with the hunting party. When one or more swollen females was present, the odds of a hunt occurring were substantially greater, independent of other factors.[18] This co-occurrence of party size, presence of swollen females, and hunting frequency led me to ask the basic question, "Why do chimpanzees hunt?"

Why Do Chimpanzees Hunt?

Among the great apes (the gorilla, the orangutan, the bonobo or
pygmy chimpanzee, and the chimpanzee) and ourselves, only humans and
chimpanzees hunt and eat meat on a frequent basis. Since neither humans
nor chimpanzees are truly carnivorous—most traditional human societies eat a diet made up mostly of plant foods—we are considered omni-
vores. The important decisions about what to eat and when to eat it should
therefore be based on the nutritional costs and benefits of obtaining certain food compared to the essential nutrients that it provides. However,
as I mentioned earlier, social influences such as party size and composition seem to play an important role in mediating hunting behavior as well.
Understanding when and why chimpanzees choose to undertake a hunt
of colobus monkeys rather than simply continue to forage for fruits and
leaves, even though the hunt involves risk of injury from colobus canine
teeth and a substantial chance they won't catch anything, has been a major
goal of my research.

In his study of Gombe chimpanzee predatory behavior in the 1960s,
Geza Teleki considered hunting to have a strong social basis.[19] Some early
researchers had said that hunting by chimpanzees might be a form of social
display, where a male chimp tries to show his prowess to other members of
the community.[20] In the 1970s, Richard Wrangham conducted the first systematic study of chimpanzee behavioral ecology at Gombe and concluded
that predation by chimps was nutritionally based, but that some aspects of
the behavior were not well explained by nutritional needs alone.[21] More
recently, Toshisada Nishida and his colleagues in the Mahale Mountains
chimpanzee research project reported that the alpha there, Ntilogi, used
captured meat as a political tool to withhold from rivals and dole out to
allies.[22] And William McGrew has shown that those female Gombe chimps
who receive generous shares of meat after a kill have more surviving offspring, indicating a reproductive benefit of meat eating.[23]

My own preconception was that hunting must be nutritionally based.
After all, meat from monkeys and other prey would be a package of protein, fat, and calories hard to equal from any plant food. I therefore examined the relationship between the odds of success and the amount of meat
available with different numbers of hunters in relation to each hunter's expected payoff in obtained meat. That is, when are the time, energy, and risk
(the costs) involved in hunting worth the potential benefits, and therefore
when should a chimp decide to join or not join a hunting party? And how
does hunting compare to the costs and benefits of foraging for plant foods?
These analyses are still under way because of the difficulty in learning the
nutritional components of the many plant foods in the chimps' diverse

diet, but the preliminary results have been surprising. I expected that as the number of hunters increased, the amount of meat available for each hunter would also increase. This would explain the social nature of hunting by Gombe chimpanzees. If the amount of meat available per hunter declined with increasing hunting-party size (because each hunter got smaller portions as party size increased), then it would be a better investment of time and energy to hunt alone rather than join a party. The hunting success rate of lone hunters is only about 30 percent, while that of parties with ten or more hunters is nearly 100 percent. As it turned out, there was no relationship, either positive or negative, between the number of hunters and the amount of meat available per capita. This may be because even though the likelihood of success increases with more hunters in the party, the most-frequently caught prey animal is a one-kilogram baby colobus monkey. Whether shared among four hunters or fourteen, such a small package of meat does not provide anyone with much food.

Chimpanzees in Predator-Prey Systems

This hunting pattern and its potential effects on the colobus population are best illustrated by my observation of one of the largest colobus hunts in the thirty-four-year history of research at Gombe. On October 7, 1992, the Kasakela chimpanzees captured seven red colobus monkeys from my main study group of twenty-five animals. I had been following the colobus group that morning, when at 11:00 A.M. the pant-hoots of two chimpanzee foraging parties rang out at close range, coming from both north and south of the colobus group and me. The male colobus began to alarm-call, and females gathered up their babies. For several minutes, these two chimp parties called; then the calls converged and moved toward us. Clearly, two foraging parties had met, become one larger party, and were headed in the colobus' direction. For several suspenseful minutes, the colobus and I waited to learn whether the chimps would encounter us.

Minutes later the vanguard of the chimp party arrived, a male named Beethoven and several of the adult females and their offspring. They were being followed that morning by two Tanzanian researchers, Msafiri Katoto and Bruno Herman. The colobus were wary and alarm calling, but such a small party was not a great risk to them. A minute later the main party arrived, with all twelve adult and adolescent males and many females and juveniles, thirty-three chimps in all. The hunt began, as usual, with Frodo climbing an emergent tree in which some of the colobus group was clustered, and for the next twenty minutes the trees shook, and the foliage crashed with the sounds of leaping and calling colobus and equally frenzied chimpanzee hunters. As the hunt progressed, I felt sure that the colobus would succeed in driving the chimpanzees away, but Frodo and the other males managed to scatter the male colobus, whereupon the rest of the group fled and became easy prey.

Just in front of me, a young colobus attempted to flee the chimpanzees by leaping onto a branch that unfortunately held a male chimp named Atlas. Atlas quickly grabbed the young colobus and dispatched it with a bite to the skull. Within seconds, an estrous female chimp named Trezia ran up to Atlas and begged for meat. Atlas held the colobus carcass away from her, and she then turned and presented her sexual swelling to him; they copulated, and only then did she receive a share of the meat. A few feet away, Beethoven had caught a young infant colobus and was engaging in identical behavior with the female chimpanzee Gremlin. The number of colobus killed, however, was difficult to know because after an hour, some chimpanzees were still hunting while others which had captured colobus sat on the ground over a fifty-yard circle eating and sharing meat.

My reaction to seeing "my" colobus being killed and eaten, one by one, before my eyes was initially excitement; I was in the unique position of observing a hunt and knowing both predators and prey as individuals. But when the final tally of colobus killed turned out to be seven, I realized that more than one-quarter of my main study group had just been eaten while I watched. Four hours later the chimpanzees finally finished their feast of colobus meat and the ensuing rest and socializing period and departed from the scene of the kill.

A hunt like this one does not occur often at Gombe; indeed, this was only the second seven-colobus kill observed in thirty-four years. But multiple kills of two or more colobus happen more frequently, twenty-one times in 1990 alone, illustrating the powerful influence chimpanzees may have as predators on the populations of prey animals within their hunting range. I estimate that from 1990 through 1993, the colobus kills made by the male chimpanzee Frodo alone eliminated about 10 percent of the colobus monkeys in the home range of the Gombe chimps.

Effects of Chimp Predation on the Colobus Population

As this hunt reveals, one chimpanzee hunting party can decimate a group of red colobus in a matter of minutes. What is the likely long-term effect of intensive chimp predation on the colobus population? Using information on the size and age and sex of the red colobus group, combined with knowledge of the hunting patterns of Gombe chimps, it is possible to estimate the impact of predation on the colobus. Based on monitoring five groups over the past four years, plus censusing a number of other groups that occupy the eighteen square kilometers of the chimpanzees' hunting range, I estimate there are about 500 colobus (plus or minus 10 percent) in the area and that chimpanzees kill approximately 75 to 175 colobus annually. I base this figure on kills that have been observed, plus the expected number of kills per day when no one was watching in the forest. The annual mortality rate in the colobus population due to chimpanzee predation is thus between 15 and 35 percent, depending on the frequency of hunting that year.[24]

While 15 percent mortality due to predation has been recorded for other species of mammals, it must be remembered that this figure represents predation by chimpanzees only and does not include death at the hands of other predators (leopards and eagles inhabit Gombe and are known predators of monkeys) or mortality due to disease, infanticide, or other factors. A 35 percent mortality rate would mean, if it happened every year, that the red colobus population would almost certainly be in sharp decline. The interpretation is that the average annual mortality due to chimp predation, taken over the past decade, is about 20 percent of the colobus population.[25]

To understand the impact of this mortality on the colobus, it is important to consider certain characteristics of the monkey population. First, female colobus appear to give birth about every two years, and births occur in every month of the year. Since chimpanzees prey mainly upon young colobus (under two years old), female colobus that lose a baby to chimpanzee hunters can begin cycling again soon afterward and produce a new offspring as soon as seven months later. These two facts—lack of breeding seasonality and mortality of immatures rather than adult animals—may well minimize the impact of predation on the colobus because a single infant lost is more quickly replaced than an older offspring or adult.

To learn whether chimpanzee predation has the potential to be a limiting factor in the size of the colobus population at Gombe, I compared the intensity of hunting by chimpanzees with the size of red colobus groups in each of the valleys of the chimpanzees' hunting range. The central region of the chimpanzees' range (their so-called core area) is Kakombe Valley; the chimps made about one-third of all their hunts there over the past decade. As one travels away from the center and toward the northern and southern borders of the chimpanzees' range, they use the more peripheral valleys much less frequently, and they also hunt less there. Only about 3 percent of all hunts take place at the northern and southern edges of their range.

I found that the size of red colobus groups also varied over the area of the chimps' hunting range. In the core region, red colobus groups averaged only nineteen animals, little more than half the average of about thirty-four at the outer boundaries.[26] In other words, colobus groups are small where they are hunted frequently, and larger where hunting is infrequent. Moreover, I found that this size variation was due largely to the different number of immature colobus in core-area and peripheral groups. In the core area, only 17 percent of each group were infants and juveniles, while fully 40 percent of peripheral groups were immature. This is a direct demonstration of the power of predation to limit both group and population size in a wild primate population. From now on, we must consider the possibility that, in addition to their other interesting traits, chimpanzees may be among the most important predators on certain prey species in the African ecosystems where they live.

Chimpanzee Hunting Behavior and Early Hominid Evolution

Did early hominids hunt and eat meat in a pattern similar to the one described for wild chimpanzees? It is quite probable that they did. Recent discoveries in Ethiopia by Tim White, Gen Suwa, and Berhane Asfaw of the fossil remains of very early australopithecines (*Australopithecus ramidus*) show that 4.4 million years ago primitive hominids lived in a forest environment that they shared with colobus monkeys and small antelope. *A. ramidus* were different from chimpanzees in two prominent anatomical features: they had much smaller canine teeth and a lower body adapted for walking on the ground rather than swinging though trees. They almost certainly continued to use trees, however, for nighttime shelter and daytime fruit gathering, as do modern ground-living primates such as baboons. In spite of lacking the large canine teeth and tree-climbing adaptations that chimpanzees possess, early hominids probably ate a great number of small and medium-sized animals, including monkeys. Large canine teeth are not necessarily important for carnivory; chimpanzees do not use their canine teeth to capture adult colobus; rather, they grab the prey and flail it to death on the ground or against a tree limb. The chimpanzees' superb climbing ability is not essential for hunting monkeys, either; once the prey is cornered in an isolated tree crown, group cooperation at driving the monkeys from one hunter to another makes a quite-efficient killing technique.

In addition to prey available in the trees, there were of course both large and small animals to find or capture on the ground. Many researchers now believe that the carcasses of large mammals were an important source of meat for early hominids once they had stone tools to remove the flesh from the carcass.[27] But the evidence for stone tools dates to only 2.5 million years ago. For the 3 or so million years of human evolution prior to that time, did our ancestors eat meat? Many researchers feel sure that they did, though the amount and frequency of meat eating are open to conjecture.

Blumenschine, for example, showed that a scavenging niche was probably available to early hominids during the Pliocene period,[28] and Marean reasoned that the presence of saber-toothed cats meant there was a ready supply of large ungulate carcasses from which flesh could be gleaned.[29] Speth, while showing that meat eating in early hominids was probably seasonal, also acknowledged that evidence of stone tools in the fossil record may indicate that meat was eaten only irregularly or infrequently during periods of drought or food scarcity.[30] While scavenging is a frequently posited mode of getting meat by our ancestors, wild chimpanzees (particularly the males who do most of the hunting) show little interest in dead animals as a food source, so scavenging may have evolved as an important method of getting food as hominids began to make and use tools. Before this time, it seems likely that earlier hominids hunted mammals as chimpanzees do today, and the role that hunting played in the early hominids' social lives was probably as complex and politically charged as it is with chimpanzees. These early hominids may have been important predators in Pliocene forest ecosystems.

When we ask the question, "When did meat become an important part of the human diet?" we must therefore look well before the evolutionary split between apes and humans in our own family tree. We study great apes not because we assume our ancestors were just like apes are today but because apes are a reality check about the likeliest range of possible adaptations in our earliest ancestors. They provide us with a window available nowhere else. They are our evolutionary cousins, cut from the same cloth, with a history that diverged from ours some six million years ago.

Why Dogs Stopped Flying

Ken Brewer

Before humans, dogs flew everywhere.
Their wings of silky fur wrapped hollow bones.
Their tails wagged like rudders through wind,
their stomachs bare to the sullen earth.

Out of sorrow for the first humans—
stumbling, crawling, helpless and cold—
dogs folded their great wings into paws
soft enough to walk beside us forever.

They still weep for us, pity our small noses,
our unfortunate eyes, our dull teeth.
They lick our faces clean,
keep us warm at night.
Sometimes they remember flying
and bite our ugly hands.

How Science and the Public Can Lead to Better Decision Making in Earth System Management

Hartmut Grassl

Hartmut Grassl is a member of the Max-Planck-Institute für Meteorologie in Hamburg. His publications include We Climate-Makers: Escape Routes from the Global Greenhouse *and "Radiation in Polluted Atmospheres and in Clouds," and he is the coauthor of* Climate of the 21st Century: Changes and Risks.

My title is very much in line with my belief that the public must be educated and engaged in international debates surrounding global environmental issues, particularly climate change. I see a major difference emerging that separates both sides of the Atlantic when dealing with global change: Europeans have assumed nominal leadership, while the United States has remained inactive. Europe has not actively sought this leadership role, but rather it has been imposed upon her by virtue of the United States' refusal to assume the responsibility that logically falls to it. This represents a significant transfer of leadership.

A logical procedure, then, is to address environmental trends now visible in the global community and their potential consequences. First of all, I want to look at the reaction by scientists, specifically how they have created global-change research programs, as well as the responses so far expressed by society. At this point, I would have to say that public awareness is slowly rising—I would emphasize the "slow" aspect. Then I will discuss the ideal structure for a productive societal debate on global change. Here I will focus special attention on the ways the scientific view of reality conflicts with political and social realities. I will conclude by both proposing steps for improved communication and recommending structural changes.

I was the director of the World Climate Research Program from 1994 to 1999, and I realized while in this position how important effective administrative structures are. This program is very successful, mainly because of its organizational structure, not its individual directors. It engages thousands of scientists worldwide in large part because it is supported by United Nations agencies and a very big nongovernment organization called the

Council for Science; this broad support makes our organization attractive to the scientific community and those around the globe who are responsible for managing public services tied to environmental change. This combination of services plus scientific communities leads to a successful program. That is why I will be emphasizing the need for the sorts of structural change that can bring the environmental debate forward through entities like the United Nations. I will provide examples of how this work has already begun to advance, and then I will speculate about the prospects for a major environmental summit in Johannesburg.

Your country has not yet energetically participated in the debates to take place at Johannesburg, and some of you may not know what I'm referring to. Johannesburg is the World Summit for Sustainable Development scheduled to take place in August and September of 2002. The entire world, with the probable exception of the United States, is looking forward to this conference. We view it as an opportunity to advise governments about the way they should deal with those parts of the environmental debate where little progress has occurred over the ten-year period since the last summit.

Let me now address the most pressing anthropogenic environmental trends. One is the increase in greenhouse gases; the other is a loss of biodiversity that is a byproduct of atmospheric change. The increase in greenhouse gases is just one of a handful of major trends, but it is the biggest, and I put it on top. The loss of biodiversity is more serious than all the other effects because if we extinguish certain species, then we have to wait millions of years until the niches they inhabited in various ecosystems are once again filled. This is extreme long-term damage.

A second point, the degradation and loss of soils, is also a long-term problem that will persist beyond fluctuations in greenhouse gases. Through our continued burning of fossil fuels, we destroy fuel-producing soils that have built up over ten thousand years in some places, twenty thousand in others. And I have heard that you had a mud rain here in Utah recently, a phenomenon that I do not believe occurs naturally in this region very frequently. This is an anthropogenic, or anthropogenically influenced, phenomenon because of the desertification process going on in your country due to counterproductive agricultural practices.

A third point, changed atmospheric composition, has already led to four global effects. Nearly all citizens worldwide know the first two; these are enhanced greenhouse effects and increases in photochemical smog. Increases in greenhouse gasses translate as global warming and stratospheric ozone depletion, which has contributed to a major debate in the United States because Americans are very scared about cancer. With good reason. Skin cancers will indeed increase when we further deplete stratospheric ozone. Photochemical smog has become a global concern as we in the developed countries of Europe deliver it into eastern Europe and central Asia. You in North America similarly deliver photochemical smog to us in Europe during the winter months. Loss of biodiversity, changes in soil composition, and biochemical fog have become global phenomena now because of the abundant production of nitrogen oxides and hydrocarbons.

Enhanced stability in acid deposition is also a serious global concern. This particular debate has calmed down in the United States and partly in Europe because of governmental measures to reduce destructive emissions, but if you go to China and India, you will discover a very serious persistence of acid deposition that is negatively influencing the entire continent.

Pollution by ecotoxicological compounds represents a fourth atmospheric change that deserves serious attention worldwide. Many countries choose to ignore this problem, but if you investigate the meat of the penguins in the Antarctic, you will discover evidence of nearly all the pesticides used in the Northern Hemisphere. These pesticides are long-lived, and their destructive influence will persist. We already have evidence of their impact on wildlife in many places, even inside our national parks.

Now to the consequences, and here I mean *observed consequences.* I am not primarily concerned with potential consequences. If you pile up what we have observed already, you realize how much alteration has already taken place and how many people are now suffering from global environmental change. And those who are suffering most are by and large not the population responsible for having caused the problem. This is a major international debate. Can you imagine what it means for an Indian—not an American Indian, but an Asian Indian—if the United States withdraws from the Kyoto Protocol? An average Indian emits a volume of pollutants one-twentieth of that generated by an average American, yet the American president tells the Indian he should make the same sacrifices expected of Americans.

Let us now consider observed consequences:

- Recent global warming and the enhanced greenhouse effect. There is no doubt that part of this change results from actions taken in the developed world; whether all are from us is a matter of current debate—we may have caused even more change than we have yet detected, as acknowledged in the Intergovernmental Panel on Climate Change report. We don't know the exact extent of the change because natural variability is large and not fully understood. We do know that we have intensified precipitation. Scientists in your country were the first to detect such change over the United States. This is, for a physicist like me, a "no-brainer." If surface temperatures warm, there is more water vapor per unit volume in the atmosphere; and if at the same time the vertical speed remains constant, there must be more intense rain. This is an entirely natural phenomenon. Everybody knows there is more concentrated precipitation per storm in summertime than wintertime.

- Higher UVB (ultraviolet B) levels on Earth's surface. This development has eradicated what used to be the gradient of UVB radiation in the Southern Hemisphere in late spring. On a sunny day, twenty-four-hour doses of ultraviolet B radiation are as high in southern Argentina as in tropical northern Australia. There is no difference because of the influence of the Antarctic ozone hole.

- Reduction in agricultural yields. Photochemical smog is dangerous for agriculture because crop yields are reduced. This has been shown in several countries. But at the same time, if we look around the world, we discover increased yields in many places due to indirect fertilization by CO_2. If a farmer gives enough fertilizer and water to his crop, he will have high yields simply because of an enhanced carbon dioxide concentration in the atmosphere, provided he raises plants like wheat and sugar beets. When farmers plant maize or sorghum, this is not the case because these plants do not react as strongly to enhanced CO_2 fertilization.

- Acidification of soil and inland waters. This was once a burning problem for the United States and Scandinavia, but it is not so great a problem now because of measures these countries have taken to reduce sulfur dioxide and nitrogen oxide emissions.

- Changes in ecosystem composition. This topic is totally neglected in public discourse. If you have plants reacting differently to CO_2 and you enhance the concentration of CO_2, the competition among plants alters, and the ecosystem composition must change. Colleagues in several parts of Switzerland have documented this change.

- Coastal erosion. Approximately 80 to 90 percent of all coasts presently experience erosion because the sea level is rising. If there were no rise in the sea level, we would have almost no coastal erosion because of naturally occurring deposits that build up along coastlines. If the rate of sea level rise is small or stagnant, then we have a buildup of coastlines, not erosion.

- Frequent melting of permafrost. This is clearly visible in Alaska and Siberia, and it poses major problems for the Siberians because they do not have the money to reconstruct houses and roads. For countries like the United States, this is not a major problem because they can divert a percentage of the gross national product to Alaska and absorb the reconstruction expenses. This is not the case for the Siberians.

- Habitat fragmentation and destruction. Soil degradation and increased land use are the main causes, which comes back to the point I made earlier about biodiversity loss. As far as potential consequences go, I have listed only three items here, though I could expand the list to five, six, or seven.
- Changed ocean conveyor belt. This is a hot topic, but it is only a hypothesis because we scientists are not able to prove by measurements that change has actually taken place; we are not yet able to observe continuously the interior of the Atlantic. Only recently, during the World Ocean Circulation Experiment, a project of the World Climate Research Program, was the first survey attempted with the aim of monitoring the entire world ocean. The United States was very, very active in this project, and now there is an emerging new observation system for oceanographers, within which NOAA plays a key role. We will soon have a fully developed observation system, but until then we can proceed on hypothesis only. How do we at this time explain such developments as the stasis of deep water within the deepest reaches of the north Atlantic—a development that has in the past occurred only when we had major changes in ice: melting or surges. Now there is not enough ice on the globe to create this dynamic. If the so-called Gulf Stream should stop, we would need another physical mechanism—a redistribution of fresh water, perhaps. But I repeat, such speculation is purely a hypothesis; it is not proven.
- Many new weather extremes. This is a giant response to all these trends and may be viewed as an obvious outcome. If we change the distribution function—shift it, broaden it, or narrow it—we will produce extremes. If we narrow the distribution function, we will reduce the probability for extremes. In the case of precipitation, we see that distribution has broadened, so we have on both sides new extremes; droughts extend for longer periods, as do periods of intense precipitation. But as this is not true for all global regions, we have to look carefully at those places where it is happening. In the United States, where the best evaluations were formulated quite early, increases in flash flooding are easily observed.
- Spreading of infectious diseases. Studies have demonstrated the spread of diseases in Africa, where measures like those taken against malaria are normally inadequate and natural boundaries to epidemics develop slowly. Here in your country, boundaries restricting the spread of malaria are in place. Why don't you have malaria? Because the health system takes measures against it; but in countries where such measures do not exist, there have been major changes in the spread of infectious diseases.

Just over a year ago, I was invited to the so-called Amsterdam Conference—the conference held last July for all the global-change research programs—to talk on water, especially projected precipitation changes caused by further global warming. Scientists now know that global rainfall averages are increasing because of an intensified water cycle. Scientists rate this knowledge under the category "we are certain." But how does my stating we will have greater rainfall globally help you in Utah? It will not necessarily be of much immediate value. You may be in an area where rainfall has actually declined because of circulation changes. The current global trend is for more rain in humid and subhumid areas, with the most significant increases in high northern latitudes. A good example of this is Norway. Despite strong warming in Norway, some of the mountain glaciers now reach the forest again because wintertime precipitation has increased by 30 to 40 percent during the twentieth century. Now there is so much snow per winter that even higher temperatures in summer and winter cannot melt it sufficiently to compete with the precipitation increase, so the glaciers advance.

In the Alps, where we have nearly stable precipitation but higher temperatures, we have a massive decline of glacierized areas. Strange as it may seem, in many semiarid or arid areas, the intensification of the water cycle can lead already dry areas to become even drier. Intense precipitation in areas with historically stable or slightly decreasing annual rates can lead to an increase in flash floods and higher erosion rates. This is a major threat for a country like China. I was recently in China, and I saw the countermeasures taken against sandstorms and desertification. In preparation for the 2008 Olympic Games, for instance, the Chinese want to plant a forest around Beijing. They have already started to reforest vast swaths of land in a tremendous attempt; not tens of thousands but hundreds of thousands of people are working against desertification. At the same time, however, the increasing numbers of farmers in inner Mongolia, which is an outermost province of China, have greatly expanded the number of cashmere goats (China is the main exporter of cashmere wool). And these goats start the sandstorms because they don't just eat the grass but deroot it. And we saw the effects of this practice when we were suddenly halted in just such a sandstorm.

Next in my list is the first response taken by the scientific community. When the question arose as to whether or not humans influence global climate, the World Meteorological Organization (WMO), jointly with the International Council for Science, called for the creation of relevant scientific unions, starting with the World Climate Research Program in 1980. In 1986 the International Geosphere-Biosphere program was created. In 1992 Diversitus was established to deal specifically with biodiversity on our planet, and in 1996 the International Human Dimensions Program on Global Environmental Change (IHDP) came into existence. And I would be pleasantly surprised if I learned that more than a handful of readers of this essay have ever even heard of these last two environmental programs. Doesn't this tell us a story? We are absolutely failing in our twin obligations to communicate major topics and ask for enough money to build the infrastructure capable of coordinating international research programs. In this context, your country plays a key role. Yours is the only country that could in principle work without the cooperation of the others because you are large enough and sufficiently developed. Much to my disappointment, I learned when I was director for the World Climate Research Program that the major research nations do not consider it productive to deal with international programs because they can manage to a large extent by themselves. But even the smaller countries are not integrated to the extent which I would like to see. For example, Austria, Germany's neighboring country, is all but absent from most of these international programs.

Fortunately, despite these disappointments, the World Climate Research Program has many success stories. Our infrastructure is solid and old enough to produce some valuable breakthroughs, like El Nino prediction or the first survey of global ocean circulation. The IHDP has also enjoyed some major successes; for example, the creation of a CO_2 flux net now operating on all continents. It is still not dense enough, but it marks the beginning of an important future observation system built entirely from research money. For this achievement, infrastructure has been critical. Diversitus lost out because of lack of infrastructure. Even though one of the funding sources is UNESCO, a huge organization, funds sufficient to support one full position working for Diversitus could not be generated. Now several countries have taken action to create an infrastructure in Paris. It is starting. Yet ten years after the creation of the program, we still have no real infrastructure for it. IHDP represents a good start, but it is still not fully accepted in all social-science communities. Natural-science communities are eager to participate in these international programs, but the social sciences are still not in the position to cooperate as strongly as the meteorologists have done for a long time. It is worth noting, however, that the meteorologists are forced to become involved because of one single geophysical parameter: the high speed of air five kilometers above our heads.

Perhaps the best example of this more or less compulsory cooperation came about as a result of the devastation by Lothar, a storm that hit Europe on the 26 December 1999. This catastrophic storm wreaked havoc on France, southern Germany, and Switzerland, producing the highest winds ever measured, but it did not appear in the German Meteorological Service forecast because of the lack of a single radiosonde measurement from Sable Island in Canada. The team on Sable Island had to restart the radiosonde because the first one, attempted under very severe conditions, did not work. The German Meteorological Service was therefore not in a position to note this later broadcast, but the French and the British were, and they successfully forecast the storm. This indicates the time-sensitive nature of weather forecasting: predicting a storm for tomorrow afternoon requires a measurement taken three or four thousand kilometers away in the western part of the Atlantic from an island off the coast of Canada. Meteorologists cooperate because they must, not because they possess superior characters.

Now the reaction by society. What has society done after learning about all the global-change problems? We see a slowly rising awareness of global responsibility, but only in Organization for Economic Cooperation and Development (OECD) countries and in most cases only in a minority of the population that does not extend to the seats of government. I am a European, so I should bash Europeans first. Looking to our southern neighbors, the Spanish, I can quickly see that they have other problems that take priority, despite the fact that they suffer strongly from desertification and a change in the North Atlantic oscillation. Global change is not an important topic for them, but for Scandinavians, the Dutch, the Germans, and the British, it is.

One serious impediment to a more active European response is a misguided early statement. We suffer from the slogan coined by environmentalists in the late sixties and early seventies which said that environmental protection requires a reduced living standard. This misperception still hampers the progress in environmental methods. *We have seen instead that technical innovation plays a key role for environmentally less-damaging lifestyles while supporting a rising standard of living.*

I can give you some examples that convey the different approaches adopted on both sides of the Atlantic:

- In European public buildings, florescent bulbs for lighting are nearly obligatory, while this environmental measure is progressing slowly in the United States, either because you have more energy or you believe you can acquire more energy.
- In Europe, natural gas is replacing coal. This was a major event for the British, who have reduced CO_2 emissions over the entire country by 6 to 7 percent since the 1990s just because they said coal was too expensive. Low-energy houses are no longer more costly. You can build a new house with one-third of the energy consumption of the standard American home and spend no more than you would pay for a less efficient home. I don't know how the prices are here; efficient homes may still be more costly.

- In Europe, CFC-free refrigerators and freezers were pushed by environmental groups, not by governments. Greenpeace created the first CFC-free refrigerator in cooperation with a company in Dresden, Germany, and now it's delivered on a global scale.
- Wind power is booming in Europe. During a typical windy night, there is at present surplus electric current. What is done with the surplus? Because we have what are called "feed-in laws," all current flows into the grid and hydropower plants in Sweden are directed to stop production when available current exceeds demand. The plants tell each other to stop because when the wind blows, they get less money per kilowatt-hour. So two renewable sources of energy "shake hands" in Europe.
- Fuel-cell cars driven by hydrogen from solar power are about to emerge in Europe. In a year or two, we will have the first examples on our roads from European and American companies. There is very strong competition among Chrysler, BMW, and Ford. They want to be the first with these cars on our roads.

What, then, is the most appropriate structure for the current societal debate on global change? First, we must agree to pursue the ideal even though we will never succeed in reaching it. Seeking the ideal is the way we do things on our planet. All our policy making, all our organization in life, is directed to approximating an ideal. In science, we need the ideal to assess new findings and determine which old and new questions to keep open. And here I see a major difference between my country and the United States. Our government would never invite only two or three scientists to a hearing before a Senate committee. The German government always consults multiple representative groups because when you are making decisions as a politician, you should base them on the best available information, and you get that type of feedback from independent groups. You don't get balanced information from those who are very near to your party.

Society should have a debate that includes representatives from all sectors, not just environmental groups, not just churches, not just the media, but a combination of all interests. We of the highly developed countries are a minority on the globe. From the point of view of the number of heads we possess, we are a real minority. And we have to deal with the Indians, the Chinese. They are the majority, and OECD countries often forget this fact.

Decision makers should be open minded. We say in Germany that we scientists have an honorable duty to serve the public. We have to tell the policy makers what we know, but they have the duty of accepting what we tell them. And both sides have to cooperate. The scientists must tell what they know, the politicians must accept what they hear, and together they must place the debate before society.

Productive innovation must take environmental concerns into account. When you create new equipment, you should not just look at your consumer; you must at the same time ask how it affects the environment. In some countries, incentives have been useful, such as offering reduced tax rates for lower levels of pollution. Unfortunately, many countries still provide a subsidy for fossil fuels. Take the Germans. We subsidize our own coal industry to the tune of three billion euros per year. This amount is declining, but we still underwrite fossil fuel. Can you imagine such a thing existing in the country that at the same time has the feed-in law, whereby any kilowatt-hour from wind and biogas has to go into the grid? Conversely, our coal-fired power plants don't pay taxes at all but rather receive three billion euros per year.

More than anything else, we must establish an agreed-upon, long-term global debate about earth system management. But perhaps you don't agree with the phrase "earth system management." I know many environmental groups that have a difficult time accepting earth system management in spite of the fact that the concept has been proven in practice. What have we done to protect the ozone layer? We have used earth system management. We found out through science what the causes of ozone depletion were, and we motivated nations to act in a global manner. This is earth system management. The Kyoto Protocol is the next attempt at earth system management. If you understand the problem, then you know what to do. At present, scientific understanding is too rudimentary to provide clear advice about how to reduce emissions. At present as scientists, we can say, "Yes, that is due to emissions," but then nations have to reduce, and the level of required reduction is debatable until the facts are in.

Think again about the meteorologists. There will soon be a very major debate over where the butterflies are. Science is good enough now to forecast weather as far as six, eight, or even nine days in advance. Computers are big enough to have so-called ensemble forecasts. So you start your model sixty-four times with slightly changed fields and then see how the forecasts deviate from each other. You will see in days three or four that there must be something happening in the near future because the forecasts diverge largely. If you run the program again and again with new information, you may find the place where additional observations are needed to distinguish between diverging forecasts. If you find this place, you then send an airplane to specific drop zones where more precise data is gathered, enabling you to revise the forecasts and conclude with confidence, "Okay, it's going this way." Isn't this a place where all people will go to find the wings of the butterfly? To slightly change the cloud cover and then let the hurricane go to Cuba instead of Florida? This may sound like an absurd overstatement, but there will soon be a debate requiring international agreements to prevent precisely these sorts of efforts.

Now the reality. Reality in science is only partially organized. The Intergovernmental Panel on Climate Change is a good example. We have no international panels for land and soils which would help combat desertification. Neither is there an intergovernmental panel on biodiversity. So these trends are not studied. We have no authoritative procedure to assess knowledge. Society suffers from both a lack of information and a reluctance to accept the knowledge it does have. Poorer countries are not normally interested in the debate we are having today. Churches are often indifferent; they could have an influence on the people, but they are for the most part not interested in addressing global change.

When it comes to decision makers, you can view Gerhard Schroder the same way you view George W. Bush: both are occupied by crisis management partly caused by neglect of global change. And lobbyists use their resources to launch disinformation campaigns. This is the typical setting. We will not avoid this, but we can exert counterpressure through sound information. This can be an effective strategy because our politicians make decisions when they see that there is sufficient minority public opinion to override the pressure mounted by lobbyists. In Germany, we witnessed a wonderful example of how this works when our government had to react to ozone depletion. This came about because conservative climatologists, among them Herman Flown, the famous German climatologist, and my colleague, Klaus Hasselman, all signed a pamphlet produced by Greenpeace and the largest environmental-protection group in Germany. Only then did the politicians agree that something must be going on; why else would these old guys sign a pamphlet produced by Greenpeace? And from this day on, the government attitude toward the chlorofluorocarbon phaseout changed dramatically.

How to improve the international response to global change? We need structural changes, as I have said, as well as international political cooperation. For this to happen, we must have international assessment agencies, as well as an environmental organization in the United Nations. At present, we have a program that is extremely unstable because it is entirely dependent on donations. For example, in March 2001 the wealthy nation Austria withdrew its support for the United Nations Environmental Program (UNEP), provoking its executive director to ask me, "What shall I do now? I have to lay people off." He is uncertain what money he will receive to fund his already-understaffed operation. Four hundred people are simply not enough to run a global environmental program. We need an environmental organization that receives payments from member countries the same way that the WMO does. In the WMO, if a country doesn't pay, it loses its voting rights. Can you imagine how the money flows in before the meteorological congress? This is the only way for a strong organization to exist.

Scientists also have responsibilities. We have to provide solid research information according to four categories of certainty: "We know"; "We calculate with confidence"; "Our best judgment is"; and "We do not know." We always have to give all four parts. Normally we start with "we calculate with confidence" and "our best judgment is." We skip the last one and the first one, but the politicians need to know what we know in a form that enables them to make informed decisions.

Finally, we must engage positively and productively with the media. I have been working to make scientific knowledge available to the public since 1986, and in the years since then, I have gathered valuable experience. My advice to scientists is to avoid specialized environmental venues. Environmentalists are already on board. Try to get onto popular TV shows watched by millions of people. Then you stand a chance of reaching the public. Set up interviews on TV, the radio, through the newspapers, and on good Web sites. There is indeed a lot to do, but you need not fear your involvement will demand all of your time. I'm giving about one-third of my entire time to public relations, like talking to the German Advisory Council for the government. I see giving advice to the government as a significant public-relations activity. And I also speak to associations of housewives in small counties throughout Germany. If I can squeeze it in, I do that because the housewives are more thankful for good information than the bosses of industry.

Martha   (1 September 1914)

Ken Brewer

—for Jennifer Price

Ectopistes migratorius Martha,
you were the last of billions,
of flocks big as cities.
You could fly 60 miles an hour.

How many shotgun shells
did it take to kill
a billion passenger pigeons?
And when we tied captured birds
upon stools to lure others,
why did we sew shut their eyes?

What did you see last, Martha?
That September sky of Cincinnati?
Or the human hand that
picked up your feathered body,
kept it on ice for the taxidermist?

In that morning light
the back of your neck
flickered from bronze to green.
Your slate-blue head, black bill,
pale cinnamon throat, white abdomen,
red iris, red legs, red feet—
Martha, you must have been
some sweet pigeon.

What Is the L.A. River?

Jennifer Price

Jennifer Price, environmental historian and freelance writer, is the author of Flight Maps: Adventures with Nature in Modern America. *She has published in the anthologies* Uncommon Ground: Rethinking the Human Place in Nature *and* The Nature of Nature: New Essays from America's Finest Writers on Nature, *and in the* L.A. Weekly, Los Angeles Times, American Scholar, *and* New York Times. *An earlier version of this piece was published in the* L.A. Weekly.

Los Angeles is gathering at the river.

What is the L.A. River? For decades, that was Angelenos' most common question about it. But during the last few years, as the movement to restore the river has accelerated faster than winter rains down the canyons, the river has reemerged on the city's mental map. At least, even if many people can't tell you where L.A.'s major river is, they know it exists. At most, the restoration efforts show that how visible you make nature in a city, as well as how well or poorly you manage nature, entails huge consequences for the quality and equality of urban life. At best, the tale of the L.A. River calls to nature writers to come to the cities where most Americans live, to see nature in these places, and to write nature newly into the American urban imagination.

What is the L.A. River? It is the river whose story tells the story of L.A.

The L.A. River is a central natural fact of L.A.

L.A. is a river basin. Just look up at L.A.'s mountains, and you can see that they have to shed water downhill. The river is fifty-one miles long and drains huge sectors of the Santa Monica, Santa Susana, and San Gabriel Mountains. The San Gabriel and Santa Ana Rivers flow through the L.A. basin, too, but the L.A. River swings through its heart—east across the entire San Fernando Valley, around the northeast shoulder of Griffith Park, and then due south through downtown and southeast L.A. into the harbor at Long Beach. The river few Angelenos can locate exactly crosses the 405, 101, 134, 2, 110, 5, 10, 105, 710, and 91 freeways and the Pacific Coast

60

Highway. Van Nuys, North Hollywood, Glendale, Boyle Heights, Vernon, Cudahy, and Long Beach all sit right on it, as do Union Station and China-town, and Universal, Warner Bros., CBS, and DreamWorks. The river flows through eleven cities in L.A. County and joins them all together in one watershed. To say L.A. has no center is a longtime act of denial.

The L.A. River is where L.A. was founded.

In 1781 the settlers from Mexico founded El Pueblo de Los Ange-les, not by the emerald Pacific Ocean or in the cool mountain air, but by the basin's most plentiful year-round freshwater supply, on the L.A. River at its confluence with the Arroyo Seco. In today's preferred navigational lingo, that's the 5/110 freeway interchange north of downtown. A lush forest of sycamores and cottonwoods lined the riverbanks, and willows choked the floodplain; big patches in the future Valley and South and West L.A. were wetlands. The city spread and leapt outward from its original spot: now, on a map of the county, it's that chaos downtown where all the freeways meet and tangle up. L.A. used the river as its major source of drinking and ir-rigation water (and its major sewage dump) for 120 years; it was only after 1900, when the city outgrew its river's water supply, that L.A. went pillag-ing for water in other watersheds. The river itself stayed put. It was polluted and pumped almost dry. But it was hardly forgotten because

The L.A. River is the most destructively flood-prone river in an American city.

Mark Twain wrote that he fell into a Southern California river and "came out all dusty." True, the river is not startlingly wet most of the year and can be seasonally dry in spots. Yet it drops 795 feet from its headwaters in Canoga Park to its mouth in Long Beach—190 feet more than the Mississippi drops in 2,350 miles from Minnesota to the Gulf of Mexico. The San Gabriel peaks rise over seven thousand feet, and during storms all three mountain ranges send torrential rains cascading direct-ly toward L.A. The crescent of land L.A. sits on can hold a megalopolis, but it's small for a river drainage. If you want to build a city in this basin—and pave over hundreds of square miles of it with impermeable surfaces—you need a plan to control floods. But what sort of plan?

The L.A. River is the most monumental public-works project in the West.

Well, you could restrict development near the river and divert floodwaters into a network of wetlands and detention basins. Or you could

squeeze the river into a concrete box. In 1938, after a series of the most
devastating floods in the city's history, the U.S. Army Corps of Engineers
expanded L.A.'s own concrete inclinations into a flood-control plan of
maximum New Deal technodreamer verve. The corps bulldozed all the
vegetation, dug the box, and straightened the river into it. This took twenty
years, with an extra ten to finish boxes for the Arroyo Seco, Tujunga Wash,
Rio Hondo, and other feeders, many of which hadn't had fixed channels
before. And eventually the county fenced the boxes off with barbed wire
and posted No Trespassing signs.

The L.A. River is one of the worst in L.A.'s long line of missed opportunities.

In 1930 the Chamber of Commerce buried a parks plan it had
commissioned from a famed team of landscape architects, the Olmsted
Brothers and Harlan Bartholomew and Associates, to respond to L.A.'s crisis of overdevelopment—the erasure of all but 1 percent of open space and
all but .59 percent outside the mountains. That beautifully ambitious plan
prescribed a wide L.A. River greenway to create parks, enhance recreation
and scenery, and absorb floodwaters. Characteristically, civic leaders instead chose a plan that made the river safe for new suburbs, freeways, and
industry within an inch of its banks—that defied ecological sense and privileged unbridled private development over public space. At a crossroads,
the U.S. city with the worst shortage of park space per capita—and perhaps
the most beautiful natural setting—turned one of its most obvious sites
for green space into a parks-free zone. A city that constructed 250- to 350-
mile aqueducts to import water turned its river into a chute that would rid
the basin of its water as fast as possible. And a city prone to carving up its
neighborhoods turned its major connective artery into a no man's land.

The L.A. River is the country's most degraded river.

A city with mounting pollution crises also engineered a new sort
of river basin where things could wash into but not out of the river—in
other words, a superbly screwed-up watershed. While the concrete box pre-
vented the river from replenishing soils with nutrients, beaches with sand,
and the aquifer with water, the county's storm-drain network emptied into
the river and its concrete tributaries. If everyone in L.A. knows that the
drains carry sewage to the ocean—which forces the unfortunate and un-
ending beach closures—many fewer realize that the L.A. River, as the central
storm-drain artery, collects trash, motor oil, human and animal feces, her-
bicides, and the hundreds more pollutants in your basic City-America-2000

toxic street stew from across a densely populated, 834-square-mile watershed and expresses it to the Pacific. People in L.A. may not know where their river is, but their lawn-care products and bits of brake linings from their BMWs and Toyotas wash into it all the time. Of course, the concrete also obliterated wildlife habitat. Fish, frogs, and birds disappeared, and steelhead trout ceased to use the river to spawn.

> The L.A. River is arguably the most extraordinary river in the United States.

In a final semantic move, the county rechristened the river the Los Angeles River Flood Control Channel and referred to it as either the Flood Control Channel or the Storm Control System. Now the Mississippi contains extraordinary volumes of water—it could float the *QE2*—and a number of other rivers rival ours for wondrous ecological ruin: in 1969 the Cuyahoga River in Cleveland was so polluted that it caught fire. What makes the L.A. River so peerlessly amazing is that its city actively "disappeared" it: we stopped calling the river a river. And it all but vanished from our collective memory. U.S. cities tended to ignore and abuse their rivers as their industrial cores declined through the 1900s. Still, can you imagine anyone asking, "What is the Colorado River?" "What is the Hudson River?" This act is unparalleled: A major American city redefined its river as infrastructure, decreed that the sole purpose of a river is to control its own floods, and said its river now belongs in the same category as the electrical grid and the freeway system and will forthwith be removed from the company of the Columbia, the Allegheny, the Salmon. In a city with a notorious, extreme tendency to erase both nature and history, arguably L.A.'s ultimate act of erasure has been not just to forget but to *deny* that the river it was founded on runs fifty-one miles—fifty-one miles!—right through its heart.

> The L.A. River is a well-known joke, and a symbol of L.A.

By the 1960s, the L.A. River was a paradox: an infamous unknown river. How could you not laugh at a river with a concrete bed and without much water—easterners like Twain had laughed at the river's flow before—in a city that was supposed to be America's new Eden? It didn't help that the channel was an excellent place to film the sort of scene in which a cyborg Terminator flees on a motorcycle from a liquid-metal alien driving a tractor trailer. *Them!*, *Point Blank*, *Escape from New York*, *Repo Man*, *To Live and Die in L.A.*, *Point Break*, *Mi Familia*: the river has served as a film set for forty-five years of scenes of urban violence and utter alienation. With smog a close second, the greasy trickle in the quality-engineered DMZ between neighborhoods became the bleakest, most laughable symbol of everything gone wrong in L.A.

The L.A. River is a fifteen-year cause, fought with tenacity and vision.

As a flood-control solution, the concrete looked final; as a river, it looked unredeemable. So in 1985, when Lewis MacAdams, an artist and writer, took a few friends and a pair of wire cutters to the river's edge and vowed to resurrect it, the response was underwhelming. People asked, "What river?" "We asked the river," MacAdams says. "We didn't hear it say no." In 1986 they founded Friends of the L.A. River. The cause seemed zany but lovely. In 1990, after the chairman of the State Assembly Transportation Committee proposed to turn the channel into a truck freeway (but only during dry season), Mayor Tom Bradley appointed a task force on how to make the river *more* riverlike, not less. In 1991 FoLAR sponsored the first conference on restoration; the nineties would see three more. The county Board of Supervisors directed Public Works, Parks and Recreation, and Regional Planning to produce a master plan, which was published in 1996. The urban foresters North East Trees planted the first trees in 1994, the Santa Monica Mountains Conservancy and Trust for Public Land opened the first new park in 1995, and the city of L.A. opened the first new bikeway in 1997—all in the Glendale Narrows stretch north of downtown. Restoration began to draw two to three million dollars each year in state, county, and city funds. County Public Works itself, and even the U.S. Army Corps to some degree, joined the cause.

In 2000 this momentum took a quantum leap as state propositions 12 and 13 (for water and parks projects) sent eighty-two million dollars-plus the river's way, Speaker of the Assembly (and Proposition 12's author) Antonio Villaraigosa championed the river as L.A.'s number-one greening priority, and Senator Barbara Boxer stood on its banks and declared that she hoped to be able to kayak down it in the near future. In 2001 the astonishingly multiethnic, multiinterest Chinatown Yard Alliance wrested an obsolete Union Pacific rail yard in Chinatown from L.A. über-developer Majestic Realty, which planned a million square feet of industrial warehouses, and into the hands of California State Parks. Taylor Yard, a second, far-larger riverside rail yard to the north, quickly followed suit: the successful battles for these two sites marked a dramatic turning point for riverside land use. The concrete river has inspired the brand-new Rivers and Mountains Conservancy (the state's first urban conservancy), four large parks in the works, a plethora of smaller parks, new bikeways, art projects, and wetlands and water conservation.

The L.A. River is one of the city's most powerful loci for visions to make L.A. more livable.

Because it turns out that when you get people together to think about how to restore the river, the conversations quickly turn not to wild fantasies but to vital agendas. Want to restore the river? Okay, here's what you have to do.

1. Green the banks.
2. Clean the water.
3. Remove concrete, though not necessarily all of it—remember that the legendary Seine runs through Paris within a concrete channel.

As you talk about greening the banks, you're inevitably going to lament that fact that L.A., of all American cities, has the least park space per capita. Parks can be vital meeting and recreational spaces—which L.A. neighborhoods are so short on. They are walkable and bikeable spaces—which L.A. is terribly short on. Trees and other vegetation clean the air: We can use more of *that*. Soft ground drains rainwater back into the aquifer: northern California and every western state would be delighted. And just as the poorest urban communities generally suffer the worst environmental problems—and L.A. is an egregious offender and a hub for environmental-justice activism—the poorer, almost entirely nonwhite communities on the L.A. River in downtown and South L.A. are among the most carved up and park starved. Maywood, a tiny, very poor, largely Latino city in southeast L.A., has a scarce 0.8 percent of its land in parks. Boston has 9, New York City has 17, and the city of L.A. has 4. The generally affluent West L.A. has thirteen hundred park acres; Southeast L.A. has seventy-five.

How do you clean the water? What people dump into the river directly is the least of it. You have to strategize how to clean up the whole stew of pollutants that washes off lawns, roads, driveways, gas stations, and parking lots into the storm drains. You have to join the increasingly mainstream efforts—as the city of Santa Monica is doing—to find alternatives to the shelves and shelves of toxic products we all rely on and that wreak such damage on human health and on the city's air, water, and wildlife. And again the worst health problems—the dumps, the spills, the EPA superfund sites—are in the poorest communities.

Can you remove concrete? Is it possible? If you dare to pursue the most heretical and hard-fought goal, you need to control floods in the L.A. basin by . . . well, *how?* The central strategy is to reduce the volume of storm water in the channel. To start, capture and use more water on-site—L.A. shoots more than half the water it gets from the sky, for free, directly to the ocean (which is measurably less water starved). And it's not a trivial amount: by one estimate, a truly heavy winter storm can pelt L.A. with a year's water supply. Also, restore small patches of wetlands to hold and divert floods—which also renews the aquifer, filters and cleans the water, and restores wildlife habitat. And it's a smart idea to use less water, too. All of which, in turn, will reduce L.A.'s fabled thirst for the water imports that drain and damage watersheds in the Sierras and the Rockies.

In short: You have to build a fifty-one-mile greenway that can be the backbone of a basinwide network of greenbelts and bikeways; clean up hazardous threats to public health across half of L.A.; and restore the health of the river's watershed, which is a huge and essential step toward reversing two centuries of environmental devastation.

Even shorter: Restoring the L.A. River is about far more than the river. It's about L.A—and beyond.

The L.A. River has become a unifying force in L.A.

A lot of agendas meet on the river. That's logical since the river literally connects this fragmented megalopolis. It is one of the few things that do. And the campaign to restore the river makes connections among causes that too often remain separate—making clear why a green-space shortage is a social-justice issue, and why a big urban area still requires ecosystem management, and how vast economic inequities are also serious environmental problems. Like an antidote to partial blindness, the river makes visible these connections up and down the L.A. basin. If you want to build new parks in Maywood, it helps if you think about parks, habitat, flood control, community, lawn care, and water economics in Sherman Oaks in the Valley.

So the movement has forged, not surprisingly, a few of the city's more remarkable and wide-ranging coalitions. The Chinatown Yard Alliance brought together players including FoLAR, the Sierra Club, the Chinese Consolidated Benevolent Association, environmental-justice advocates Mothers of East Los Angeles, and the architects and planners of the Latino Urban Forum. The Los Angeles and San Gabriel Rivers Watershed Council, founded in 1998, brings dozens of stakeholders—water agencies, FoLAR, the mayor's office, cities north and south, the EPA, the nonprofit TreePeople, the U.S. Army Corps, County Public Works, the Forest Service—voluntarily to the same table to coordinate water-related projects in L.A. (and what isn't one?) and to work toward an integrated approach to sustainable watershed management. Like the council, the new Rivers and Mountains Conservancy, created to purchase, preserve, and improve lands for open space in the San Gabriel and lower L.A. River watersheds, joins disparate interests—city governments, environmentalists, water managers, county supervisors—that to anyone familiar with L.A. politics looks more like a recipe for a Molotov cocktail than a viable working alliance. All of these coalitions, however, have proved that they can make on-the-ground progress to reform L.A.'s worst habits.

The L.A. River could be a vital, beautiful urban river.

To resurrect it means to return it not to its past but to a state of health. A restored L.A. River would be an unapologetically urban river. Chicago, Portland, San Antonio, Denver, Milwaukee, New York, Cleveland: a growing number of cities are re-greening and cleaning up their rivers to redress the urban crises of health, environmental quality, and social cohesion that the twentieth century created. A fifty-one-mile rehab of such a devastated river will take two decades or more. But if L.A. succeeds, the river will be the "anything is possible" of a more sustainable L.A., and of river restoration and urban revitalization nationally.

In *Them!*—the 1954 sci-fi classic and the first film set in the concrete box—gargantuan mutant ants use the L.A. River's storm drains to stage an invasion of the rest of the world. For a sunnier metaphor, how about the 1997 *Volcano,* in which smart-thinking Angelenos guide the lava into the channel and the L.A. River saves the city? What is the L.A. River? Advocates for its restoration would like to turn it into a major social and environmental asset. A river that shows what a city can do with its river. A river that recreates the ultimate symbol of what's gone wrong in L.A. as a symbol of things done right. It's hard to imagine a swan in the social and ecological landscape of L.A., but the L.A. River, if restored to health, could be, in the future, an exceptionally lovely duck.

The River Blind

Ken Brewer

Before sunrise,
he gathers thin
dead branches,
pokes them upright
in the mud
among the reeds.

He strings brown
camouflage netting
along the stick points,
then drapes his pack,
guncase, thermos.

He kneels at the edge
of the river and waits.
He calls across the water,
listens for the heavy wings
of the dark angel he would kill.

And the angel flies
from the eye of the sun
to where the hunter kneels,
and pellets, like prayer beads,
fill the sky, strung
from eye to eye.

The Unexpected Environmentalist
Building a Centrist Coalition

Ted Kerasote

Ted Kerasote's books include Bloodties: Nature, Culture, and the Hunt; Return of the Wild; The Future of Our Natural Lands; Navigations: One Man Explores the Americas and Discovers Himself; Heart of Home: People, Wildlife, Place; *and* Out There: In the Wild in a Wired Age, *which won the 2004 Natural Outdoor Book Award for Literature. His work has appeared in more than fifty periodicals and a dozen anthologies, including* Audubon, Outside, National Geographic Traveler, The Nature of Nature, *and* The Best American Science and Nature Writing 2001. *He has written the environment column for* Sports Afield *since 1987.*

Since its beginnings in the late 1800s, the movement to preserve nature has been divided into two camps: the strict protectionists and the more liberal utilitarians. As a way of illuminating that division and proposing a way to heal the rift between the two camps, I would like to tell a story about two of the movement's leading figures, whose differing beliefs continue to shape our views about our place in the natural world.

In August 1897, John Muir, fresh from a trip in southeastern Alaska, stepped off his steamer at the dock in Seattle and headed for his hotel, where he picked up a newspaper. Scanning the columns, he found an article about the nation's new forest reserves, the predecessors of what today are known as national forests. His jaw clenched, his blue eyes narrowed in anger, and then—in one of those synchronicities that determine the future of land and people and animals—he looked up and saw Gifford Pinchot, America's leading forester, standing across the lobby. It was Pinchot's words, quoted in the newspaper, that had so angered Muir.

The two men were already well acquainted. Both had been members of a National Forestry Commission the previous summer, created by the secretary of the interior to investigate the condition of the nation's western woodlands. Also among the eight-man panel was Arnold Hague, an engineer from the U.S. Geological Survey and a member of Theodore Roosevelt's newly formed Boone and Crockett Club. A hunting and conservation organization, the club had made protection of the nation's forests one of its primary goals. Charles Sprague Sargent, the grand old man of American botany and the director of Harvard University's arboretum, was also on the commission, and so was John Muir, already famous for his explorations of the mountains of California. He was now president of the four-year-old Sierra Club, which, like the Boone and Crockett Club, had placed forest preservation at the top of its agenda.

The group zigzagged throughout the West, Sargent and Muir quickly taking a preservationist stand and arguing that the nation's new forest reserves, initially created by President Benjamin Harrison in 1891, be given full protection. Hague, a political animal who was well aware that western timber interests were horrified over withdrawals of federal land from the public domain to create the reserves, and Pinchot, trained in the French and German schools of tree farming, campaigned for opening them to regulated grazing and logging.

Despite their differences, a grudging respect developed between Muir and Pinchot. While camped on the rim of the Grand Canyon, the forester listened in wonder to the explorer's tales of Yosemite and Alaska and was amazed that Muir, in all his wanderings across America's backcountry, had "never carried even a fishhook with him."[1] Muir, who was running his father-in-law's fruit ranch in Martinez, California, in addition to traipsing around the Sierra, found himself praising Pinchot as a man of practical forestry, one who had shown that state woodlands don't have to "lie idle" but can be made to "produce as much timber as is possible without spoiling them."[2]

Nonetheless, the commission remained split along its initial philosophical lines, Sargent and Muir advocating total *protection* of the forests by army patrols, Hague and Pinchot urging the creation of a civilian forest service which would oversee the *management* of the reserves. They struck an uneasy compromise: the commission's report supported military control only until a federal Forest Bureau, subject to civil-service regulations, could be established. Impressed with the document, President Grover Cleveland withdrew another twenty-one million acres of forests into the reserves during the final weeks of his administration.

Westerners, witnessing what they understood to be the theft of their land by the federal government, went berserk. A bill restoring all forest reserves to the public domain passed the day it was introduced to the Senate, and Pinchot, seeing his dream of managing the nation's forests slipping away, closeted himself with Hague and John F. Lacey, a congressman from Iowa. A longtime naturalist, hunter, and angler, Lacey had authored the Yellowstone Protection Act of 1894, which made the park an inviolate wildlife refuge. He was a protectionist but one with strong pragmatic leanings.

Together the three men fashioned House legislation that authorized the secretary of the interior to protect forest reserves as well as allow timber sales and mining leases within their boundaries—very much the national forest system as it stands today. The purists cried shame; Congress adopted a version of the Lacey bill; Cleveland addressed it with a pocket veto; and the new president, William McKinley, was handed the entire boiling pot.

Pinchot and his cronies in the U.S. Geological Survey—Hague, and, more significantly, the survey's director, Charles Walcott—went into hyperdrive, lobbying Rocky Mountain and West Coast legislators with the message that forest reserves, properly managed, could be a tremendous asset to their regions. The subtext was obvious: if the forests remained open for lumbering and mining, what difference did it make if they were called forest reserves or public domain?

Muir, watching from his California ranch, vacillated. After all, he was making more than a substantial living doing a branch of tree farming, growing grapes and pears while driving himself so hard that he was chronically tired and plagued with an unrelenting bronchial cough. The only way he could restore his health was to repair to the wilderness for several months each year, and his essays from that time, written for *Harper's Weekly* and the *Atlantic Monthly,* reflect the balance he was trying to strike between an aesthetic and a utilitarian appreciation of nature. At one point, he waxes elegiac: "The whole continent was a garden, and from the beginning it seemed to be favored above all the other wild parks and gardens of the globe."[3] At another, he sounds like a chamber of commerce and an apologist for his ranch: "I suppose we need not go mourning the buffaloes. In the nature of things they had to give place to better cattle, though the change might have been made without barbarous wickedness. Likewise many of nature's five hundred kinds of wild trees had to make way for orchards and cornfields."[4]

The rancher in Muir finally won. He suggested that through selective logging, woodlands could "yield a perennial supply of timber . . . without further diminishing the area of the forests. . . ."[5] Nevertheless, he was still Yosemite's most caring son and made a distinction between good ranchers like himself and "wealthy corporations" that were using the needs of poor settlers as a smoke screen to open the forests to unbridled use. Muir was also furious that prospectors and stockmen continued to torch the woodlands to lay rocks bare for excavation and create trails for sheep. "Let right, commendable industry be fostered," he thundered, "but as to these Goths and Vandals of the wilderness, who are spreading black death in the fairest woods God ever made, let the government up and at 'em."[6]

His words came a little too late for the legislators. The day before his *Harper's* essay appeared, and while his *Atlantic* essay was still in manuscript, Congress passed the Forest Management Act, suspending all but two of Cleveland's reserves for nine months pending further study. Secretary of the Interior Cornelius Bliss appointed Pinchot to carry out the investigation, and with Pinchot's approval, Bliss let sheep into the Oregon and Washington reserves.

It was this news that so infuriated John Muir as he passed through the doors of his Seattle hotel. Not only did he detest sheep more than any other creature, calling them "hoofed locusts"[7] for the way they had destroyed Yosemite, but he was also now stunned that Pinchot had been quoted as saying sheep did little harm. Spying the forester's aristocratic form at the other end of the lobby, Muir strode toward him, brandishing the newspaper.

"Are you correctly quoted here?" he demanded. Pinchot could only nod, and before he could muster a reply, Muir lashed out. "Then, if that is the case, I don't want any more to do with you. When we were in the Cascades last summer, you yourself stated that the sheep did a great deal of harm."[8]

Pinchot tried to backpedal—both to Muir as well as in print. "Overgrazing by sheep does destroy the forest," he agreed after his next fact-finding trip to the Southwest. "Not only do sheep eat young seedlings, as I proved to my full satisfaction by finding plenty of them bitten off . . . but their innumerable hoofs also break and trample seedlings into the ground. John Muir called them hoofed locusts, and he was right."[9]

But did the smarmy Pinchot then ban sheep from the reserves? Hardly. When "young trees are old enough," he went on to explain, "grazing may begin again."[10] For Pinchot, protection on one hand, use on the other, was the ultimate win-win solution: the resource could be sustainably harvested, commercial interests could be served, and the greatest good for the greatest number could be achieved. As for the question of forests maintaining a complex age structure of trees, solitude, and a large array of flora and fauna (the term *biodiversity* had not yet been coined), Pinchot gave a succinct and utilitarian answer: "Forestry is Tree Farming. Forestry is handling trees so that one crop follows another. To grow trees as a crop is Forestry."[11]

Muir did not take this sort of language sitting down. In his next essay for the *Atlantic*, he sounded a panegyric to aesthetic, nonutilitarian values: "Thousands of tired, nerve-shaken, over-civilized people are beginning to find out that going to the mountains is going home; that wildness is a necessity; and that mountain parks and reservations are useful not only as fountains of timber and irrigating rivers, but as fountains of life."[12]

From this moment on, men who had considered themselves united by a love of nature hardened their stances over the issue of how wildlife and wild landscapes should be passed on to future generations: the multiple-use conservationists on one side of the divide and the forever-wild preservationists on the other. Pinchot's ideas became institutionalized in the U.S.

Forest Service, and, with the help of Theodore Roosevelt, in the National Wildlife Refuge System and the Bureau of Reclamation. Muir's legacy took shape in organizations like the Sierra Club and the Wilderness Society. Today the divide that separated the two groups remains in place, pierced by valleys through which some of us travel, continuing a century-long tradition of negotiating a détente between these two factions and uniting them in a common cause—a healthier natural world.

In my own work, I've used three approaches to try to bring about the end of this impasse: first, recounting the lives of historic figures, like Theodore Roosevelt, who embraced both sides of the fence; second, trying to demonstrate the existence of like interests between the two groups; and third, creating stories about wildlife that dissolve ideological barriers by appealing to one of the most fundamental of human emotions—sympathy for fellow beings who are caught in what the nature writer Henry Beston called "the splendour and travail of the earth."[13]

I'd like to spend the rest of this essay to describe each approach in more detail to further discussion among other writers, educators, environmentalists, and politicians. Through our joint efforts, we may be able to motivate individuals who, though thinking differently about the natural world, can nonetheless form a political coalition whose power to preserve that world would be enormous.

✳   ✳   ✳

First, let's consider the legacy of environmental protection that hunters and anglers have left us. Even though a large part of the public would point to the 1960s and 1970s as the birth of environmental consciousness—a time that saw the publication of Rachel Carson's *Silent Spring* and Congress's passing of the Wilderness and Endangered Species Acts—hunters and anglers had been at work preserving nature for seventy years before this epochal time.

George Bird Grinnell, who helped found the Boone and Crockett Club, was not only an avid hunter and ethnologist but also the founder of the Audubon Society and one of the chief movers behind the creation of Glacier National Park, the protection of Yellowstone's wildlife from poaching, and the inauguration of forest reserves themselves. His accomplishments might be more widely recognized if his contemporary Theodore Roosevelt had not been such a giant in the field: doubling the size of the national forests and setting aside five national parks, sixteen national monuments, and fifty-free national wildlife refuges, some at Muir's request after the two men camped together in Yosemite.

On the heels of Grinnell and Roosevelt came Aldo Leopold—angler, hunter, forester, wildlife biologist, and ecologist—whose work and thought has formed one of the most well-traveled valleys between the protectionist and utilitarian camps. An advocate of protecting roadless land, Leopold convinced his superiors at the Gila National Forest in New Mexico to set aside 574,000 acres as a wilderness area in 1924, the nation's first. He then went on to work for the Sporting Arms and Ammunitions Manufacturers' Institute, producing a national survey of game conditions, a study which led to his publishing *Game Management* in 1933, a book that remained the standard text of the wildlife manager into the 1960s. Yet, while advocating the sustained yield of upland birds and deer for the hunter's gun, Leopold counseled that predators, especially wolves and grizzlies, be left alone. A founding member of the Wilderness Society, Leopold made his most notable contribution in *A Sand County Almanac,* a book whose themes began to change, as Leopold put it, "the role of *Homo sapiens* from conqueror of the land-community to plain member and citizen of it."[14]

Olaus Murie, the great wildlife biologist of Alaska and Wyoming and one of the founders of the Wilderness Society . . . Sig Olson, who fought to save Minnesota's Boundary Waters . . . Stewart Udall, secretary of the interior during the Kennedy and Johnson administrations and a constant wilderness advocate . . . and Jimmy Carter, who added fifty-six million acres in Alaska to the National Wilderness Preservation System—all these individuals were hunters. In addition to the efforts of these luminaries to protect habitat, the rank-and-file members of hunter/angler organizations have also contributed significantly to preserving North American landscapes. In fact, in the last seven decades, these groups have set aside 112 million acres of land, 18 million more acres than in the National Wildlife Refuge System. Individually, Ducks Unlimited has spent 1.4 billion dollars to protect 10 million acres; the Rocky Mountain Elk Foundation, 154 million dollars to buy or enhance 3 million acres; the National Wild Turkey Federation, 120 million dollars for 2.2 million acres; Pheasants Forever, 70 million dollars for 2 million acres; The Ruffed Grouse Society, 7.2 million dollars for 450,000 acres; Quail Unlimited, 6 million dollars for 400,000 acres; and Trout Unlimited, 4.94 million dollars, and the Izaak Walton League of America, 75 million dollars for the restoration of thousands of miles of streams.[15]

Concurrently, the Federal Aid in Wildlife Restoration Act (commonly known as the Pittman-Robertson Act) has taxed firearms, bows, and ammunition. The Sport Fish Act and its Wallop-Breaux Amendment have taxed sportfishing equipment, electric trolling motors, and motorboat fuel. Together these excise taxes on sportsmen have generated billions of dollars for habitat purchases and restoration, wildlife research, and education.

Strict protectionists, of course, criticize this brand of conservation because of its self-serving nature—hunters and anglers are only preserving habitat because it generates more wildlife for them to shoot and catch. Though this is partly true, one must consider that protecting habitat for one species like elk, ducks, or trout protects it for other species like sage grouse, badgers, whitefish, sandhill cranes, avocets, and beaver. Protecting ruffed grouse habitat simultaneously protects a home for golden-winged warblers, common yellowthroats, and towhees.

And habitat protection hasn't been the only legacy of hunters and anglers. Before the Endangered Species Act was ever a legislative notion, sportsmen of the early 1900s set about to rectify the staggering slaughter of wildlife for the market that had taken place in the previous century. Their restoration efforts helped to take elk, numbering fewer than 41,000 in 1907 to 1.2 million animals today. Turkeys, down to 30,000 birds in 1890, now have a population of 5.6 million. Bighorn sheep had been reduced to fewer than 10,000 individuals in 1900—there are 230,000 today. Deer, down to fewer than half a million animals in 1899, now live from coast to coast and at 36 million animals have become so numerous as to be nuisances and hazards in many suburban and urban places. Trout, salmon, and bass have also been reintroduced to countless bodies of water.[16]

Again these efforts can be looked upon as self-serving and sometimes mistaken, for example, introducing brook trout from the East and rainbow trout from the West into Rocky Mountain waters where they were not native. Yet I would suggest that those of us who are not hunters or anglers— who only like to hike in undeveloped country and watch wildlife—have richer lives today, in part, because of the work sportsmen did during the last century.

Recounting these kinds of stories, I believe, does two things: first, protectionists may see that they haven't cornered the market on caring about nature and that consumptive users of wildlife may actually be allies in the fight to preserve nature; in turn, hunters and anglers may realize that they have a rich history of habitat protection and that they have made a contribution to preserving and restoring ecosystems as well as to growing more targets for their guns and rods. This is a message that hunters, in particular, need to hear. Beleaguered by bad press and shouldering a substantial amount of guilt for the scofflaws in their midst, many of them have retreated to a paranoid and uncooperative position vis-à-vis what they think of as "environmental groups." Validated, they can come to the table with something more than suspicion and a poor self-image.

On the political front, some have taken these ideas and turned them into a proactive campaign. One has been Tim Richardson, a media and political-affairs consultant, who in the 1990s pulled together an unlikely group of organizations ranging from the Sierra Club and Audubon Society on one side and the National Rifle Association and Safari Club International on the other. The group signed off on a plan to protect 376,000 acres of privately owned wildlife habitat in the Kodiak Archipelago using money from the Exxon Valdez spill fund. Under their fiduciary responsibility to turn a profit from these lands, Native corporations had planned to develop this key salmon and brown-bear habitat with luxury hotels and fishing camps.

At the tail end of this unprecedented achievement, Richardson and conservationists from sporting organizations like the Mule Deer Foundation, the Rocky Mountain Elk Foundation, Trout Unlimited, Wildlife Forever, and the Wildlife Management Institute thought that they could use a similar approach on national-forest issues by conducting outreach to fellow sportsmen. The organization Richardson and his colleagues created was named the Theodore Roosevelt Conservation Alliance (TRCA) after America's first conservationist president. The Pew Charitable Trusts endorsed the concept behind TRCA—anglers and hunters being rallied to protect wild country and wildlife habitat in national forests—and came through with a two-year, 2.3-million-dollar grant that has since been renewed for a third year. More than eight hundred affiliate organizations and sixty-five thousand individuals have joined, and today more than 50 percent of the public comments from hunters and anglers on recent forest plans across the nation have been generated by TRCA. Last August Forest Service Chief Dale Bosworth received a letter signed by more than four million TRCA hunters and anglers during the public comment process on amending the Roadless Area Conservation Rule, a landmark effort conceived under the Clinton administration that would prevent road-building in 58.5 million acres of the agency's roadless areas that haven't been designated as wilderness. The Conservation Rule has not been supported by the Bush administration.

Should we be sanguine about TRCA and its efforts to preserve wildlands? Isn't it just another Johnny-come-lately among the hundreds of nongovernmental organizations that have blossomed under the Save-the-Something banner? Richardson, one of the more astute political analysts around, suggests that TRCA, as well as another public-lands sportsmen organization, Wildlife Conservation Partners, should be watched very closely. He explains,

> The margin of partisan control in the 107th Congress is more narrowly divided than in any other Congress in the nation's history. Democrats control the Senate by 1 vote out of 100. The GOP margin in the House is 6 votes out of 435. All Senate and House committee chairmanships—in other words, control of the entire congressional agenda—can change overnight with the change of 7 out of 535 seats in the Senate and House. This unique set of circumstances affords extraordinary leverage to *any*

political faction that can tip the balance. In other words, small changes
will mean large results.[17]

Enter the sportsmen vote. Classic swing voters, nonaligned and non-
partisan, sportsmen are populists: against big business as much as against
big urban politics. They can also be blue-collar independents and eccentric Bubba-Thoreaus, predominantly white and male, bringing along their
voting spouses and children. Finally, they can be Reagan Democrats, but
they know that the traditional Democratic establishment's fixation on in-
ner-city homicides makes it hostile to the rural use of firearms for hunting.
Thus, their affiliation goes to the NRA. However, if the issue of gun control
can be put to rest, sportsmen's votes are up for grabs.

The most recent demonstration of this scenario took place in the 2001
Virginia gubernatorial race, where a Democrat, Mark Warner, won a Sun-
belt governorship by championing gun rights and thereby keeping the
NRA out of the election. The NRA backed no candidate because it had
nothing to fear from this Democrat. In a race won by around 4 percent, the
sportsmen vote, particularly in Virginia's southwestern, ancestrally rural
Democratic counties, was enough to determine victory.

Richardson goes on to say that the results of the Virginia gubernatorial election were hardly a fluke, and he offers a reasoned "proof," based
on simple electoral mathematics, why its outcome could be repeated in
other close races across the nation. Hunters and anglers, he notes, make
up 17.5 percent of the U.S. population or fifty million individuals. But giv-
en their older-than-average-median age and predominantly white racial
background, the voting presence of sportsmen represents more like 22 to
25 percent of the voting population nationally. In rural areas, the hunter/
angler constituency represents between 30 and 50 percent of the electorate.
Indeed, the sportsmen swing vote was a bigger factor in defeating Al Gore
than was Ralph Nader's candidacy. This occurred because sportsmen were
motivated by fear of gun control. If pro-environment Democratic candidates could soft-pedal this issue, the 80 percent of sportsmen who support
keeping roadless areas undeveloped would vote Democratic. This in turn
would lead Republicans to compete for their votes by promoting far more
moderate environmental positions than are found in the Bush administration. The result would be the reliable election of conservation-minded
candidates no matter their party affiliation.

If one looks at House and Senate seats where the victor won by 56 percent of the vote or less, and if one also factors in how many of these seats
could be determined by a 7.5 percent turnout of sportsmen (the number
of hunters and anglers who might be termed truly "activist"), one has to
admit that Richardson's electoral mathematics are compelling. In 2002, for

instance, 73 House seats out of 435 and 23 Senate seats out of 34 could be decided by what he calls a virtual "third party" of sportsmen. Forty-eight of these swing House seats are rural, and all 23 Senate seats have significant rural election turnout. There's one more factor to consider. Thirty-eight of the forty-eight predominantly rural swing districts lie east of the hundredth meridian, crowded places where hunters and anglers have realized that the biggest threat to their pastimes is the loss of wild places.

I offer Richardson's analysis of environmental politics in such detail because his coalition-building tactics provide us with a model that could break the current legislative stalemate between out-of-power preservationists and in-power utilitarians, the latter viewing unrest in the Middle East and worldwide terrorism as perfect opportunities to take energy profits from the nation's public lands, despoiling them in the process. He also refocuses our attention on preserving wildlands when some of that endeavor's energy has been siphoned away by the environmental-justice movement, birthed in 1982 when the state of North Carolina tried to build a PCB dump site in a rural and mostly African American county. Five hundred people protested what they defined as the state's environmental racism,[18] and their actions inspired the creation of numerous grassroots environmental-justice organizations around the nation. Ten years later President Clinton formed the Office of Environmental Justice under the EPA, outlining its charge as the "fair treatment for people of all races, cultures, and incomes, regarding the development of environmental laws, regulations, and policies."[19]

During the subsequent decade, environmental justice has evolved into a broad-based coalition of organizations representing people of color, church and civil-rights groups, Native Americans, and unions. They have directed their attention to toxic wastes, pesticides, occupational safety and health, Native land rights, networking with solidarity and human-rights movements abroad, and the effects of corporate globalization on the environment. As one exponent of environmental justice put it, "While there is no doubt that ecological problems would be much worse absent the mainstream environmental movement and current system of regulation, it is also clear that the traditional strategies and policy solutions being employed are proving to be increasingly limited." This author, Daniel R. Faber, the director of Northeastern University's Philanthropy and Environmental Justice Research Project, goes on to say that no other force within grassroots environmentalism offers the same potential for bringing new constituencies into environmental activism while creating "innovative and comprehensive approaches to environmental problem solving."[20]

I think it's important, though, to bear in mind that many of the constituencies that make up the heart of the environmental-justice movement are not focused on preserving natural landscapes. They emphasize the disproportionate negative effects of toxins on the poor and people of color. While we need to support this fight, we also need to be clear that a society that respects both human rights and natural landscapes won't be created solely by the environmental-justice movement joining forces with traditional environmental-advocacy organizations. Between the two remains a vacant niche, occupied by many of the readers I often address in magazines like *Sports Afield* and *Bugle,* the journal of the Rocky Mountain Elk Foundation. These individuals lack affiliation with either environmental-justice or environmental-advocacy groups; by and large they are not concerned with issues of human health, equity, or the preservation of wild places for their beauty, peace, and harmony.

Yet, like Tim Richardson, I believe this group of people could be instrumental in protecting wild places, particularly when their environmental cohorts are either making little headway in that endeavor or not directly addressing it. In this regard, I've shamelessly milked the connection between healthy wildlife and healthy wild places, pointing out to these sportsmen that they won't continue to enjoy their favorite shootable or catchable species without undeveloped wildlands. After this nod to their hedonistic self-interest, I've also tried to demonstrate how all of us, whether we're land preservationists, wildlife conservationists, or human-rights environmentalists, have similar stakes in the natural world. I've done this by writing about *ecological services,* that is, the natural processes and species that sustain human life, and how expensive they are to replace by technological fixes. These services include purification of air and water, mitigation of floods and droughts, detoxification and decomposition of wastes, generation of soil, pollination of domestic crops and wild plants, control of agricultural pests, moderation of temperature extremes, protection from ultraviolet rays, and maintenance of biodiversity, from which we derive a great variety of indispensable agricultural, medicinal, and industrial products.[21]

This may seem like a simplistic approach for those who take for granted that the idea of our utter dependence on the natural world has embedded itself in the cultural consciousness. Perhaps, as an abstract notion, it is becoming part of the zeitgeist. But if we ask ten people in Los Angeles where their tap water comes from, I bet not more than two can answer that some of it comes from the Green River above Pinedale, Wyoming, not all that far from where we gathered for this symposium. Connecting urban people—whether they are preservationists, conservationists, or neither—back to the nearby and distant wildlands that support them is a way of building a common language and concern about the environment.

The notion of connection has also figured in the work I've done as I try to nudge sportsmen toward a more holistic environmental position. Using terminology with which they're familiar, like *habitat fragmentation* rather than *land preservation*, I've introduced the ideas of the Wildlands Project, an organization that is working to maintain and enhance the connections between still-functioning ecosystems like the northern woods that stretch from Maine to the Adirondacks, and the basins and mountains that lie between Wyoming and the Arctic Ocean, a project known as Yellowstone to Yukon or Y2Y. For sportsmen, the motivation for supporting these initiatives is better hunting and fishing, and the language they find most compelling highlights restoration rather than preservation. In places like the Great Plains, now emptying of people, this sort of language can be an attractive tool, motivating sportsmen to literally roll up their sleeves, take down fences, and help bring back free-roaming antelope, bison, elk, and perhaps, in another generation, even wolves and grizzly bears.

The idealists among us may balk at joining forces with these sorts of unexpected environmentalists, people who will then shoot or catch what they've just preserved. But the bottom line of the matter is that these individuals can help protect habitat, which then safeguards populations of wildlife if not individual animals themselves. The nonhunter John Muir recognized that this was sometimes a necessary bargain to strike. While unhappy with his friend Theodore Roosevelt for going off on an African safari after his second presidential term, Muir nonetheless kept Roosevelt's photograph hanging on the wall of his study above his desk.

It is this fundamental life choice—how each of us treats animals—that I believe can often be one of the more divisive elements among people who call themselves lovers of nature, in particular between hunters and anglers on one hand and animal-rights supporters on the other. To soften the animosity between these two groups, I've tried to demonstrate that we're all consumers of sentient beings. Some of us do it quite directly, by hunting and fishing. Some of us do it secondhand, by eating domestic meat. Some of us do it third hand, by being vegetarians and supporting an agricultural system that inflicts death and mayhem upon all sorts of wildlife through pesticides, cultivation, harvesting, and transportation. None of us are exempt from participating in this ongoing cull, and some forms of taking life, for instance, hunting and fishing locally, can have more positive ecological consequences than importing domestic meat or vegetables from afar. Elk and deer, for example, grow themselves without the addition of fossil fuels, don't produce feedlot wastes, and don't change natural landscapes into rows of monoculture vegetables. To site one graphic statistic, an average feedlot steer will consume in his lifetime 284 gallons of oil, most of which was used to grow the corn that has fattened him.[22]

Individuals who are deeply committed to protectionist animal-rights positions will of course not suddenly turn around and support hunting and fishing after hearing arguments such as these. But if they're willing to listen to a rigorous examination of hunting and fishing along these lines, it becomes much more difficult for them to stereotype hunters and anglers as knuckle-dragging Neanderthals out solely for the kill or amusement.

With the playing field thus somewhat leveled by appealing to the record of history; the like interests of all people, regardless of their stances on the environment; and the ecological costs of our various lifestyles, I've tried to strengthen a centrist coalition by telling stories about wildlife, especially mammals, that show how human and nonhuman animals share many traits and behaviors, including, as Charles Darwin noted, "love and the distinct emotion of sympathy."

One of my favorites stories has been about watching a pack of four wolves in Yellowstone National Park kill a recently born elk calf. The calf's mother comes to its rescue a few seconds too late, and over the space of an entire day, she exhibits virtually all the reactions humans display when faced with the loss of a loved one: denial, anger, depression, and acceptance. The only stage of grief she omits is bargaining with the wolves. Instead, she expresses her anger by attacking them. They drop her calf and retreat to a safe distance; she sniffs at the carcass, and, overwhelmed with what any of us would instantly recognize as profound grief, trots off, dazed, only to have the alpha male make a risky dash to the carcass and grab it.

As I say in my original essay:

> [The wolf] runs several hundred yards before slowing and coming to rest in the grass. Glancing over his shoulder, he begins to nip at the calf with tender little bites. The mother elk stares at him, then retraces her route up the hillside, sniffing here and there before coming to the spot where blood stains the bunchgrass. She stops directly over the site of the kill, looks back to the wolf, and begins to grunt mournfully, her sides contracting and her muzzle elongating into the shape of a trumpet. A moment later her bellow of loss and frustration floats down the hillside to us. Again and again she calls.
>
> The black wolf glances one more time at the grieving elk before standing and getting the calf set comfortably in his jaws. He trots in a straight line toward the forest and his den. He has made his meat, and six new pups are waiting to be fed.
>
> We watch the elk watching the wolf disappear into the trees, and she continues to cry out, turning this way and that, sending her dirge in every direction as the morning heat rises and the light becomes glaring. I would like to see how long she remains there, but we have to head downvalley to locate other wolves.

On our return at sunset, fifteen and a half hours after her calf was taken by the Druid Pack, we see the mother elk standing on the very spot it was killed, a monument to fidelity in a natural world that barely blinks at such recyclings of protein. She looks weary and beaten, her head at half-staff. She also appears immovable in her resolve to guard the site, or stand witness to what has occurred, or to continue to hope for her calf's reappearance. Who can know what is in her mind, except perhaps another mother elk? Perhaps a wolf, determined to bring meat back to his pups, might know.[23]

My hope in telling such stories is that hunters and anglers will come to see wildlife as creatures with intricate emotional lives and decide that if they are going to take these lives, whether they be an elk, a trout, or a wolf, they ought to have very good reasons. On the other hand, my hope for pro-tectionist readers is that after reading such stories, they may have a better understanding of nature in all its interplay of light and shadow: sometimes Edenic, sometimes a place of violence where accident, tragedy, and death come to all its citizens, just as in human life.

For both sides, I hope to point out that in North America the wild and the civilized have increasingly porous boundaries. The Rockies are being avidly settled, bringing people close to cougars, grizzlies, and wolves. The East and the Midwest are seeing a florescence of Canada geese, snow geese, sandhill cranes, moose, and deer.

In this more highly mixed human/wild culture, one great challenge will be to find language that convinces the hunter and angler descendants of Pinchot to support vast habitat-protection schemes that eliminate some human use, particularly motorized access. Our other great challenge will be to convince those who have followed in John Muir's idealistic footsteps that hunters and anglers hold one of the more important cards for land preservation on a national scale. Note carefully the terms of discussion I've used for each group: habitat protection, land preservation. They're differ-ent languages but have a common theme: creating a world where people can join the wild without overwhelming it, protect it without becoming mere observers of its creatures and their lives.

Dermatophagoides

Ken Brewer

In extreme density perhaps 3,500 mites
live in a gram of dust, like angels.
They feed on flakes of skin, hair,
all the detritus we shake away.

Not even the air around us is empty.
Dust mites have their own detritus.
Invisible pellets of mite feces float
like balloons on the slightest whisper.

At Cloudy Pass
The Need of Being Versed in Human Things
Louis Owens

Louis Owens (Choctaw/Cherokee/Irish), who died in 2002, was a distinguished writer and critic of American Indian literature. Among his many books are I Hear the Train: Reflections, Inventions, Refraction *(2001) and* Mixedblood Messages: Literature, Film, Family, Place *(1998) (essay collections/memoirs);* Wolfsong *(1995),* The Sharpest Sight *(1992),* Bone Game *(1994),* Nightland *(1996), and* Dark River *(1999) (novels); and* John Steinbeck's Re-Vision of America *(1985),* American Indian Novelists *(1985),* The Grapes of Wrath: Trouble in the Promised Land *(1989), and* Other Destinies: Understanding the American Indian Novel *(1992) (literary criticism).*

In my office at the University of California at Davis, I have a small, much-battered cedar sign, brown with faded white paint routed into the wood. It reads, Cloudy Pass—Foot Travel Only. I didn't steal the sign. In the late summer of 1976, if my fading memory is correct, one of my jobs as a ranger in the Glacier Peak Wilderness was to remove old signs, replacing some with newer signs and leaving some unreplaced. Our goal was to reduce the size of the human footprint in the wilderness, a goal I bought into enthusiastically. I had loved the Cloudy Pass sign from the first moment I saw it in its rocky alpine saddle very close to the Cascade crest. So that sign came home with me and has followed me around for a quarter century.

It was natural, of course, that when asked to speak at Huxley College, I would think of the Glacier Peak Wilderness nearby, where I worked for several years, first on trail crew and later as what back then we called "wilderness guard." And it may be just as natural that Cloudy Pass asserted its important position at that moment, for Cloudy Pass was nearly as remote and perfect as a place could be for us on trail crew and for me roaming around with a backpack up there. Cloudy Pass meant eleven miles up the Suiattle Trail, then seven miles of switchbacks up Miner's Ridge, and then several tough miles along the ridge through the Bear Creek mining claim to the pass. "Foot Travel Only" meant no horses or mules. The government was trying to minimize impact on that fragile subalpine and alpine zone, never mind the mining operation just a few miles back.

At the tail end of the 1960s and throughout the first half of the '70s, I worked seasonally in various capacities for the U.S. Forest Service. On trail crew, I helped build and maintain trails through the Glacier Peak Wilderness, heading out with a string of philosophical mules with such names as Kansas City, Kitty, and Festus; with diamond-hitched packs, double-bit axes, pulaskis, two-man crosscut saws, hazel hoes, and shovels—sometimes even dynamite, blasting caps, and plastic explosives—with the purpose of grading trails as flat and smooth and generous as we could make them, removing windfalls that might bar a horse or strain a backpacker, or turnpiking wet places and building beautiful hand-split cedar bridges over streams and marshes. Our job was to make it easier for human beings to access what the federal government had defined in 1964 as "wilderness." Paradoxically, we were paid to let people into a place valued precisely because people had been kept out by resistant nature and the whims of history.

After I left trail crew and took a job as a ranger, I found myself guarding the wilderness against a nemesis I would without hesitation have unthinkingly named as humanity, and I felt good and not a little smug about that, though had I sat thinking on one of those isolated ridges long enough, I would have come to the disquieting conclusion that I was guarding that wilderness against my own presence. Nearby, a three-sided log shelter had been built in a lovely pass, just off one shoulder of the magnificent glaciated volcano called Glacier Peak. Eleven miles from the nearest trailhead by deep forest trail and killing switchbacks in one direction and even more miles from the nearest road in any other direction, the log shelter was securely deep inside the official wilderness area.

In the summer of 1976, I was dispatched from the Darrington District Ranger Station in the Mount Baker Snoqualmie National Forest to a place called White Pass with a job. I was to burn the shelter that had stood in the saddle of the pass for many more decades than I had been alive. It had buckled under heavy winter snow, and the roof had collapsed. The Forest Service had a new policy dictating that man-made objects be removed from wilderness areas, and the shelter had to be erased. The agency was striving for minimum footprints inside official wilderness—while selling timber hand over fist and bulldozing logging roads with hysterical speed right up to the borders of those same wilderness areas.

I arrived in the midst of a late snowstorm to dismantle and burn the shelter, which I did—an experience I've written about elsewhere and won't go into here, except to say that after five days of fire, no sign of it existed. While the snow raged, I took down the old logs and burned them until no coal or cinder remained. I bagged and cached the hand-foraged spikes in

gunnysacks out of sight for later removal by mule, and I spaded and re-
planted the packed earth with plugs taken from secret, hidden spots along
the ridge. The meadow soil that had been beaten down and packed hard
and tracked for nearly a century by man and horse and mule and mouse
(and every other creature that had sheltered between the log walls) was
restored, the impact erased. When I finished my task, it was impossible
to tell that a human construction had ever been there, that man had ever
come to this spot and erected a small monument to his will within what
we call wilderness. As I surveyed the snow-streaked meadow, I was proud
of what I had accomplished. I knew that by fall nature would take the pass
fully back into its fold.

I packed up my camp and headed out, but a mile or so down the first
long switchback, I met two old women, two Native Upper Skagit sisters
who looked to be in their seventies. They explained that they were hiking
those wrenchingly hard eleven miles of river trail and switchbacks to camp
in the log shelter their father had built at White Pass before they were born.
For the Upper Skagit Indians, the pass had been an ideal place to hunt and
gather berries. In late summer and early fall, the meadows between the pass
and the slopes of Glacier Peak were thick with miles of blueberries. The
two women had lifetimes of memories of camping in the beautiful shelter
their father had built, and thousands of backpackers and horse packers had
also shared it, protected from the kind of bone-chilling weather through
which they were now hiking.

My meeting with those two ladies unhinged and rehung the way I
looked at the world and began a process of thought that continues to this
day. I realized then that I had been seeing only a small part of the picture.
I had learned to self-righteously feel myself and all things human to be
profanations of this thing called wilderness. In minutes, with smiles and a
few words, the sisters at White Pass had taught me all that was wrong with
what I had come to believe. One needed to be versed in human things, I
realized as I followed the North Fork trail to my car, to know that people
might weep for the vanished shelter, and that it was right and necessary for
them to do so.

For the past twenty years, in several American universities, I have taught
Native American literature, and I have lectured on that subject throughout
the U.S. and Europe. In my classes, we read novels and poems and stories
written by authors who identify and are identified as descendents of ab-
original Americans. We talk about that impossibly vague and infinitely varied phenomenon called *traditional value,* the system of belief that comes to
us through stories and tells us how to live in the world. It is dangerous and
wrong, I always say, to generalize about Native Americans. There are today
more than five hundred distinct Native cultures articulated throughout the

oldest stories. Most important among those values are human responsibility and reciprocity. The oldest stories teach us, in all Native American cultures (and likely all Native cultures around the world), that we are related deeply and inextricably to and with the world we inhabit. We have a natural place within the natural world, just like the mountain goat and marmot and black bear. We belong here, and there.

I tell my students now, all these years since I burned the White Pass shelter, the truth that the shelters we build, the footprints we leave, the very thoughts that form within and around us are natural and acceptable and even, at times, beautiful strands woven into the natural fabric. As we all recognize more and more clearly with every year that passes, through our presence, through our very thoughts and words as well as deeds, we affect and alter our world. If we value the world we inhabit, we must also value our places in that world. If we fail to realize this, we may construct in our imaginations something called "wilderness," gather up and remove any human beings who may be native to that space, and then symbolically wall humanity out, leaving it vulnerable to the ravages of whatever devastating forces manifest themselves from the maelstrom of civilization.

Long ago, with some wonderful people who are attending this symposium, I helped build and maintain trails into and through Glacier Peak Wilderness. In long retrospect, I now believe that what we were doing was attempting to direct humanity both toward the beauty and natural wealth that is the birthright of each human being and away from that which is fragile and too easily perishable. We were engaged in implementing choices: I will build for you this eighteen-inch-wide strip of earth to trod, to impact, to lay barren with the mark of your passage through life so that you will see and know and value that which lies off-trail but of which you are, vitally and inextricably, a part. The trail, ideally, will preserve this invaluable part of you from the mark of your own crucial passing. Something will be given so that something may be withheld, and the withholding must be the fruit of mutual assent, reciprocity, and respect. This is the bargain we must learn to make: I will touch the earth with my passage because I must pass and can do no less, but in passing I will leave unmarked all that I may.

Today birds visit the meadow at White Pass, and I'm sure none of us would be foolish enough to believe that Nature ever wept for the burned shelter. However, today I understand as I could not understand so many years ago that something valuable, something perfectly human and therefore perfectly natural, disappeared with the vanished shelter. One needs to be versed in human things to understand why the sisters must have wept.

Trying Not to Lie

Ken Brewer

A good person will not learn the wiles of art.

—Czeslaw Milosz, "Reading the Notebook of Anna Kamienska"

Language itself is a lie.
The words become thieves,
spoken or written; even
when we think them,
words steal the truths
of our lives like shoes.

Words walk from our
voices, our pages, our minds.

Yet, I cannot imagine
my life without words.
Even if they stood beside me
and I reached round
their shoulders, squeezed
them to my side
trying not to lie,
I would think
"Ah, my friends,
again you have
fooled me."

Tuttle Road
Landscape as Environmental Text

Kent C. Ryden

Kent C. Ryden is an associate professor in the American and New England studies program at the University of Southern Maine. He is the author of Landscape with Figures: Nature and Culture in New England *(University of Iowa Press, 2001) and* Mapping the Invisible Landscape: Folklore, Writing, and the Sense of Place *(University of Iowa Press, 1993) and is currently working on a manuscript titled "Knowing Who and Where You Are: Region, Place, and Identity in American Literary Landscapes." He has published articles and reviews in fields ranging from cultural geography to regional literature and ecocriticism.*

When I first started thinking about the topic of this year's Tanner Symposium, "The Search for a Common Language: Environmental Writing and Education," it occurred to me again, as it often has in the past, just how language bound, how linguistically mediated, my relationships with the environments around me tend to be. One of the great things about my line of work is that people pay you to sit around and read books, getting smarter and smarter (ideally) about the world around you. So there I sit between four walls, cut off from external distractions, honing my head to a finer and finer point as I peruse and digest works of historical ecology, environmental history, nature writing, and ecocriticism. If I had a daughter, she would find Take Your Daughters to Work Day a huge and boring anticlimax. She would probably soon wander off to find something more exciting to do—probably outside.

But then, suitably sharpened, I go off to my classroom to share with my students some of what I've read and discuss their thoughts about and reactions to the words we read together as that week's assignment. I've even been known to commit a few words to paper myself from time to time. And, all flippancy aside, I'm sure readers of this volume agree that the shared possession and work of "common language" and "environmental writing," and "education" as pursued through those linguistic means are crucially important, today perhaps more than ever. There's good and vital stuff in those books—and not just information about how humans have thought about and interacted with the natural world in the past and present but potential applications of that information to our own lives and times: moral lessons, good and bad examples, opportunities for new and better ways of thinking and acting. If my nonexistent daughter tugged on my sleeve and asked me to go for a walk in the woods, I'd explain to her not only that Dad has a class tonight and quickly needs to figure out just what on earth he was thinking when he put this book on the syllabus but also that my reading and writing and teaching are some of the most important things I do.

But I'd also really want to go outside with her—and not only because I am a highly trained procrastinator who is always eager to practice his craft but also because the landscapes around us are rich and complex environmental texts in their own right in much the same way that the books are. They may not be as easy to read as books, may not always be fully legible, may be more suggestive than definitive, but in their form and composition, our everyday landscapes not only provide information about what has happened in a particular environment in the past but also take that important additional step of suggesting why what happened matters. When we're thinking about education, about taking in and passing on information and ideas about the world around us, it has always struck me as a little artificial and counterproductive to separate conceptually the human, cultural space contained within the four carpentered walls of my reading room from the ostensibly natural space in the woods, and similarly to privilege the linguistic over the nonlinguistic excessively as a means of gaining insight into environmental history, attitudes, experiences, and ethics. I prefer to see continua between spaces and between linguistic and material texts, not frontiers.

One of those books that I like to read, Robert Finch's *The Primal Place,* contains a nicely self-aware moment when Finch describes the same sense of continuity between the spaces inside and outside his house on Cape Cod, between the meanings he finds on that sandy peninsula and the words that he derives from those meanings, that I intuit in my own life and practice. Noting the mazelike quality of the woods around his house, Finch remarks that "what I wanted, what I was seeking here, was entrance, or rather re-entrance, into that maze."[1] Having realized this, Finch enacts his desire while sitting at his writing table:

> I take the sheet of paper, half-filled with sentences, out of the typewriter and hold it up before my eyes. Turning the sheet sideways, I look over its edge out the window to the trees beyond. When I do, the vertical lines of black ink begin to blur into the dark, rising bars of the trunks. It is

a self-conscious gesture, but perhaps that is what it takes—a deliberate change of perspective, a loosening of focus, and a bending of your lines of sight to what it is you would see.[2]

Finch's gesture erases the boundary between indoors and outdoors and also symbolically demonstrates the continuity between words and the environments that inspire them, with each taking on equal presence and importance as part of a single dark line of significance. In an irony which Finch seems to fully recognize, his book, this product of his human brain, this repository of chewed-up trees, this manufactured artifact is meant to draw readers out of their own reading rooms and into that natural world in which words and artifacts and human minds seem not to matter very much—a contrast which, as it turns out, may not be as firm as may first appear.

At least, that is the way I experience it. When I go outside, the landscapes that I walk through pluck at my sleeve as insistently as my nonexistent daughter. Without language, they whisper to me, try to tell me things about themselves, about who they are and what they mean and why they look the way they do and how they got that way. Landscapes are complexly authored texts, rich blends of natural and cultural process, deeply suggestive artifacts, material culture carrying within it the evidence of the many hands and minds that have shaped it over time. Any scene we sweep our eye across, from the shaggiest forest to the most densely developed suburb, has taken on its form and content because of actions that past humans have decided were possible, appropriate, and right for some combination of economic, technological, aesthetic, and ideological reasons. Sometimes these decisions turned out to be environmentally inappropriate, humans withdrew, and new green growth now stands where once animals grazed or buildings stood. Other times these decisions seemed to be so good that people decided to reproduce them again and again, creating environments that seem almost completely and irrevocably humanized; only time will tell how good these decisions ultimately happen to be.

But no matter where we look, at long-abandoned New England farmscape or metropolitan Phoenix, we see before us an environmental text. And it is a primary text at that: landscapes comprise firsthand archival evidence of how human minds guided human hands to build what amounts to a material embodiment of their cultural relationship to the natural world, and of how that embodiment—and, behind it, that cultural stance—fared once it was released into time and history. There's a valuable education available out there, an education in not only how past humans have related physically and imaginatively to their environments but in how well both humans and environments have adapted to, if not survived, those

relationships. As we contemplate our collective future, we can learn a lot
from the presence of the pasts which surround us every day.

When I was starting to think about composing this essay, I went out for
a walk one afternoon down a rural Maine road, planning to do little more
than clear my head and enjoy an early spring day. I should have known
better: to me the rural New England landscape is a fascinating historical
document. When I spend time there, my imagination is usually spurred
rather than lulled, as I find myself surrounded by both material and floral
evidence of activities that happened there in the past, evidence that challenges me to fill in the temporal gaps between past and present as best I
can. Any landscape that we see is not a complete and finished thing but
rather stands at a certain point on an arrow of time. Landscapes are cumulative rather than designed whole; they evolve piecemeal as different
episodes of natural and cultural activity, of human intention and ecological process, are brought to bear on them. What we see when we walk down
the road can best be thought of as a sort of freeze-frame snapshot in a
much longer process of change, one that looks the way it does because
of combined material and imaginative relationships that people have had
with the natural surface of the place in the past, and one that will take on
new forms in the future as people decide to either keep manipulating the
landscape or leave it alone and let wind and water and plant succession
take over the heavy lifting again. This is true of anyplace we look, and so
it occurred to me that my three-mile walk down Tuttle Road in Pownal,
Maine, a walk taken almost at random, would be as good a place as any to
think out loud about reading everyday landscapes as environmental texts,
for both what they can tell us about the past and what they can suggest to
us about the future.

From one direction, anyway, Tuttle Road actually starts out as Beech
Hill Road in the town of Freeport, that well-known New England shopping
mecca. If you've ever seen the dozens of outlet stores surrounding the huge
L. L. Bean retail complex in downtown Freeport, you know that the town
speaks volumes for the ways that coastal Maine has changed both on the
ground and in the mind over the last several decades. Beech Hill Road itself
has a few private roads trailing off it, each leading to a cluster of large new
homes for people who likely commute each day to nearby Portland. But as
you walk past the last of these roads and go farther inland, you can be for-
given for indulging the illusion that you've strolled out of the realm of recent history represented by the outlet stores and new construction and into
a place where different, slower laws of time apply. For the remainder of its
extent in Freeport, the road passes a small handful of nineteenth-century
houses, some with barns attached in the distinctive northern New England, connected-farmhouse style. Behind the houses on each side extend

the meadows of a dairy farm, with woodlots ringing the entire landscape in the near distance.

After a half-mile of this stereotypically and reassuringly bucolic New England scenery, Beech Hill Road crosses into Pownal, becomes dirt rather than paved, and undergoes a name change to Tuttle Road. Not much else changes about it for the next mile or so, though. The houses become fewer, but the fenced-in pastures of another dairy farm continue to create open space between the road and the woods that attempt to encroach on each side. That farm's two houses, one an old small Cape and the other a full, two-story Federal structure, crowd the road where it curves down to meet a small brook also used as a stock pond.

The farmers aren't the road's eponymous Tuttles, though. In fact, the only Tuttles I came across on my walk were Joseph and Dorcas and their children, Willie and Margaret, all of whom now help fill a small neighborhood cemetery across the road from the farmhouses. Willie and Margaret died in childhood, Willie in 1851 at six months and Margaret in 1856 at two, but their parents enjoyed a long adulthood, with Dorcas dying in 1888 at fifty-seven and Joseph following her in 1893 at eighty-one. (Joseph's first wife, Elizabeth, was not so lucky; she passed away in 1846 at thirty-three.)

So far, so timeless. When you're in the mood for it, it's always heartening to walk down a dirt road in the opposite direction from the modern world and hang out in a nineteenth-century cemetery next to a farm where the cows still drink straight from the river. But this therapeutic sense of timelessness is, of course, a willed illusion. The road from Freeport represents a continuum within a landscape shaped and reshaped by history, not a border crossing into a world that history obligingly passed by. The difference on Tuttle Road, of course, is that the biggest evidence of change today comes from human absence rather than presence, from things that people have ceased to do rather than from the frenetic accumulation of new buildings and traffic. The Tuttles aren't the only family in that old cemetery after all. It's crowded with several other collections of husbands, wives, and children as well: Soules, Cushings, Davises, McDonalds, Toothakers. And Mr. and Mrs. Tuttle seem to have outlived most of their neighbors as most of the death dates on the cemetery's headstones are from the 1850s and 1860s. It was quite common in nineteenth-century rural New England for bodies to be interred in small neighborhood cemeteries rather than churchyards or the new parklike garden cemeteries being designed in the region's cities, and so the old Tuttle Road graveyard amounts to a sort of ongoing census of its immediate social surroundings, suggesting to us the ghostly presence of a far busier and more populous past landscape whose heyday was a good 150 years ago.

Just past and uphill from the brook, the woods thicken and crowd the road on either side for the remaining half-mile or so of its length, but their form and composition also suggests the shaping hand of a past agricultural community. Judging from the size and spacing of their trunks, these trees largely constitute an even-aged hardwood forest, which began to grow together after the cessation of some past human disturbance on open ground. Their long skinny stems, their general lack of lateral branching except on the sunny side of those trees adjacent to the road, and their bushy crowning tufts of foliage indicate that these shade-intolerant trees were not growing individually in the open but were spending all their energy competing with each other to get up into the sun and not be trapped under the developing canopy. This being northern New England, where dairy farming surpassed crop raising in the nineteenth century to satisfy the region's need for the perishable milk, cheese, and butter that could not be shipped like other food crops from the fertile Midwest, it is likely that these woods were at one time extensions of the grazing lands which still lie just down the road, an impression bolstered by the stone walls that border the road on either side and occasionally form a right-angled line into the forest. These walls mean that livestock once had to be kept either in or out of the lands that they enclose, and since they are made of a single course of rock, they likely surrounded pasture lands; walls enclosing fields under cultivation in New England were generally double ones containing an infilling of the smaller stones that had to be plucked from the open fields each spring after the previous winter's heaving frosts. In another common regional pattern, it is also possible that these old fields originally grew up after their initial abandonment to white pine, which then was logged off, releasing the hardwood seedlings growing in its shade to dominate the forest in their turn, but I don't see any evidence of old decaying stumps from where I stand.

At any rate, my eye and mind have been caught by what I can only think of as the textual aspect of the Tuttle Road scene. Far from being an unaltered slice of the nineteenth century, when the Tuttles and their neighbors built their houses and barns and fields for later residents to maintain and preserve as best they could, this pastoral and wooded landscape carries within it the marks of its own shaping history, having acquired its current form because of the deliberate cultural and material choices made by its human residents in the near and more distant past. Some spaces along the road are quite clearly humanized, designed and engineered and fenced and mowed and built on, while others in their green and shaggy state quite clearly conform to what we conventionally describe as "natural." But all in one way or another look the way they do because of—and therefore provide evidence of—the same combined mental and physical process of selecting a sequence of material actions (or deliberate nonactions) from among what seems ideologically, economically, technologically, aesthetically, and legally possible and feasible in a particular environment, a process that produces fields and, eventually, forests just as surely as it produces houses and barns.

I eventually came to the end of Tuttle Road where it T-intersectioned into another rural lane that looked just like it and gazed across at what appeared to be a near-solid wall of trees with a rough path leading into it. I tend to find the allure of rough paths impossible to resist, and so I crossed the road intending to sneak onto whosesoever's property it was for a few steps and take a look around. I soon noticed a small cardboard sign tacked to a tree, though, informing "park users" that hunters frequented these woods on Sundays during the appropriate seasons. While I was dressed in my usual mud-colored wardrobe, singularly lacking in anything resembling blaze orange, a quick check of my mental calendar assured me that I was not likely to get shot, and so I continued on into what I had determined was one of the outlying edges of Bradbury Mountain State Park, a popular local destination for hiking and camping. And the path was as mud colored as I was, sometimes running over exposed bedrock ledges, sometimes trickling with the remainder of the spring's runoff.

But despite my having seemingly crossed over a physical and conceptual frontier from cultural space to natural space, from graded road surface to chaotic rock and mud, it quickly became clear as I picked my way along that I was now walking on an extension of Tuttle Road, one that had been completely abandoned for some time by farmers and residents but had once formed part of a busy rural transportation network. The stone walls which bordered the old right-of-way on either side hinted to me about just how bustling and well traveled this stretch of road might once have been. When laying out roads, rural New England surveyors usually made them a certain whole number of rods wide for ease of measurement, with two-rod roads the most common. The stone walls lining the abandoned Tuttle Road were a good four rods apart, leaving plenty of room for two wagons to pass each other with ease. The walls are now crumbling and overgrown, the road impassable to anything but foot traffic, but that road's scope suggested to me not only how much work and thought had gone into its construction, not only how much the structure and form of today's green space depended on the ways that rural Mainers had shaped that same space in the past, but also how drastically the landscape had changed since the time of the Tuttles. A scene of work and social life and rigidly managed agricultural spaces had been essentially walked away from and allowed to revert to whatever unplanned growth was suited to replace it, given the condition of the landscape that the people left behind. I was walking through not a timeless natural scene but the end point of a historical process, the point B that follows point A, and it was the distance and movement between those two temporal points, and the reasons for that distance and movement, that occupied my thoughts as I continued up Tuttle Road.

Sometimes in the New England woods, you can get the same sort of feeling that you get when you walk through a long-abandoned house. The presence of old lives is what strikes you in either case, even when that presence is now obscured under either dust and decay on the one hand or a regrown hardwood forest on the other. You're always coming across something—an old pot or tool in a house, a wall or foundation in the woods—that reminds you that people lived complex lives here, engaging in their daily round of activity, embedded in culture as well as landscape, creating and being created by the world around them. Even the form of the forest shows you past minds at work, decisions being made, landscapes being designed and made useful. At one point, I stepped over the wall and dawdled in a small parklike stand of pine that stood at the edge of a downward slope. There was little undergrowth here, and the trees spread their branches luxuriously, evidently having stood unmolested long enough to weed out the weak and shade out the competition. The land down the slope, though, was dominated by the same tall skinny hardwoods that I had seen earlier along Tuttle Road, evidence of past clearing and regrowth. The edge between pine and hardwood represented not just a transition between different kinds of woods but also a past decision, a deliberate choice to clear some lands and not others: perhaps the hilltop was too inconvenient to plow, perhaps grazing animals avoided it, perhaps it was part of a remnant woodlot, perhaps something else. Regardless, within the economic calculus of farming in this past neighborhood, it evidently made sense to use certain pieces of the landscape in some ways and not others, and so the present landscape is patterned according to the lives and minds of its past residents.

That same patterning is even evident in some individual trees. As I explored the hardwood forest on the path provided by an old farm lane that wandered away from the road, I noticed many trees that were coppiced—that is, they had many individual trunks growing from a single stump. In New England forests, this pattern generally means that trees have been cut down in the past, but their root systems have been left alive to send up multiple shoots. Here, too, decisions were made: certain trees in certain parts of the landscape were logged off in the past for certain purposes. While the sequence and detail of the history made evident in the landscape are not always fully clear or legible, and while I have confined myself here to the visual and imaginative impressions I garnered during my walk down Tuttle Road and have not delved into the available archival evidence, it's clear that there is a history here that you can catch glimpses of wherever you look, a temporal sequence of shaping, use, and abandonment, the advance and withdrawal of human agents making the land over so that it would most clearly match the efficient, useful form that they carried in their heads.

But this isn't the only kind of history that's evident here; the landscape has been shaped by changed thinking as well as altered activity. On the one hand, the land along the old Tuttle Road seems to have been abandoned when it no longer made economic sense to use it for farming. But deciding *not* to use land is just as active and culturally conditioned a choice in our culture as deciding to use it, and the fact that this landscape has been allowed to revert to a green shaggy state over the past decades is in large part due to the fact that the way that such land has been valued and defined has itself shifted over time. What at one time looked to Mainers like little more than lousy farmland appears through a newer, differently ground cultural lens to be valuable open space, and so the landscape has been protected by the state and permitted to become wild looking again according to its own schedule, conforming just as closely and surely to a prevailing visual ideal as did the ordered agricultural lands that it replaced.

Like any landscape—to switch metaphors for a moment—this patch of earth has remained immobile in one place while different meanings and sets of meanings have flowed and ebbed over it, and the scene that we see today is the cumulative result of the material actions that people have taken while guided by those meanings. And high on the list of those motivating meanings are the environmental values and perceptions that human actors have held. Walking the physical and historical length of Tuttle Road demonstrates how, while agricultural and other economic endeavors still rank high among the most strongly endorsed cultural uses of land in New England, new elements and categories of cultural landscape—the state park, the marked walking trail, the camping area—have been more recently invented and applied to this place to reflect a belief in the value of preserving environments for recreational as well as productive use. Not without irony, though: it can certainly be argued that to replace the old Tuttle Road farm neighborhood with Bradbury Mountain State Park is simply to switch one framework of human perception and use for another, not to recognize any inherent right of the nonhuman landscape to be left alone.

And, to be sure, as I continued on my walk, I found that before long the abandoned Tuttle Road intersected another old road that is marked and maintained today for snowmobiles and all-terrain vehicles, machines which all too often degrade environments in the ironic name of outdoor enjoyment. And, of course, there's William Cronon's famous "the trouble with wilderness" argument, whereby setting lands aside in parks implicitly gives us permission to continue messing up the fallen landscapes not sanctified by park boundaries. Still, the material effects of one aspect of what we call environmentalism, or environmental awareness, are as evident along the old Tuttle Road today as the tumbledown stone walls that once helped tie the landscape into a network of markets and production.

What interests me most here, though, is not only the stories that the material text of the landscape is trying to tell me but the lessons and applications that we can draw from those stories—particularly lessons about the ways that people have related, and can relate, to the environments where they live, and how those lessons can help us think about our *everyday* environmentalisms, our patterns of thinking and acting in the world along the graded and lived-on Tuttle Road, not just the abandoned one turned over to hikers and snowmobilers. I've been talking a lot here about humans as agents of historical change, using their brains and tools to reengineer landscapes however they want, but keeping our focus on people tells only part of the story. Nature also has historical agency. Human culture and technology are powerful things, but they must always necessarily operate within particular environments, sets of natural conditions which offer both opportunities for and constraints on human action. Nature is more than just a stage set upon which human dramas play out; it also helps write the script, makes certain plots more feasible than others, and is a close partner in arranging the set design. Any landscape, regardless of how much engineering has been brought to bear on it, is a collaboration between the processes of culture and nature, the end result of the overlap between the plans and patterns that people carry in their heads and the material environs where they decide to bring those plans and patterns into physical being.

We are surrounded everywhere by enactments of cultural relationships with the natural world, by historical artifacts made through collaboration between these two realms, and so when we read a landscape, we should be prepared not only to contemplate what happened in a particular place in the past but to evaluate the environmental relationships and assumptions that that landscape reveals and the thinking that lay behind its creation and modification. Any glance in any direction invites us to consider the implications of the history we are shown, to try to learn from the past to think more critically and with more self-awareness about the landscapes we build and inhabit in the present and the future, that world that we continue to make and remake in our heads and with our hands.

The old Tuttle Road landscape is particularly suggestive in this regard since I think it teaches humility. It tells a story not only of human modification of a particular environment but of an eventual recognition of natural limits. It is a scene where nature's agency was allowed to retain its power and influence in the end, not denied or engineered ruthlessly into submission. As such, perhaps it stands as an emblem, a reminder that our lives are in fact specifically located whether we want to admit it or not, that we ignore our collaborative natural partner at the peril of both of us. The second-growth woods that I enjoyed on my walk represent one small piece in a much larger regional story: the widespread abandonment of marginal farmlands in New England, especially the northern part, in the mid-to-late nineteenth century and early twentieth century. As more and more settlers moved into northern New England following the end of the French and Indian War in 1760, they attempted as best they could to rebuild the worlds that they had left behind in the southern part of the region, clearing forests for fields and pastures, constructing new houses and barns and farm spaces according to old culturally sanctioned forms and patterns, unquestioningly reproducing a familiar agricultural economy, ecology, and landscape in as-yet unfamiliar spaces.

But nature had a great deal to say about the success of this enterprise. The thin rocky soils and short growing season of Maine, New Hampshire, and Vermont meant that productive agriculture there was always a strenuous and difficult proposition at best, and once the larger and more fertile farms of the Midwest were connected to eastern markets by canals and railroads during the nineteenth century, farming became as economically unfeasible as it was ecologically tenuous for many families. In response, some individuals and families moved west to start over on what they hoped would be better lands, while others moved to the many burgeoning mill towns and villages that were sprouting along New England's rivers. Much of the land they left behind, as on Tuttle Road, now looks once again like forest primeval, its straggling stone walls providing the only obvious hint of its agricultural past. It's tempting to think that nature "won" in much of New England. The landscapes shaped by farmers proved to be untenable given the natural constraints of the region, revealing people's imperfect understanding of what the environment would and would not let them do over the long term, and so, rather than continue to endure failure, the people withdrew, leaving the land to do what it does best: grow trees.

As I say, I think there's a lesson here. Those farmers didn't expect to fail, didn't know that with every stroke of ax or plow they were carving onto the earth a material confession of their environmental miscalculation, didn't expect their children to have to move away to make a living. But that's exactly what happened. Tuttle Road shows us that things change, that landscapes evolve according to shifting cultural and natural conditions, that regardless of our best intentions, we'd be best off doing what we can to conform our actions to the limits inherent in the environment, not making the environment conform to the dreams of our unlimited imaginations. Everyplace is Tuttle Road in the end, even those places which seem unimaginably different from these quiet tangled woods.

True, if the Pownal end of Tuttle Road looks like a place where nature has won, the Freeport end looks like a place where humans have dominated the field, where the relationship between nature and culture has been adversarial rather than collaborative—which is, of course, the assumption that many of our landscapes today seem to reveal. Any cultural landscape is an embodiment of an environmental ethic, a set of assumptions about what is right and proper to do in, and to, the natural world. And much of what we see around us today seems to reveal an unquestioned ethic of subjugation and domination. We seem in large part to be living more and more in what I think of as a "postnatural" world, where location, and the importance of location, seem not to matter. Transportation and communication networks have annihilated the natural constraints, and even the felt experience, of time and space. Energy is assumed to be unlimited; we don't even need to locate factories next to rivers anymore, and we feel assured that there's always another oil field somewhere out there to be tapped. Enormous cities sprawl all over the deserts of the American Southwest, bringing in water from remote rivers and aquifers to support populations much, much larger than could have lived there even in the relatively recent past. Vernacular landscape traditions collapse under the weight of a homogenized national taste. Everywhere we look, we see landscapes that basically tell us, "I don't have to be here, you know. I could have been built anywhere."

And to that, I guess my response is, "Just wait." Phoenix is basically just a big old New England farm, a place where landscapes that worked in the past are assumed to be viable indefinitely into the future—and we know what happened to most of those New England farms. I'm not trying to be unduly apocalyptic here, and I'm certainly not saying anything that lots of people haven't said before me. But what I am doing is trying to encourage a certain way of seeing and understanding the world around us. More so than through written texts, our everyday landscapes are sites where people directly enact and reveal their understanding of and assumed relationships to their local natural environments. Not everyone writes books or essays, but lots of people build houses, landscape house lots, unquestioningly accept the patterns of movement and thought and behavior that their built surroundings enforce on their lives every day. We all shape and navigate our worlds daily, revealing culture through unreflective acts of making and doing.

The landscape is the most democratic, representative historical resource we have—and, as I've said, the history it reveals is one where natural process is inextricably interwound with cultural process. And if that intermingling, that mutual agency and determination, doesn't seem evident in the current appearance of a place, a Phoenix or a Freeport, I think it will in the future. We need to keep Tuttle Road in mind. Doing so, reading it for its stories and the implications of those stories, for the way it brings natural presence and power firmly into what we tend to think of as an exclusively human narrative, allows us to see any place as a reflection of who we are and how we relate to the environments around us—and, more importantly, lets us think critically about how we want ourselves and those environments to further our collaboration and continue our mutual story far into the future, hopefully with a happy ending.

The Tarantula Hawk

Ken Brewer

Not a hawk at all,
the blue and orange wasp
hovers above desert milkweed,
dips its legs into the milky hoods
where pollinia weep for love
and latch onto those thin limbs
for a whirling lift away
to be dropped like Ophelia
into another milky stream,
a dream of flight, an explosion
of pollen.

       All the spring while,
we drive in our machines,
stop at desert inns to sleep,
sometimes joining, wet and heavy,
upon dark beds, our thin skins
glistening, our wings and hoods,
petals, sepals, pistil, stamen.

Begin with a River

Annick Smith

Annick Smith has lived for more than thirty years on a homestead ranch in Montana's Blackfoot River valley. Her books include In This We Are Native: Memoirs and Journeys, Homestead, *and* Big Bluestem: Journey into the Tallgrass. *She was coeditor of* The Last Best Place: A Montana Anthology *and edited* Headwaters: Montana Writers on Water and Wilderness. *Her essays and stories have appeared in numerous publications, including* Audubon *and the* New York Times. *Smith's work as a film producer includes* Heartland *and* A River Runs Through It. *A founding member of the Sundance Institute, she has also produced a series of documentaries—*The Real People*—about Native Americans in the inland Northwest, and a film portrait of poet Richard Hugo, and she was associate producer of* Peacock's War, *a documentary about grizzly bears for* Nature *on PBS.*

Begin with a river, and you are guaranteed a story will follow. Perhaps river talk is our common language as riversheds are our common homes. John Wesley Powell saw correctly that the life of the West is organized around watersheds. Scarce water is the life-giving source in arid lands, and where water is plentiful, river valleys have always been our main avenues of settlement and connection, which is one way of saying *stories.* Connection. Settlement. Source. Obstacle. Flux: words that describe or characterize rivers also describe the processes of life and so describe the way narrative works—art imitating life. And rivers are powerful metaphors. They offer a natural form and a natural subject—actual and symbolic at the same time (for stories often shape our minds and cultures).

Rivers are also instructors. They can teach us how a story works. Begin with beginnings. All rivers have a real beginning, a source, a spring from underground, a joining of waters. Tributaries flow into larger veins and become the thing they flow into—larger, like subplots in a narrative. This often happens in the troublesome middle of a story. Anyone who's tried to write a story or a book knows that the middle is the worst part. The middle of a story is the venue for obstacles. Think of the varieties of complexity and change the river model offers: calm pools, rapids, backward-flowing eddies, waterfalls, rock slides, beaches, snags, logjams, ice.

That's just the beginning. Rivers have currents. Some run underground for a time. They carry seeds dispersing and colonizing. They are avenues for great runs of fish that can fertilize whole ecosystems. They also carry detritus and waste. Rivers may be poisoned. They may spread disease. They destroy with floods. They create floodplains. Sometimes they run dry. But eventually rivers, like narratives, reach the third act, the climax, the ending. All rivers have endings. They end in deltas. They open in mouths. Always in the process of transformation, even their endings are transforming. For in the end, rivers become something else, something larger: a lake, a sea, an ocean, clouds in the sky.

But beyond the language of metaphor, rivers also carry our actual stories, our voyages—a voyage being one of the great forms of narrative. Think of the river narratives of America. Here are just a few of them: Louis and Clark on the Missouri and the Columbia River; Mark Twain's Mississippi; Ann Zwinger's Colorado River; Annie Dillard's little Tinker Creek; Norman Maclean's Blackfoot, which is also my river of possession; John Graves's Clear Fork of the Brazos in *Goodbye to a River*. I could go on; so could you. Think of the river stories and the larger sea stories and the ocean stories. Think of stories flowing like water.

Flowing water can be the text, subtext, texture, but it is sure to hold many of our stories. Which leads me to a subject more political. For stories that are true to human experience and true to place can act as powerful agents for environmental change. Rivers in a storyteller's heart may be associated with pure water, wilderness, animals—like Ted Kerasote's story of the wolf and the elk, a really compelling story. Stories like Ted's incite readers to connect their stories to wild places, to the wild places that they know—because that's what storytelling does; it connects. Nobody cares about *your* story. They care about *their* story. And if you tell a really good story, a reader will connect to his or her story in a new and invigorated way. That's why we even bother telling our stories, because we are hoping to incite other people to imagine their stories freshly. So, when somebody tells a story about wilderness and somebody else reads it and connects the experiences that they've had in the wild, they begin to value wilderness more. The stories inhabit their imagination and their hearts, and the wilderness becomes sacred. People who read stories about pure rivers, pure wildlands, and the great stories that happen in them, may want to preserve those places themselves and also preserve the possibility that the next generations will be able to find their sacred stories in the same sacred places.

Of course, rivers in a storyteller's heart are not necessarily pure or wild. They can be like Jennifer Price's Los Angeles River and the Chicago River of my childhood, which runs backward as well as being polluted. Such rivers speak of degradation and loss, which are also great subjects for stories. They offer hope for renewal. Wherever there is loss or degradation, there is hope for renewal. So possibilities for change and transformation are often connected to rivers and places that have been degraded. Remember Dickens's prescription for a good ending: a death and a wedding—you can't lose.

Fear of loss, hope of renewal, joy of preservation—these are the emotions of our common river language. Writers seeking to help some particular environment or endangered places in general have recently found a new format, a tool if you will, that may move readers to reconsider their own stories and revalue their own sacred places. I think there's a new form of publishing that's happening. Maybe some of you can give me some previous examples, but I've only noticed this phenomenon in the last ten years or so. My companion, Bill Kittredge, defines sacred as those things we cannot do without. Each one of us has a sacred story of identity, or spirit, or connection, and each sacred story takes place or is animated by places that we also know are sacred. We cannot do without the stories or the places. If we fear they are going to be lost, we will fight to protect them. So writers and publishers have lately joined in creating collections of nonpolitical personal stories, essays, and poems about *places* that hold their stories.

The writers whom I'm going to be talking about don't write environmental stories; they're not writing propaganda. They're writing the true and important stories that happen to them or their characters in certain, very special kinds of places, and their stories connect to those places. Later, publishers may take those stories and put them together and say, hey, look at all these stories about this river, or this wood, or this mountain; let's see if we can publish this collection and thereby help protect those places by enabling readers to connect with them.

The first book that I know of this kind is *Testimony*. Put together by Terry Tempest Williams and Steve Trimble, it was an effort to try and convince federal legislators to save the southern Utah desert. And they asked writers such as Bill Kittredge and Barry Lopez—twenty writers in all—to write essays or publish already-written essays that could be used as an argument for saving the southern Utah deserts. Williams and Trimble put this book together with grant money and distributed it in a limited edition to Congress, to policy makers; then it was picked up by Milkweed Editions in Minneapolis, which also publishes a wonderful series of books called *Credo*, about what writers believe and value, and another series of books called *The World as Home*. My first book, *Homestead*, is part of that series. Milkweed Editions is a nonprofit, educational, literary publishing venture, and the money that it makes selling the series goes back into other nonprofit books, and sometimes part of it goes directly to the cause itself.

Testimony inspired me to try to publish a similar kind of book in Montana because my beloved river, the Blackfoot, was in danger of being killed off at its headwaters by a huge, cyanide heap-leach gold mine. And I thought, well, let's try and get a whole bunch of Montana writers together to write stories that have to do with the Blackfoot River—very short pieces because we wanted to influence state legislators, not federal, and Montana state legislators have a very short attention span. So we asked for five pages as an optimum length. I started to circulate queries to friends of mine— there are so many writers in Montana—and I was overwhelmed by the response. Forty-seven people sent material. Then we got a grant from an anonymous contributor to finance publication of six thousand copies, and Russell Chatham, a very fine western artist, donated artwork. Everybody donated everything; nobody was paid a cent. Finally, we gave those books away free. We gave them away free to the legislature that was sitting in session at the time. We called the anthology *Headwaters.*

During the editing of the anthology, I was bereft because my father had just died, and Bill and I were looking for consolation at the seashore in Santa Barbara when I got a call from the Associated Press stringer in Helena. And he asked, "Did you hear what happened to your book?"

And I asked, "What?"

And he said, "Well, they passed it around to the legislature, and one guy started reading in it, and he got to page seventeen where there are some really dirty words. And so he alerted the speaker of the house, and the speaker of the house got the sergeant at arms to confiscate all the books and put them under lock and key." Which is why our anthology became a cause célèbre. Newspapers picked the story up, and people wrote letters to the editors about freedom of expression, and those six thousand copies just disappeared. They're a rare item now.

Headwaters was followed by a book put together by Carolyn Servid and Hank Lentfer, which, like *Testimony,* was printed and distributed through Milkweed Editions. It includes little stories and testimonies that have to do with the Arctic National Wildlife Refuge from people as varied as Native Indian people who live there and native Alaskans who've connected their lives to that place, and people who haven't been there but value it as a sacred place in their imaginations. So *Arctic Refuge* was printed and distributed and sent to opinion makers and lawmakers.

Another similar but not overtly political book of this kind was edited by my friend Mary Clearman Blew, a wonderful writer from Montana and Idaho, who teaches at the University of Idaho. Blew was struck with people's stories about rivers, and she put together a collection called *Written on Water: Essays on Idaho Rivers*—which came out in 2001 from the University of Idaho Press, another nonprofit publisher. This book will be followed by a collection of writings on fire.

Finally, I want to mention *The River We Carry with Us,* published by the Clark Fork Coalition, an environmental group in Montana that deals with the various branches in the Clark Fork River: the watershed, the Blackfoot, the Bitterroot, and the Clark Fork. Like the other collections, this book includes all kinds of pieces by well-known writers, stories that connect with the watershed. Clark City Press, Russell Chatham's press, in Livingston, Montana, printed it, and its sale will help to finance the efforts of the Clark Fork Coalition to preserve those rivers and riversheds.

I know there will be more collections of this sort coming soon, and I bet some of you can tell me about similar books that you know that I'm unaware of. For example, on my to-call list when I get back to Montana is to respond to a call from an ex-governor of Wisconsin, who heard about these kinds of books through a magazine that I was featured in and wants to know how he can do an anthology in Wisconsin to save his troubled, endangered watershed. I don't know how politically effective this book tool is, but it is a way for writers to engage in the common language, the common purpose of helping the environment by doing what they do best. Most writers aren't great organizers. They don't chain themselves to trees; they're not good at listening to meetings that go on and on. But they *can* write stories, and then they can try and get their stories out.

I'd like to give you some examples of the kinds of stories or poems that appear in these collections, stories about rivers or places. Let's begin with a poem by my great friend Richard Hugo, who was a wonderful poet from Washington and Montana. This one is called "Plans for Altering the River."

Those who favor our plan to alter the river
raise your hand. Thank you for your vote.
Last week, you'll recall, I spoke about how water
never complains, how it runs where you tell it,
seemingly at home, flooding grain or pinched
by geometric banks like those in this graphic
depiction of our plan. We ask for power:
A river boils or fails to turn our turbines.
The river approves our plan to alter the river.

Due to a shipwreck downstream, I'm sad to report
our project is not on schedule. The boat
was carrying some mint for our concrete rip rap
balustrade that will force the river to run
east of the factory sight, through the state-owned
grove of cedar. Then, the uncooperative
carpenter's union went on strike. When we get
that settled and the concrete, given good weather
we can go ahead with our plan to alter the river.

We have the injunction. We silence the opposition.
The workers are back, the material's arrived
and everything's humming. I thank you
for this award, this handsome plaque I'll keep
forever above my mantle. And I'll read
the inscription often, aloud to remind me
how, with your courageous backing, I fought
our battle and won. I'll always remember
this banquet, this day we started to alter the river.

Flowers on the bank? A park on Forgotten Island?
Return of cedar and salmon? Who are these men?
These Johnnies-come-lately with plans to alter the river?
What's this wild festival in May
celebrating the run off, display floats on fire
at night and a forest dance under the stars.
Children sing through my locked door, "Old, stranger,
we're going to alter, to alter, alter the river."
Just when the water was settled and at home.[1]

At our symposium, we rejoiced that the Arctic Refuge was saved, at least for
now, so I include a piece from the *Arctic Refuge* book by John Keeble, a very
good writer and teacher of writing at University of Washington in Spokane.

> At Prudhoe Bay I had a guide supplied by Arctic Oil to show me around.
> It seemed a little unbelievable, the astonishing place I'd flown into com-
> ing over the Brooks Range upon the vast plain. The powerful expanse
> between the edifices of extraction heightens the sense of remoteness and
> exquisite menace. It seemed to level the very brain. Impressive as it was,
> both the topography and the insulations, with their gas plumes alight
> back into the land as far as one could see. It was impossible not to con-
> sider the damage caused by that infrastructure. Out there, propping up
> our infrastructure of greed down at home, there the soiled wetlands, the
> heaps of drill tailings, the 40,000 gallons of oily waste generated each day,
> the gravel pits, the dumping pits, the 250 oil spills a years, seeping into the
> sea. The litany could go on and on.
>   As my Prudhoe Bay guide and I sat in a GMC Suburban at the end of a
> spit one evening, looking out upon the gray Beaufort Sea, four arctic foxes
> materialized from the ditch. I rolled down my window to see them better.
> "Don't get out," my guide said. "Rabies." To me, the foxes didn't appear
> rabid in the least. They barked making a sound much like a cat's meow
> then edged closer to the Suburban one at a time. They hunkered down

until they laid flat on the ground, then passed their tails up along side their bodies and covered their noses. It was a delicate, studied and graceful motion. A long-held response to cold. I was thinking about oil, the deliquescent remains of life itself, the quintessential substance of all the last century. At that moment I was also thinking about the long controversy over Anwar. I remember the words of a native woman, a Gwich'In from Arctic Village explaining the oil battle. And yet it is like we are still lost somewhere, lost somewhere, that is how it seems to me.

Alongside the Suburban the four foxes moved again, rising, edging forward, stopping and curling their tails over their noses. I suddenly realized why they were here. This was a favorite overlook for workers; the foxes expected food to be tossed out the windows. They'd been habituated into a new dependency. They were pets. This remains mysterious to me and troubling, as I myself feel lost. We keep bombing Iraq to protect our oil interests. We keep driving our gas-guzzlers. We keep drilling and despoiling. While other choices for conservation and renewal of power generation exist, we keep doing the same thing over and over. It's as if groping in the tunnel of our own making, we're caught in an entropy of the imagination, too habituated to our ways to consider the alternatives. Meanwhile, the tunnel is collapsing all around us.[2]

An important new writer who we'll all hear a lot more about, Debra Earling, who teaches Native American studies and creative writing at the University of Montana, provides a very different kind of story. Earling's first novel, *Perma Red,* was published in 2002 to rave reviews and has received many prizes. This piece, eventually printed in *The River We Carry with Us,* was first published in *Big Sky Journal,* which is what some of us women in Montana call "Big *Guy* Journal." This very personal essay is another way of telling stories about rivers. Its title is "River Home."

Rivers tell us stories. My parents had been looking to buy a house and when my mother saw the house along the river she wanted it. A house we could afford and yet a house far removed from the trailer life we had once known. A house with a carved wooden banister, a riverstone fireplace; a sleepy house perched above the green tangled currents of the Spokane River. It was the house of my mother's dreams, a luxury house with hard wood floors, a sunny kitchen with a pantry bigger than the room my brother and sister and I shared. I remember my mother and father walking through the open rooms, the gleam of our faces in the picture windows. They surmised that the house was haunted because it was so affordable. It was the home they would raise us in, they told themselves. A safe home with room to grow where we would all find certain happiness.

My parents didn't buy that house. They didn't buy that house, my mother told me, because when they stepped outside to look at the lawn that stretched down to the deep river's edge they saw me enter the water. "You were fearless," my mother tells me even now. "We know we would have lost you to the river." And when she tells me this story, I see myself as a child wading into the cool, embracing waters, knowing the story my parents had told themselves was true.[3]

And then, a little later on in her essay, here is the dark story that did become true. I won't quote the renewal, but, trust me, there is renewal.

Years before, in the summer of my twenty-seventh year, I had come back to the Flathead Reservation with hopes of living a life that embraced all I was, or perhaps all that I thought I was. I am Indian, I told myself, though my skin was lighter than my mother's, lighter than my brother's, and lighter than the Indians I knew on the reservation. I was searching to affirm my identity, to find the story I knew would define me and I walked the rivers that summer listening for the story they would tell me. I would put on my high boots and walk through rattle snake grass, beside the jackal; I would spend long evenings at the car damn sight, standing high on the banks, to stare down into the deep carving river of the Flathead. I would stay until twilight listening to the churning water below me, believing the rivers had a story to tell me.

I did not know that the man I had married as a child of seventeen and divorced as a child of twenty-one; the man I would let slap me, punch me until my breath left me; the man who knew my thoughts; the man I held through long winters of blue moon nights and white frosted windows; the man I had lost not just once, but hundreds of times to swallows of beer and an old grief I could not translate; the man I loved, the man I loved beyond death, beyond the deer rifle he lifted to my head at the age of nineteen—that *that* man, horrible and wonderful, would jump off a bridge and hit the water so hard he would shatter the sweet cage of his ribs, that he would swallow the river and the river would swallow him like heartache and he would sleep in the hissing water of the Spokane for seven days.[4]

Ian Frazier, who lived in Missoula for years, wrote quite a different, lighthearted piece about a local view called, "A View of the Clark Fork." He writes often for *The New Yorker,* and published a wonderful book several years back called *Great Plains.*

When I lived in Missoula, I used to walk along the Clark Fork River almost every day. Sometimes I stared at it, the way you stare into the flames of a campfire; sometimes I checked it again and again like an emerging story on the TV news. Sometimes I just idled and fooled along its banks with lack of purpose that approached pure waste of time. I like to fish but I seldom fished in the Clark Fork. Fishing it would have been too utilitarian some how. Better to stand on the Higgins Avenue bridge in early spring as I used to do, dropping pennies in an attempt to get one to land on the paperback and placemat-size cakes of ice floating past. Better to sit on the riprap embankment behind the Missoulian building at dusk in early winter looking at the town's Christmas lights reflected in its wide flat stretch of river just up stream. The current runs close to the bank here and it makes spirals on the surface like a thrown football. Better just to look at that than to do a lot I can name.

I should thank the river; throw wads of tens and twenties to it, not just pennies, for all the pointless fun it gave me. Smashing ice with my son, for example. A fact you learn when you have kids is that once they get to be about four, they can smash ice for any amount of time. He and I used to go to the little side channels by the railroad bridge on the west side of town and smash ice in the shallows until not a pane remained. Then we'd take the biggest fragments and throw them to smash smaller ones. When there was no ice, we would hit things with sticks. Throw sticks and rocks in the river and build small forts in the sand and smash them.

Once we were down there smashing and whacking, when we came upon a young man with a black Labrador at the river's edge. The Labrador was just coming out of the water with a large riverstone in its mouth. The Lab went back in, dove, found another rock on the bottom, surfaced, and swam back, struggling stoically against the current and the rock's weight. He already had a couple dozen similar rocks slowly drying in a pile along the riverbank. The young man said this was just what the dog liked to do. We put aside our weapons and watched while the Lab, answering a higher call, dove and returned and dove again.[5]

Like Frazer and others, I've also written about a river important to me. This is the end of a piece about the Blackfoot River.

Connecting with a river means learning to float. You think you know where you're going and then you encounter an unexpected turn, a current or flood. You are swept under. You emerge transformed by the act of surviving danger. The river hides rocks and deep snags and drowned creatures. And it is this secrecy that draws me—the tension between what's on the surface and what lies beneath. I believe we are more like rivers than we are like meadows.

Floating on my back down the Blackfoot on a dog day in August, I
like to point my toes downstream and look up to cliffs and clouds. A
red-tailed hawk sails above me; I float past silver-plumed willows; blue
dragonflies hover above a riffle; a kingfisher with his crested, outsized
head dives for a minnow. Immersed in liquid light I find relief from self
and time. Each of us has memories we sing over and over again like a
song in our inner ear.

If your place of memory and connection is the Big Blackfoot River,
you are blessed as I am, you will want to do what you can do to save the
river so your grandchildren can float its green waters and fish its native
cutthroats and bull trout. You will teach them to dive into deep pools,
touch stones that go back to the beginnings of time. The river is not dead
yet. Boys and girls should make love on its banks.[6]

I'll finish this recitation with one of the funniest poets in the world, Greg
Keeler. He is a wonderful poet and humorist who teaches poetry and creative writing at Montana State University in Bozeman and writes amazing
songs. So this is a poem that Greg wrote for our *Headwaters* book called,
"Your Waking Thoughts of Quack."

When weather won't hold and clouds
turn snake down skies too bright
to stay, you blame the ducks and
think bad ducks then fisting skyward
shout bad ducks at Vs that waver
but don't quit coming.

When rivers turn dreamside down
and thicken to the green of marmalade
in a schoolgirl's twisted fantasy,
you blame the ducks and think
duck guilt where they capsize
in backwaters to peck scum
from rocks and moon the sky
with their pointy duck butts.

When you wake to duck quacks
and time flags down your
waking thought of quack and
quack again, you blame
the ducks for last night and
the night before and scatter
them wobbling down the bank
toward the fat confetti
of their reflections, shouting
beat it, bad ducks. Take this luck
and scatter on the sky for good.[7]

How to Train a Horse to Burn

Ken Brewer

—for Dan Flores

One method always works.
Tie the horse in its stall
and pile the old straw high.

Douse the straw, the stall,
all the wood, all the tack.
Open all the windows for a draft.

Stuff cigarettes up your nostrils,
cram cotton in your ears,
light a match and run.

Horses hate fire.
They whinny, snort, scream.
They buck and kick.

Flames grow in their big eyes,
smoke chokes them,
the hooves and flanks heat up.

Then the shoulders, the neck, the withers.
The tail begins to burn like a torch
whipping the barn-dark, then the mane.

Takes a long time
to teach a horse to burn.
They never get used to it.

But no record exists
of one horse
burning another.

The Natural West

Dan Flores

Dan Flores, writer and professor, divides his time between places in the Bitterroot Valley of Montana and along the Galisteo River outside Santa Fe, New Mexico. Born in Natchitoches, Louisiana, he has lived in the West for twenty-five years. He holds the A. B. Hammond Chair in western history at the University of Montana, where he specializes in the environmental and cultural history of the West. He is the author of seven books, most recently Horizontal Yellow *(1999),* The Natural West *(2001), and* Southern Counterpart to Lewis & Clark *(2002). His work on the environment, art, and culture of the West also appears in magazines such as* Southwest Art, The Big Sky Journal, *and* High Country News. *His books and essays have been honored by the Western History Association, the Western Writers of America, the Denver Public Library, the National Cowboy Hall of Fame, the Oklahoma Book Awards, and the Texas Historical Association. He is currently writing a general history of the American West for McGraw-Hill. This essay is distilled from* The Natural West, *published by the University of Oklahoma Press in 2001.*

On an invigorating autumn morning in Montana's Bitterroot Valley, with the first big snow of the season draping the sagebrush and the sun angle yet low enough that, as frost settles out of the intense blue, the heavens seem to be raining glitter, I strap on skis, whistle for my wolf hybrid to join me, and set out across the foothills of the Sapphire Mountains to look for elk. It is one of those incredible daybreaks that in late-twentieth-century human description (or so the thought hits me) would come across, frankly, as so beautiful that it's almost corny. It's sunrise. It's the Rocky Mountains, with all their associations. We're looking for elk, an animal with a peculiar history in this part of the world that I can conjure with just a little concentration. I'm in Montana, with a meaning different from anywhere else, skiing literally out the door of my house, with big, official wilderness areas in view, accompanied by an animal whose ancestry is three-quarters wolf and acts like it. It's the American West at the turn of the twenty-first century, and all those names and thoughts have cultural associations in my head that are coded into the synapses. I can't get them out if I want to.

We move—I glide; Wily lopes, bounds, and sniffs—our way across foot-hills covered with Idaho fescue, sagebrush, rabbitbrush, and ponderosa pines, and as I continue my thoughts about this flux we call nature, naming things and experiencing emotions that are equal parts personal and cul-tural, I happen to glance at Wily, who appears to be devouring the morn-ing as avidly as I am. We are connected, this part wolf and me, by more than personal history, and skiing along, I begin to tick off the ways. We are both native earthlings, for one, both vertebrate mammals of peculiarly social species with more in common—more DNA, skeletal, and chemi-cal similarities—than not. We're also both male. We share a hunting past and adaptive plasticity. Our apparatus for apprehending the surrounding world—our sensory organs—are exactly the same, even if our separate evolutionary streams have caused him to rely more on smell, me on sight. But the biological drives bequeathed us by natural selection have meant that as species we both have manipulated the world for reasons we barely comprehend. What does it mean, then, that when I look out at "nature" this bright morning, my cultural associations are richer than his? What does it mean to our experiences that I am densely cultured, and he (relative to me) is not? And what meaning can be divined from the fact that I, after all, am only his rather more reflective cousin—that I, too, am an animal?

"Dreams and beasts," Emerson once wrote, "are two keys by which we are to find out the secrets of our nature."[1] In entire deference to Emerson—and to Freud and Darwin, who certainly took him to heart—I sometimes wonder if there's not a bit of myopia in that aphorism. As any advocate of past as prologue may ask, where does *history* fit into Emerson's equation as an avenue for exploring human nature? Dreams indeed are something of a pathway, and not just to our aspirations and hopes but back to our animal selves. But what of the historical dream, particularly the one that involves humans and nature and animals all yoked in common to places with great power in our imaginations?

I'll return to the themes of dreams and beasts, but perhaps history is the place to start to rethink the Natural West. I wrote the preceding paragraph in my hand-built, adobe-style home looking out on the Bitterroot Valley, one of the state of Montana's storied Rocky Mountain paradises. This is a place where the Old and the New West confront one another daily in often-bizarre ways. There are ranches in the foothills around me that still make nostalgic use of big draft horses in their haying operations, and fami-lies with logging (and bar-fighting) traditions going back to Marcus Daly's

time at the turn of the last century. (It is still all too easy for the masoch-
istically inclined to get themselves beaten to a pulp in a Bitterroot Valley
bar.) Meanwhile, at the turn of this new century, among other neighbors
of mine are famous writers, intellectuals, and ex-politicians living dot-com
lives in what recently was a very remote valley. You know your place has
been discovered when it turns out that even the Dalai Lama has been pok-
ing around, looking for a Bitterroot retreat!

I confess I'm a sort of new westerner myself. Because of relatively recent
inventions like solar panels, satellites, cell phones, composting toilets, and
four-wheel-drive vehicles, I'm able to live where no one has since the Salish had this valley. So maybe this is the New West we're experiencing. Or
perhaps it all just seems new because the prism through which we're ac-
customed to view the history of the region has only recently been polished
sufficiently to permit a deep view.

Ten miles from here, in 1841, the Belgian Jesuit—Father Jean Pierre
DeSmet—founded the first Christian mission in the northern Rocky
Mountains. In terms of conventional history in the American West, that's
pretty early; in terms of the deep view back through this ancient homeland, though, DeSmet is barely yesterday. Even in the conventional terms
of history-beginning-with-white-settlement, the Bitterroot Valley has a
rich story, to be sure, similar in outline to that of much of the rest of the
plains and Rockies. But like most western history, the conventional narrative is a lumpy one. It's a story that glosses over a great deal of meaningful
change to focus on "event history": the appearance of Lewis and Clark and
DeSmet, the removal of the native Salish people, the arrival of railroads,
irrigation and logging and town building, booms in sheep, busts in apples.
Read the histories of the counties anywhere in the West, and settlement, local politics, participation in the nation's wars, and schemes to make money
dominate.

So in one way, we know how to fit the so-called New West into this kind
of history because in truth the New West just exchanges the old settlers,
and extractive industry, for new arrivals and tourism and real estate, the
whole now based on scenery and an amenity lifestyle in a mountain paradise. Stir around a bit beneath the surface, and it truly seems that David
Brooks's *Bobos in Paradise* isn't all that different from Jesuits in search of
souls, Mormons in search of a desert to convert into Eden, or miners on
the road to El Dorado. To me the New West just doesn't seem so alarm-
ingly different from what's been going on across the region for the past
150 years. Only now the victims have changed, and the angst has shifted.

Thinking these thoughts under the blue skies of Rocky Mountain days a couple of years ago, when by all that's proper in life I should have been out climbing mountains instead, I've sporadically revisited the idea and tried to reimagine the history of my homeland valley. What I'm hoping for is a history, if you will, that digs into the stratum below the ones that carry wars or political affairs, although ultimately this isn't a kind of history that can ignore politics altogether. Although the basis for such history is old, many of the questions are new. Locally, as well as on the grander scale of the American West, they have to do with our interaction with the ecological landscape, with what we might call the "Natural West," as both idea in the mind and tangible, touchable rock, grass, and flesh, which of course it is.

At the dawn of this new century, apparent global warming has us all mesmerized by the weather. Yet in most western history until now (perhaps Canadian or Dakotan history is different), we've mostly ignored the role of climate. What, for instance, have been the major climatic cycles in the West since the Wisconsin glaciations, and what have they meant for the Natural West in which our cultures are now so embedded? *Longue durée* western history, in fact, is rife with human drama that seems to have been precipitated by climate change, from the Altithermal, the greatest of all the droughts at least since we humans have been on the continent, to the Little Ice Age of the fifteenth to the nineteenth centuries, to droughts that exposed the weaknesses of Chacoan and Anasazi civilizations, to gullying episodes across the Southwest early in this century, and on down (more recently) to the Dust Bowl of the 1930s, which may have switched off climate as a historical catalyst for us because of our sense that we defeated it with technology.

There are other great ecological revolutions in the big story of the West that ought to interest us, too, for the ripples of ecological transformations in the western past extend into our own time. How long, after all, have Indians been setting fires in the West and to what effect? Peat-bog core samples in the Bitterroot Mountains across the valley from me indicate that airborne charcoal deposits increased fairly dramatically about 2,500 years ago, an indication of more frequent fire and quite likely a marker for the entry of full-time Indian residents. Countless historical documentation of the Indians' use of fire to transform the world around them is now resoundingly seconded by repeat photography across the West, revealing a far more open Western landscape 150 years ago than the one we Euro-Americans have produced with our land-use practices.

As just one example, ecologists along Utah's Wasatch Front have documented an eightfold increase in the areal extent of Utah juniper since the Mormons took over much of the state from the Utes and Paiutes. Everywhere from the Colorado Front Range to the Sierra Nevada to the mesquite plains of Texas, the same principle—a savannah West becoming engulfed in forests and shrubs—is playing out in our time. Unquestionably, lightning fires that Native people didn't, or couldn't, put out were a major factor in the fire ecology of the ancient West. But Indians seem to have set virtually all the fires that burned in the autumn, winter, and early spring months.

The use of fire is one big and obvious change in the way peoples with different cultures have managed the West, but there are others we're only now questioning. How did thousands of years of plant gathering by Indian women, or animal hunting by men, help fashion essential local western ecologies? It shouldn't surprise anyone that we know rather more about the effects of hunting than of gathering, and what we're beginning to understand is that our deeply internalized impression of a pristine West—Lewis and Clark's upper Missouri River paradise of 1806 is the touchstone of those assumptions—requires some rethinking.

Rethinking because the presence (or absence) of animals in the explorers' West had a great deal to do with human decisions. An article published in the journal *Conservation Biology* three years ago argued that human causes—specifically tribal conflict among the Blackfeet, Mandans, Crows and others over access to the upper Missouri—explain why Lewis and Clark could travel from the Mandan villages to the Lemhi Valley of Idaho in 1805 without meeting a soul, and that human absence caused that Eden of animals they saw there. Indeed, all across the West Indian intertribal diplomacy routinely created buffer zones between tribal territories that allowed animal populations to build up.

Or, in the postcontact period, the size of animal populations could have depended on whether disease epidemics had cut down Native populations enough to release prey animals from human hunting pressure. Or, as the nineteenth century wore on, whether particular tribes had or hadn't succumbed to hunting for the market. If they had, it made no difference whether it was a Euro-American mountain man or a Nez Perce hunter who killed a wolf for its pelt. When the global market came to town, the result on animal populations was the same no matter whose finger pulled the trigger.

Another effect that ecology has studied but the traditional history of the West has usually ignored is the impact of exotic introductions. In the West, we celebrate cows and cowboy history without ever stopping to think that the bovine object of all our attention is as foreign as tumbleweeds and dandelions, and in mountain valleys west of the Continental Divide, like the Bitterroot Valley (where the bunchgrass did not evolve with large, trampling, native herd animals), such introductions have been a source of significant ecological change. In a human sense, that change was not as traumatic as the similar introduction of human disease pathogens cultivated in Old World conditions. And yet there are direct correlations between all these introductions and the depressing reality of a modern West that, as we look on, is losing its ancient biodiversity to an onslaught of Old World weed infestations. Somehow a West composed of cheatgrass, spotted knapweed, sulphur cinquefoil, Saint-John's-wort, dalmation toadflax, Russian thistle, Siberian elms, and Asian tamarisk just doesn't have the same romance—or appeal to the native communities that evolved here over hundreds of thousands of years—as a West of buffalo and grama grass, paintbrush and shooting stars, aspens and cottonwoods.

The more you pay attention, the longer the litany of questions about this kind of western history grows. Here's a basic one: If aridity as we well know has shaped the history of the Great Plains and the southwestern and Intermountain deserts, you have to wonder what influence a physical (but unexamined) reality like *slope* has had on Rocky Mountain history. Plenty of thinkers, from John Wesley Powell to Walter Prescott Webb to Wallace Stegner, have ruminated on the importance of the word "arid." But who has paid attention to slope, despite the obvious pressure on human adaptation that living in mountainous landscapes implies? I once compiled a list of technological adaptations to mountain living that rivaled Webb's well-known list of institutional adaptations to plains life assembled in his classic, *The Great Plains: A Study in Institutions and Environment.* Consider this list of mountain adaptations, and it's only partial: vertical transhumance, water manipulation via stream irrigation and eventually transmountain diversions, narrow-gauge railroads to ascend mountain grades, new snowplow designs for mountain railroads, ranching technology like the Beaverslide haystacker for coping with high-elevation winters, and extractive industry innovations like aerial tramways and more recently aerial logging for areas roads can't penetrate. Aridity, sure. But the above are mostly changes wrought by *mountain* living: existence in a vertical and snowy country.

Then there's this question, as close to where we live today as technological innovations and almost as old. Globalization, historians well understand, is not a new phenomenon. So what has it meant for ecological history that for two hundred years now, the global market has been extracting the juice out of the Rocky Mountains and the Great Plains, too? Someone once remarked that with the collapse of Communism, environmentalism was primed to become the lens through which we could critique capitalism. Observing how the inland West has fared under market influences almost seems an obvious and, further, a politically charged exercise. Yet, as D. H. Lawrence once observed of something far more abstract—"spirit of place"—we should not ignore such "great realities" when we think about the West.

* * *

And speaking of great realities, surely it's intriguing (or maybe inspiring, or maddening, depending on your politics) that the mountains standing over Rocky Mountain valley floors belong to the American people as a whole rather than the local communities near them. I have two communities in Montana, one of which (the Bitterroot Valley one) clearly finds this historical development maddening in the extreme. My other community, the more urban Missoula one ("the valley of the liberals" it's called in Montana), thinks national ownership of the western mountains is one of the great inspirational developments of western history.

Most so-called new western historians, with their gender and multicultural interests, would be intrigued by the class and rural versus urban dimensions of that difference in viewpoint. But I find myself more interested in the origins and ultimate ecological implications of the system. How did that form of ownership come to pass? What were, and are, the alternatives to it? Does national ownership and federal management of the high mountains of the West make the Rockies unique in the world? And what have been the ecological consequences?

Next in my litany of essential questions to ask about the Natural West, consider the charismatic native animals with which we've shared the region. How has human culture fashioned perceptions about our animal kin, and why do those perceptions (and the values attached to them) often appear so different from one group of people to the next? Indeed, why do places like Hispanic New Mexico, Mormon Utah, and Rocky Mountain Montana strike us so differently when the natural world seems so similar in all three? (Or—a question I'll return to—are they actually all that different?) What does it mean about our arc across time that wolves and grizzlies, ancient natives that we Euro-Americans tried mightily (and largely successfully) to extinguish across the West, are now back, or at least on their way? Or that having been nearly erased by a complex array of nineteenth-century causes we're only now coming to understand, buffalo are reappearing in larger numbers every year out on the great, expansive plains? Perhaps most important as a question to ponder: Is the wildlife reinhabitation of the West telling us something important about the evolution of human environmental sensibilities?

*   *   *

Restoring the West to its "natural condition" seems likely to be the great environmental crusade of the twenty-first century, and here again it strikes me that a less traditional history can help us understand what we think about it. When we talk about "restoring" the West, what in fact are we trying to recreate? This question is, of course, one of those marvelous postmodernist catch-22s that asks us to assess whether what we think is a great *reality* may not actually be a great *construction*.

Thinking about restoration poses a *really* good question: Whose Natural West was this, initially, anyway? Was it evolution's superorganism, which we Euro-Americans have so long called "wilderness"? That has served as the classic opinion, among historians, the public, even ecologists, for most of the history of the U.S. Or, as many of us are coming to ask more recently, did the United States actually inherit a continent shaped by a very long previous human inhabitation that our value systems and ideas conspired to have us mostly ignore?

Many of us who read and think about western history have come across two great debates that are even now coloring how we think about *longue durée* history in North America. One has to do with just how long and just how many people were here before Europeans arrived five centuries ago. And the other involves Indians' abilities and willingness to alter the world. No real consensus about either question has surfaced yet, but the directions are clear. If it helps as a way to fold these questions into your view of history, just consider these two apparent facts that have emerged from the debates. One: Using recent middle-of-the-road estimates of approximately ten million Native inhabitants in 1492, if you add up the generations of Indians who were in the present United States and Canada in the previous thousand years before we got here, the number is roughly the population of the United States according to the census of 2000. Second: With that many people on the continent at least since the spread of agriculture two thousand years ago, Indians probably produced more far-reaching ecological change on the continent than Europeans were able to during the entire colonial regimes of England, France, Spain, and Russia.

*   *   *

Only since the advent of the United States and Canada as nations have our accumulated changes exceeded those the Indians made in North America. That simple but powerful alteration in perception comes through very clearly, I believe, from an interpretation of western ecology in the careful scientific work that Dr. Peter Custis did on Thomas Jefferson's "other Lewis and Clark expedition" into the southern Louisiana Purchase. Custis's fine-grained work shows us a West extensively lived in and shaped by the previous Indian presence.

Which is a point that finally allows me to circle back to my opening, and to a very fundamental question that history rarely considers: Are all our desires and the things we value *purely* cultural, springing entirely from our Mormon or Hispanic or Comanche or Pueblo or capitalist traditions? Or is there something else, more universal, that our richly layered cultures disguise, perhaps something as essential as an evolutionarily derived "human nature" that influences the way we—*all* of us—see and interact with the flux we call the natural world?

The Human Genome Project has demonstrated that as a species we spring from a founding population of only about sixty thousand individuals and that we all descend from a single female who was alive 170,000 years ago and a single male who lived 59,000 years ago. Not quite Eve and Adam since a 111,000-year age difference would strain any relationship, but close. Across the global human population, 99.9 percent of our thirty thousand genes are identical! So the assumption that we all share a human nature that is part of our universal biological inheritance simply can't be dismissed anymore. History ought to take notice of this effect, which in our new genetically grounded "century of biology" is certain to become widely acknowledged and understood.

To me the reality of our evolutionary origins argues, for one thing, that the human past in all its specific variations of culture and place belongs not just to (say) the Blackfeet or the Mormons as a unique kind of group possession but to all of us. So I'm interested in everybody's particular stories in the West. The whole of the past ought to be ours, as a species, to learn from since in truth everybody's story is our own. And to take another step toward acknowledging who we really are, biological history argues that we humans cannot be considered separate from the Earth of our evolution. We, too, are "natural." Which does not mean, of course, that our every act is sanctioned. We seem fully capable of maladaptive decisions, foolish insensitivity, and disregard for the rest of the world. Indeed, some of that kind of selfishness, the "selfish gene" idea that makes us care most about ourselves and our close kin, is built into our very evolution, which perhaps helps explain the genesis of capitalism as an institution in the modern world.

In environmental terms, what may be the legacy of our long and ancient evolutionary origins? *Steppenwolf,* the German writer Herman Hesse's surrealistic novel written in the post-Darwin 1920s, sums up the dilemma of the protagonist this way:

> He calls himself part wolf, part man. . . . With the man he packs in every-
> thing spiritual and sublimated or even cultivated to be found in himself,
> and with the wolf all that is instinctive, savage and chaotic.[2]

In terms of our classic understanding of human nature, Steppenwolf's
situation seems that of humankind as a whole. According to Genesis, in
the Judeo-Christian religious tradition, nature was benign in the beginning. Then humanity discovered its animal passions, and sin came into the
world along with evil, followed by the fall from grace. Perhaps that view
colored the early interpretations of Darwinism, wherein the religious sins
of gluttony, lust, greed, envy, anger all became stripped-down expressions
of impulses emerging out of evolutionary natural selection and the operation of the selfish gene. This is the so-called dark view of human nature; it
grants us little hope.

But there is a more sophisticated, more current understanding of our
evolutionary heritage as well, and it came about as an effort to grasp
how—if the entire biological world is blueprinted around replication of
the selfish gene—we can explain the emergence of altruism and human
morality. Are they, as Steppenwolf seemed to think, purely the result of
culture? In fact, as game theory researchers have famously demonstrated,
human morality evolved as part of our nature, too, from the success of
reciprocity as a human strategy. Reciprocity in nature enhances individual
success through cooperation with others, an arrangement that human societies buttress with an ethical code (the social contract). The evolutionary
strategy that seems to have produced reciprocity, altruism, and morality in
a selfish-gene world? What else but "tit for tat," or "Do unto others . . . ."

I go into all this because it has a significant bearing on the history of
the Natural West. Along with our evolutionary willingness to engage in
reciprocity, the "bright view" of human nature also argues that our long
evolution as part of nature has bequeathed us, as beings who recognized
our kinship to the natural world and our dependency on it, a love of life
and of a rich biological diversity in the world—Henry David Thoreau's
passion for "an entire heaven and an entire earth."[3] This evolutionary impulse within us E. O. Wilson calls "biophilia."[4]

What might be called human nature is probably visible at every level of
Big-Picture western history. As one example, it seems that irrespective of
our cultures or ethnicities, we've all found the West a magical place. Think
of the Great Plains and Rocky Mountain West, a kind of "dream landscape"

in American history. Can that dreamlike power have something to do with our intrinsic sensory impressions and ancient responses to a vast, open country of wind-whipped grasses with outsized blue mountains standing above the horizon, a country saturated in yellow light, domed by dramatic skies? In our art, many of our expressions of popular culture, and our collective historical memory, we tend to see the West as it was two centuries ago, full of immense herds of big animals and big predators.

Consider this description of the Great Plains of western North Dakota (now robbed of its ancient power by industrial agriculture and so denigrated as "fly-over country" by sophisticates on the coasts). Painter John James Audubon penned it in his 1843 Missouri River Journal. [5]

> At the report of the guns, two Wolves made their appearance. . . . Harris saw a gang of Elks, consisting of between thirty and forty. . . . We passed some beautiful scenery . . . and almost opposite had the pleasure of seeing five Mountain Rams, or Bighorns, on the summit of a hill. . . . We saw what we supposed to be three Grizzly Bears, but could not be sure. . . . We saw a Wolf attempting to climb a very steep bank of clay. . . . On the opposite shore another Wolf was lying down on a sand-bar, like a dog. . . . I forgot to say that last evening we saw a large herd of Buffaloes, with many calves among them; they were grazing quietly on a fine bit of prairie. . . . They stared, and then started at a handsome canter . . . producing a beautiful picturesque view. . . . We have seen many Elks swimming the river. . . . These animals are abundant beyond belief hereabouts . . . [and] if ever there was a country where Wolves are surpassingly abundant, it is the one we now are in.[5]

Audubon closed a letter to his wife after these experiences with the admission that he had to stop since he was "too excited to write."

✳ ✳ ✳

You have to wonder if that dreamlike North Dakota doesn't seem reminiscent of a place important to all of us—the Serengeti or the Masai Mara plains, where our early hominid ancestors blinked into consciousness. The western writer Zane Grey once wrote that, alone in the western landscape, he experienced "fleeting trances that belonged to the savage past. I was a savage. I could bring back for a brief instant the sensory state of the progenitors of the human race."[5]

✳ ✳ ✳

By reason of considerable residence in two very different parts of the West—the blue-green Bitterroot Valley of Montana and the sere, brick-hued Yellow House Canyon at the head of the Brazos River on the Texas plains—a good bit of my interest in the West's environmental history has tended toward wonder at the regional distinctiveness of the place. The Great Plains and Rocky Mountains do not comprise the whole of the West, of course, and even their boundaries intergrade, one with the other. The adjoining tall-grass and oak prairies to the east of the plains, and the great, varied deserts west and south of the Rockies, make up as large a share of the West, and there's also the Pacific Rim and Alaska, of course, all with their peculiar ecologies and historical arcs. But for two causes that go beyond anyone's affection for home ground, the plains and Rockies of the West make, I think, an especially compelling stage for thinking about western environmental history. One cause is that the history of the Great Plains might be called the origin for environmental history. Walter Prescott Webb, James Malin, and more recently Donald Worster have all made the Great Plains the subjects of big, important books about some of the fundamental issues of western nature. For many writers in the twentieth century, from Webb to the 1937 Committee on the Future of the Great Plains to Frank and Deborah Popper, the Great Plains is the ultimate proving ground of environmentalism's doomsday predictions for the modernist experiment in a massively altered western landscape. Whether contemporary Great Plains culture can survive the implications of its twentieth-century history is a question almost nobody asks about any other part of America. But if you know something about *longue durée* history and groups of folks called Clovis and Folsom, you know that today is not the first time surviving has gotten discussed on the plains.

Interest in the Rockies derives from another source. These two regions, not merely adjacent but anciently spooled together in a kind of ecological yin/yang interlock, have startlingly different environmental histories. I mean less that trail drives are associated with one and miners with the other than that human history has bequeathed a strikingly different land-ownership pattern in the two settings. The Great Plains is western America's great experiment with privatization, the Rockies our historic communal-land experiment. That we're now entering the second century of these two radically different land-use strategies coexisting side by side makes their comparative environmental history interesting (I almost said "critical") to ponder. What happens in the next century will eventually tell us what we think about these two grand western laboratories. Naturally I have some ideas about that. Comparing the current state of environmental health in the two regions makes me think that the communal Rockies strategy is going to serve as a model for the future of the West, and that the Great Plains—while it won't abandon privatization—are likely to borrow from the Rockies more than the other way around.

I haven't so far indicated what straightforward conclusions I expected readers of the book from which this essay is distilled to draw. But quickly sketched, the big story looks something like this: First, every western cultural group I've studied seems to have pushed the natural world to the brink at one time or another. Second, we have done better by nature when we've emphasized communal effort (our natural reciprocity again) than when we've allowed pure self-interest to dominate. And third, what we seem to require from a culture is that it allows—even encourages—our intrinsic evolutionary love of life processes and biological richness to flower. And yet, as the history of groups as disparate as the Clovis people, the Comanches, New Mexico's Hispanic pioneers, Mormons, and Montanans demonstrates, that is not enough. Equally important, our cultures need to teach us how nature works and the more sophisticated the knowledge, the better. And that includes the most important lesson of all: *Who we actually are.*

Thus my view: If contemporary human cultures (which now know more than humans have ever known in all our long history about how ecological processes work) can just accept the stunning Darwinian insight—who we are and our kinship with the rest of life—and can take steps to allow our evolutionary biophilia to express itself, then the Golden Age of environmentalism lies in our future, rather than in our past.

Unlike, say, quantum physics or poststructural literary criticism, history—and it may be that this is particularly true of environmental history—has no business (or reason for) cloistering itself away from public rumination. The real target of questions like the ones I've posed is the ordinary resident of the modern West, the interested general aficionado of western nature and western life who is going to have a say in how the continuum plays out. For those of us intrigued with the West who have looked at the surrounding world and wondered how it came to be so, these are the kinds of questions that, perhaps, can provide a start in making history relevant to everyday life. And if not, then perhaps they may at least work as a revision of Emerson's idea about dreams and beasts and human nature.

Sheep

Ken Brewer

—for Ellen Meloy

The Virgin River vanishes
in canyon rock
leaving tear stains
for the mountain sheep
who graze on stone,
who know the earth is steep
in every direction, who know
geometry is merely
the shape of stone,
empty space,
memory of hooves.

We want to ask
"How can you live here?"
But we drive fast
past their answer,
our attention always
ahead of us.

Separation Anxiety
The Perilous Alienation of Humans from the Wild

Ellen Meloy

Ellen Meloy's The Anthropology of Turquoise *was one of two finalists for the Pulitzer Prize in nonfiction, a* Los Angeles Times *book of the year, and winner of the Utah and Banff Mountain Book Awards. In 1997 the Whiting Foundation honored her with a Whiting Writers' Award. Other books include* The Last Cheater's Waltz *and* Raven's Exile: A Season on the Green River. *Pantheon will publish her next book,* Eating Stone, *in fall 2005. Meloy uses memoir, wit, and natural history to guide readers through landscapes of pure sensation—"There is no desert writer of greater depth," wrote one reviewer. Ellen Meloy died suddenly in 2005.*

It has been said that human joy is inseparable from wild places and wild things. A pessimist might add that, with our radically diminishing experience of the natural world, we shall soon become a joyless species. About this descent into lives of blissless artifice, conservation biologists and artists may be among the most fretful and vocal. Their anxieties about loss and separation—for one group, the loss of biodiversity and the declining health of life support systems, for the other, the alienation from mystery and experience—appear to be finding a common voice, one that is often shrieky with desperation but increasingly unified nonetheless.

To bring together such disparate fields is no easy task. Try to pry the scientist from his or her research or the writer from the desk and you might get bitten. However, I have created a metaphor for their emergence from their lairs and into joined public discourse. I call it coming *out of place*. We meet on common, perhaps exotic ground, we feel a bit awkward, and we bring much of our homes with us.

In my life as a writer and artist, "out of place" bears a double meaning. First, the sense of a misfit. Second, a voice that speaks *from* a place, a certain geography—in my case, the remote quarter of Utah's slickrock desert. This makes me somewhat of an anomaly because unlike many "nature writers" who are urban and leave home for inspiring, natural settings—or, as someone said, they "drive to their poems"— I do not live in a city. My neighborhood mixes the collective presence of coyotes, cacti, and cotton-woods; bighorn sheep, bobcats, peregrines, and people; red rock, dry wash-es, and roaring river. It is, relatively speaking, a wild place.

The word "wild" can immediately plunge us headlong into a million toothy pitfalls. Indeed, both the word and the place may lie in the eye of the beholder. The range of definitions is vast and we will strain to agree on them. Here is a short list:

"The wild" is land where natural forces still operate in relative auton-omy, with human presence albeit the lightest of human influence; not a pristine ecosystem but one that is essentially still under nature's control. (Based on that definition, and my own exploration in the field, I am here to report that these places shrink daily and that we must fight furiously to protect, restore, and expand them.)

For our nation's leaders, "wild" are the places you hand over to the in-dustries that helped you get elected.

"Wild" is a cultural concept called *wilderness*. The wilderness concept is rich fodder for the corporate barracudas who give us *product*—lurid al-pine calendars, whale-noise CDs, and my personal favorite, a forty-minute video of a crackling campfire.

Wilderness is a therapeutic device. Not long ago I met another hiker in a backcountry canyon near my home. "I came here to get away and unwind," he told me as he dialed a cell-phone call to his personal investment banker. This "wild" is the bag-a-peak, ego-buffing wild, nature simply out there to make us feel better—"wilderness as car wash."

Let us abandon this thicket of subjectivity and use the simple pragma-tism of a certain Londoner, who described nature as "a damp sort of place where all sorts of birds fly about uncooked."

More than I worry about semantics I worry about separation. Environ-ments of our own design increasingly shape our perception of the world. We have more contact with inventions of the mind than with creations of the planet. Nature is mediated and modified, secondary and barely expe-riential.

Time and distance no longer match our own biology. We seldom move at the speed of thought (walking) or rely on our sensory intelligence to feed our spirits. Our hominid bodies are Pliocenic, still profoundly timed to the universe. We still grow food in dirt and we still breathe through the grace of trees. Yet in less than a hundred years we have surrendered several million years of intimacy with the earth. We have relegated nature to scraps of tiny, crowded real estate loaded with our hopes for solace and reconnec-tion.

I fear grave consequences for this estrangement, for the loss of attentiveness, the atrophy of awareness. I try to think of this not as a terminal condition but as a stuckness. We are like a bunch of desert tortoises lined up on our backs, unable to flip over and live in the world again.

Obliquely, "nature writers" have been assigned the role of soothing the separation anxieties, of reunifying our lives with our landscapes. Our words are meant to remind people of the primary rhythms of life. We map the wild places and sometimes write their obituaries. We are the ones to help flip the turtles over again. Indeed this is a heavy burden.

An intriguing offshoot of this role is a kind of literary cross-dressing between fiction and nonfiction. As a great deal of fiction goes minimalist and indoors, into the terrain of culture and psyche, writers of nonfiction have become keepers of the deeper metaphors of wild places. They hold that nature, not just the mind, is the medium in which all life transpires.

With exceptions such as Gabriel García Márquez, whose novel *Love in the Time of Cholera* is one of literature's great river stories, writers of creative nonfiction appear to be heirs to a mantle of traditional fiction, the fiction of Melville, Hardy, Faulkner, and others for whom *place*, as Eudora Welty wrote, is "the ground conductor of all currents of emotion and belief and moral conviction that charge out from the story in its course."[1]

Although the genre of nature writing is best cast in the broadest terms (in my mind, writing about the natural world offers an easy excuse and wide latitude to write about anything), critics, readers, and writers themselves have acquired certain expectations. We assume that art and activism are joined at the hip. Words must be deployed in nature's defense. For every poetic wallow in a sunset, the wielder of the nature pen must also fire off letters to politicians and other moronic invertebrates. We must come "out of place" and use our art and our ferocity to affect social policy.

I accept this responsibility. Yet the best a person can do to change the world is to write from experience. Because I live where I live, the richest experience lies in the canyons and mesas outside my door. I can explore what it means to be human even as the world's basic humanity seems to be unraveling. Thus, my two definitions of *wild* are the ground beneath my feet and the wild of ideas.

So here we are, we poor nature writers. You want us to write like Melville *and* save the Arctic National Wildlife Refuge. Blithering self-pity aside, this is precisely the kind of schizophrenia the world so desperately needs. As loud as their differences may glare, science, art, and activism arise from the same source: *passion*. Thus, into the symposium's discussion of "common language" I would like to insert a plea for raw instinct, the uncooked act of creativity.

More than a year ago the editor of a literary journal asked me to combine art and advocacy, to pen an essay in service of a cause. Write it in the form of a letter, she said, a letter to anyone of your choice. Her request came shortly after the 2000 presidential election, when attention was riveted on the alarming schism in American civil life, on the national epidemic of nastiness. In my neighborhood the discord came as a frightening intolerance, a vitriolic hatred—often fought in a bumper-sticker war—of anyone who held different points of view, especially about the use and future of public lands.

At first I did not want the assignment to draw me away from my own demented little work world and force me to actually do something worthy and useful. Then out of nowhere I received an anonymous message. The message was about ants.

The ant message prompted me to write the piece and put it in the form of a sermon. Some may think it's a diatribe, but I wrote it so I get to call it a sermon. This story illustrates the pull between the private fires of creativity and one's public duty, the necessary duplicity of being "out of place" in search of a common language—out of science into art, out of self-interest and into community, out of silence and separation and into conversation.

Brain Damage

Received by fax, source unknown:
I'm not afraid of insects taking
over the world, and you know
why? It would take about a
billion ants just to aim a gun at
me, let alone fire it. And you
know what I'm doing while
they're aiming it at me? I just
sort of slip off to the side, and
then suddenly run up and kick
the gun out of their hands.

Dear Suddenly Runs Up,

Your fax came today. At first I thought you were wayward spam. Now I know you are a mentalist. Somehow you obtained an article of my clothing then held it to your forehead and squinted into the depths of the spirit world. You pronounced: This woman is caught in a rip tide of chickenshitness. And so you sent the warning.

You cannot recruit me for the revolution. You cannot pick on me like this. I wish I could offer medical reasons. I wish that someone would believe me when I say that I have evacuated my wits. I have lost my edge. I fit nicely in the company of head injury people. I have stopped waiting by the mailbox for my MacArthur grant. My god, the expectations of genius! No wonder they all spend their award money on Prozac and psychiatric help. One of them bought a Cadillac. If I had that kind of cash I'd run out and buy a Cadillac too, a self-bailing Cadillac. I would self-bail my Swiss cheese intellect straight into the delusion of wisdom—she hasn't, uh, slipped, people will say in awestruck whispers, she is not terminally confused. *She is a visionary.* When you're a visionary you're no longer required to cope with such mystical concepts as shoelaces or the Denver Airport. You never tie them, you stumble off the plane and ask the pilot why the hell he landed in Kansas. Everyone thinks it's poetry.

The brain fog wreaks havoc on my work. I lose my way two inches into a thought. I have developed a Byzantine neurosis about the width of my salsa-spattered notebook pages. If they are not precisely five and five-eighths inches, I start licking light bulbs. All of my stories look back, I risk chloroforming anyone in my path with the weight of memoir. The present flits away. Bits of the past float to the surface like detached kelp.

I remember a stuffed bear that was my best friend and all the teeth marks in its face.

I remember barricading myself in the bathroom because I was thirteen years old and eight feet tall with insubordinate hair.

I remember Keds with half-moon rubber toes and red canvas faded to soft pink, a lot of years being in love with Alan Bates, a vigorous interest in electroshock therapy, a D. H. Lawrence, Gaulois-smoking phase fired by a snappy Zippo cigarette lighter engraved with the word "Bliss," gift from a friend who went to Vietnam and did not came back.

I remember an all-night hike across a playa in Death Valley, walking on snow-white, moon-drenched salt crystals from one jagged mountain range to another. I remember standing atop a Sierra waterfall in the bright summer sun, the heavy heat rising from the river, hummingbirds hovering near my fingertips, the feel of the air on the soles of my feet as they left the rock to make the leap.

Memory is like both feet stuck in cement-filled paint cans. It is oh so heavy, it has distracted me from my defense of nature and justice.

I am no longer capable of striking down Orrin Hatch with an essay. I wince at the cosmic squish that co-opts nature writing: the sensitive ATV riders, the mountaineers with laptops, the vegetarian dogs, the sacred pen-raised elk, the reincarnation fantasies—coming back as a wolf or an eagle with absolutely no self-esteem problems whatsoever—hell, I want to come back as Aretha Franklin. The globe is being jerked off its axis by stratospheric sludge and melting polar caps. Rivers have been reengineered beyond their tolerance. The entire planet is zoned commercial. Viagra sales are skyrocketing in polygamist colonies. Dr. Science thinks he is Elvis. The rest of us think we're reinventable. What an ingenious way to silence cries raised against the madness of power: suffocate them in self-help books.

"The resources available to us for benign access to each other, for vaulting the mere blue air that separates us, are few but powerful: language, image, and experience,"[2] writes Toni Morrison in her essay, "Strangers." More than others, it is said, artists have the capacity to seal themselves away in a private world, to retreat into a forest of mental forms which ordinary humans cannot penetrate, there to explore all that it means to be human. Without an unwavering fidelity to humanity—to language, image, experience—the creative process is bankrupt of its fire.

When we writers wake up and stop working in our pajamas all day, when, as a friend of mine advised, we put on our fleece neck gaiters to hide the claw marks we gave ourselves over the Bush-Gore election, when we realize that the profound questions of existence cannot be easily settled, we will be free to go out and do kind, practical things.

You are right, Mr. Not Afraid of Insects, it is time to put the brain fevers to good use. It is time to go out and commit acts of aggressive beneficence.

I am not the only one who wore Keds or watched *King of Hearts* ten times. I am no better than all the other selfish bloodsuckers who, in middle age, have let the terror of our impending demise distract us from dissent. We are a thousand voices, in Whitman's vision, voices like and unlike our own. Each of us finds in love and life great squalls of the heart, and this grand and tender fellowship of emotion calms us. Most of us would gladly stop conversing in bumper stickers and start talking to one another about remapping the world with our better selves, sending across the blue air a gesture as light and sure as a spider's thread. And there in the transformation of something rigid into something supple, we might begin to see the notion of expansion.

Why we are drawn to the odd things that we love? Like poetry and bowling, moonlit salt pans and romantic grief. Or ants. Billions of them. Abruptly startled, their little ant hands raised mid-aim and suddenly very, very empty.

Largest Living Organism on Earth

Ken Brewer

Imagine a honey mushroom
the size of 1,665 football fields
beneath Oregon's Malheur National Forest.
This *Armillaria ostoyae*, this fungus,
more animal than plant,
sends its rhizomorphs to suck
the water from trees.

A mushroom can have 36,000 sexes.
Imagine a mushroom high school
in the hallway between classes.
Imagine the combinations, the cliques,
the gametes, the spores, the std's,
the constant fusings,
the constant sound of sucking.

Going South

William Kittredge

William Kittredge, professor emeritus from the University of Montana, is the author of Owning It All, *and* Who Owns the Sky *(essays);* Hole in the Sky *(a memoir);* We Are Not in This Together *and* The Van Gogh Field and Other Stories *(short fiction);* Balancing Water: Restoring the Klamath Basin, Taking Care: Thoughts on Storytelling and Belief, *and* The Nature of Generosity *(nonfiction), as well as numerous periodical pieces. He was coeditor of* The Last Best Place: A Montana Anthology, *coproducer of the film* A River Runs Through It, *cowinner of the Neil Simon Award from American Playhouse for his work on the script for* Heartland, *and winner of the Frankel Award from the National Endowment for the Humanities.*

I can't believe that I'm billed as a nature writer, even included in nature-writing anthologies. If I said to anybody in Missoula, "You know, I'm a nature writer," they'd look at me flabbergasted. I don't want people to ask me questions about activism because I'm not much of an activist. I tend to be pretty scattered. The title of this piece is supposed to be "Storytelling and Belief," and I'll probably hit on it somewhere. Think of this more as a meander than an essay. You can always tell how hard your writing is to classify when you publish a book—the editors put some kind of name on it: it's essays or a memoir or a meditation. You're talking about increasing levels of incoherence as you go down that list. Meditation tends to be fairly incoherent. I've published a couple.

I'm going to include passages from a new book called *Southwestern Homelands*. It's about escape, being on the move. Then I'll move to pieces I have written about storytelling, some sketches about belief, and then some more from *Southwestern Homelands* toward the end.

Going south is a pervasive notion in the northern Rockies. It has to do with fleeing winter. Often we go to the American Southwest: arid lands, bounded by watersheds, the Colorado and Rio Grande Rivers. Seeking warmth and sunlight in a land where spicy food, music, and frivolity are understood to be ordinary human needs. Our moods lift as we go. Flight involves reinventing the sweet old psychic self. Our species evolved on the run. Part of us yearns constantly toward nomadism. We're emotionally hardwired to hit the road every once in a while. As my old pal, the poet Richard Hugo, said, "The car that brought you here still runs." It's an ancient dream: walk out and, as you go, listen while the world and its intricacy sing and hum; the child on its mother's lap listens as she moves through the world and speaks the names; a southwestern litany might go badger, quail, cotton fields, ocotillo, coyote, kachina, roadrunner, expressway.

Entering my seventh decade, I usually opt for quiet pleasures and diversions. No more nonstop drinking and driving. I like to contemplate the stars and planets surrounding a cup of moon in the night sky over Arizona. Or ease along the banks of Cave Creek below the reddish cliffs on the eastern edge of the Chiricahua Mountains in the quick presence of hummingbirds. I want to love my beloved unreservedly and fool aimlessly around while it's still possible. At the same time, without purpose we wither. So it's useful to understand that travel is not altogether an indulgence. Going out, seeking psychic and physical adventure can reawaken love with a shifting presence of the so-called ten thousand things we find embodied in the wriggling world.

Travel, then, is a technique for staying in touch, a wake-up call, not a diversion but a responsibility. Journeying is ideally a move toward reeducation, but it's also a try to escape from our insistent homebound selves; from boredom, or too much to do, or not enough quiet; from the mortal coil of who we've lately been. Where were you last night? Out. What were you running from? Mechanical civilization, I want to say, and its sources of discontent: the stuck-on-the-wheel-of-repetition disorder, or temporary blindness, or what might be called the yearning-for-other-points-of-view-and-variety anxiety.

Overwhelmed by the intricacy of our relationships, we turn resentful and cranky, constantly aware of what's called "the bastard unfairness of things." There come times when we dream of afternoons of reading on a verandah, overlooking Mediterranean islands or a mountain lake; or fantasize about nights spent dancing down Bourbon Street with strangers. We're not by nature always entirely at ease with nonstop domesticity. I'm not advocating infidelity; what I've got in mind are other forms of psychic renewal. Don't mistake me; the virtues of a rooted life are real. It's just that, as with agriculture, they can be practiced too intensively and deplete the soil.

* * *

The poet C. K. Williams came to Missoula and spoke of narrative dysfunction as a prime part of mental illness in our time. Many of us, he said, lose track of the story of ourselves, which tells us who we're supposed to be and how we are supposed to act. It doesn't just happen to people; it happens to entire societies. Take, for instance, the United States during the Vietnam War. Stories are places to inhabit inside the imagination, and places are understood in terms of stories. I've always said—and it's kind of a wisecrack, I guess; it's partly true and partly not true—that for a long time many of us in the West got invited to a lot of conferences, which were called "sense of place" conferences. Nobody ever knew exactly what in the world he or she was talking about. I finally resolved it by thinking of place in terms of stories, all kinds of stories: scientific, geological, whatever . . . familial. Anyway, the stories we know, stories connected to a place. I think we understand place in terms of stories. I really do.

We all know a lot of stories, and we're in trouble when we don't know which one is ours, or when the one we inhabit doesn't work anymore and we stick with it anyway. We live in stories. We do things because of what is called character, and our character is formed by the stories we learn to live in. Late in the night, we listen to our own breathing in the dark and rework our stories, and we do it again the next morning, and all day long before the looking glass of ourselves. Reinventing our purposes. Without storytelling, it's hard to recognize ultimate reasons why one action is more essential than another.

Aristotle talks of recognitions, which can be thought of as moments of insight, or flashes of understanding in which we see through to coherencies in the world. We are all continually seeking such experiences; it's the most commonplace thing human beings do after breathing. One day I may wake up in the morning and start thinking about how I'm supposed to stand up and give a talk, and it's not very well organized, and I'm worried, and suddenly I'm a little flustered, and I'm continually trying to reinvent myself all day long. And some days I've also got to give readings in the evenings—Oh, my God. But we do it. And we reinvent ourselves all day long. As I said, I think it's about the most commonplace thing we do after breathing.

We're like detectives, each trying to discover and define what we take to be the right life. It is the primary, most incessant business of our lives. We figure and find stories, which can be thought of as maps or paradigms where we see our purposes defined. Then the world drifts, and our maps don't work anymore; our paradigms fail, and we have to reinvent our understandings and reasons for continuing. Useful stories, I think, are radical because they help us see freshly. That's what stories are for: to help us see and reinvent ourselves. If we don't see clearly, if we don't see freshly, if we imagine the world's going to hold still for us, we're probably going to get in trouble. If we ignore the changing world and stick to some story too long, we are likely to find ourselves in a great wreck.

It's happening all over the American West right now, to many of us and our neighbors, as they attempt to live out rules derived from an outmoded model of society. Old stories—for instance, the one about radical independence, which is so beloved out West and seminonsensical in the light of our continued colonial status—are attractive because they tell us we are living the right life. But they also reconfirm our prejudices. We get to see what we want to see. They may provide consolation, but it's not consolation we need. We need clear fresh insight; we need coherent purposes and intentions; we need to know what we're up to and exactly why.

✳ ✳ ✳

Down by the slaughterhouse, my grandfather used to keep a chicken-wire cage mounted on a sled so it could be towed off and cleaned for trapping magpies. His cage worked on the same principle as a lobster trap: the iridescent black-and-white birds could get in to feed on the intestines of butchered cows, but they couldn't get out. Those magpies would flutter around in futile expirations, then give in to a sullen acceptance of their fate, hopping around, picking at leftovers, and waiting. My grandfather was Scotch English and a very old man by then, but his blue eyes never turned watery and lost. He was one of those dead-set desert men, heedless of most everything outside his playground, which was livestock and property, a game which could be called accumulation. But the notes were paid off; he didn't owe anybody any money. You would think he might have been secure and released, eased back into wisdom. No such luck. He had to keep on proving his ownership. This took various forms like endless litigation, which I have heard described as the sport of kings. But the manifestation I recall most vividly was killing magpies.

About once a week, when a number of magpies where gathered in his trap, maybe ten or fifteen, my grandfather got out his lifetime twelve-gauge shotgun and had someone drive him down to the slaughterhouse in his dusty gray Cadillac. He looked over his catch and got down to the business at hand. Once there the ritual was slow and dignified and always inevitable, like one shoe after another. My grandfather sat in the Cadillac gazing at the magpies with his merciless blue eyes; the magpies stared back with their hard black eyes. The old man sighed and swung open the door on his side of the Cadillac, then climbed out, dragging his shotgun behind him, the pockets of his gray gabardine suit coat bulging with shells. The shotgun stock had been broken and was wrapped with fine brass wire, which shone golden in the sunlight while my grandfather thumbed shells into the magazine. All this without saying a word.

In the ear of my mind, I want to imagine the radio playing softly in the Cadillac, something like "Room Full of Roses" or "Candy Kisses." But there was no radio. There was just the ongoing hum of insects and the clacking of the mechanism as the old man pumped a shell into the firing chamber. He lifted the shotgun, sighted down a barrel with bluing mostly worn off into the eyes of those magpies, and then killed them, one by one. Taking his time, maybe to prove this was no accident. After an explosion of feathers and blood, the booming of the shotgun echoing through the flattened light, the old man muttered, "Bastards"; then he took his time about killing another. Finally, he was finished, and he turned without looking back and climbed in his side of the Cadillac, where the door still stood open, ready to ride back up the willow-lined lane, through the meadows, to the ranch house and the cool living room, where he would finish his day playing pinochle with my grandmother and anyone else he could gather, once in a while taking a break to retune the Zenith transoceanic radio.

No one knew any specific reason why the old man hated magpies in his old age. "Where's the difference," I asked him once. "Because they're mine," he said. I never did know exactly what he was talking about: the remnants of entrails left over from butchering or the magpies. But it was clear he was claiming absolute lordship over both, and me, too, so long as I lived on his property. We believed we owned the property, morally and absolutely, because of our history. Our ancestors had brought law to a difficult place; they had suffered, and shed blood, and survived. They had earned this land for us. Their efforts had surely earned the right to absolute control. We could do as we saw fit.

East of Warner we summered cattle on a million acres of public land: lava rock and sagebrush deserts—country where we owned most of the water, a few acres around each seep spring. But we really felt we owned it all. The government was as distant as news on the radio. Western history has been one resettlement after another, haunted by dreams of possession. For my grandfather's life and for most of mine, the idea of property as absolute seemed like a law of nature, even though it never was. But that old-folk way, call it a dream, is pretty much irrevocably dead, and many westerners feel something invaluable has been lost, and they are angered by its going. But in our best minds, we know that things have always been like this: changing. It's hard to imagine that a man will ever again think he owns the birds. Truth is, we never own anything absolutely or forever. As our society becomes more and more complex and interwoven, our entitlements are less and less absolute, increasingly likely to be legally diminished. Our rights to property will never take precedence over the needs of society, nor should they. We must agree in our grudging hearts that ownership of property is always a privilege granted by society and revocable.

A few years ago, I went back to Warner with a couple of filmmakers from NBC. The footage ran on *The Today Show.* Sitting in an antique GMC pickup alongside a great reef of chemically contaminated cow shit, which had been piled up outside feedlot pens where fattening cattle existed like creatures in a machine, I found it in myself to say the valley should be given back to the birds and turned into a wildlife refuge. It was a way of saying good-bye. I was saying that the biological health of the valley was as important to me as the well-being of the community of ranchers who lived there. I'd gone to grade school with some of them. People in Warner mostly understood that as an act of betrayal. Some eggs were broken, but I had at last gotten myself to say what I believed.

I'm a little different now. I've come to think we've got to preserve both community and ecologies. I think human ecologies and wild ecologies are pretty much the same thing. And we've got to take care of both. I don't think that we get to do one or the other. It's complicated, and the problems are difficult, but we have to address them at the same time. Nobody will pay to watch you juggle one ball at a time.

✳ ✳ ✳

One Sunday, while living in the heart of the French quarter of New Orleans, Annick Smith and I were out walking in the rain when we realized we were hearing echoes of someone singing—a vivid, unaccompanied voice in the narrow street, maybe three blocks away when I first heard her. A black woman with her eyes closed and face open to the rain as her voice rose and fell to "Glory! Glory! Hallelujah!" She shone in the gray light. I almost couldn't look and wondered if she cared what anybody thought as I dropped two folded paper dollars into the coffee can at her feet. She didn't look at me.

I can still hear that woman. Her life looked endlessly more difficult than mine. Her courage and passion were evident in singing, even if it was a street shuck for money. And I envied her. I felt like weeping for myself. And I was afraid of it. Like something in me might break. There I was, living near some of the best eating and drinking and music in the world; in a place where I never heard so many people—black, white, Cajun, Creole—laughing so much of the time, and I was awash in sadness. Maybe it was because I had never lived so close to so much violence, which was the other side of things. Everything was carpentered. My shuttered door was one in a wall of shuttered doors. The light seemed to rebound from the walls, illuminating wet bricks.

During Mardi Gras on Rampart Street, a little more than three blocks from our door, some lost tourist was shot every night—killed and robbed. Every week or so, there was a schoolyard killing. Perpetrators of these crimes were often young men from the projects, publicly owned housing for the poor. Those young men were alienated and angry because they saw correctly that their situation in society was hopeless. They were essentially uneducated, their schools were war zones, and their chances of finding jobs—much less meaningful and respected work—were nil. A friend who grew up in New Orleans said, "They've no place to go, there's no ladder up, there's no ladder out. They're left with nothing but selfishness. It's the second lesson," he said, "you learn on the streets." The first lesson, according to my friend, is that nobody is bulletproof.

In the American West, we should consider the ways the projects and their capacity to generate hopelessness are so much like so many of our failing towns and Indian reservations. We should consider the rage generated by disenfranchisement and the way it looks when it gets to the streets. The process starts with broken promises. In the West, people came thinking they had been promised something, at least freedom and opportunity and the possibility of inventing a new, fruitful life. That was the official mythology. When that story didn't come true, as so often happened, the results were alienation, ignominy. When people are excluded from what their society has defined for them as the main rewards of life, when they sense that they are absolutely out of the loop, as a lot of Americans do in the rural outback and the deep heartlands of the cities, they sometimes turn to heedless anger. A lot of people in our streets are staring back at us, the enfranchised, with a hatred we all know to be at least partway justifiable. Fewer and fewer of them are willing to stand singing in the rain, waiting for a few dollars to accumulate in the tin can at their feet.

Many of us live with a sense that there is something fundamentally wrong with our society. Many of us feel our culture has lost track of the reasons why one thing is more significant than another. We are fearful and driven to forget basic generosities. We anesthetize ourselves with selfishness. Many live insulated lives, as I do most of the time. In New Orleans, I like to walk down a couple of blocks to the Bombay Club and disassociate my sensibilities with one and then another huge, perfect Bombay martini. In Las Vegas, I like to stay at the brilliantly named Mirage, amid those orchids and white tigers. What I don't like to do is walk the streets and look the other side of my society in the eye. I want to think I deserve what I get. I don't want to consider how vastly I'm overrewarded or think of the injustices around me. I don't want any encounters with the disenfranchised. I want to say, "It's not my fault."

But it is. It's mine and ours. And we better figure out ways to spread some equity around if we want to go on living in a society that's at least semi-functional. Doing so fulfills a fundamental responsibility to ourselves. We inhabit a complex culture that is intimately connected to societies all over the world: vividly wealthy, while increasingly polarized between rich and poor; increasingly multiethnic, multiracial, predominantly urban, sexually ambiguous, ironic, self-reflexive, drugged up, dangerous, and resounding with discordant energies; a selfish, inhumane society without a coherent myth to inhabit. Many citizens do not believe in our society anymore. They don't vote. They withdraw from the process of governing themselves. On C-SPAN all day long, we see the other end of that society: privileged, long-faced citizens, trying to figure out what to do about our global troubles without foregoing any of their privileges.

We are a society without much idea of how to proceed. In the United States, the index of social health recently hit its lowest point in seven categories. They are these: children living in poverty, child abuse, health-care coverage, average weekly earnings, out-of-pocket wealth, care for the elderly, and the gap between the rich and the poor. We're developing a world society increasingly split between vast hoards of the disenfranchised and an elitist first class. There are twenty-five million ecohomeless people in sub-Saharan Africa; wandering, starving people who'd be coming after us, the most privileged society in history, if they had the strength. And who can blame them? What are we going to do in the future? Build nuclear fences? A society which defines selfishness as a main way of proceeding is embracing both heedlessness and irresponsibility. It can be considered, quite literally, sociopathic.

Good societies work on a sense of mutual affection, which is ordinary in our species. Citizens in such societies think of responsibilities, then of rewards, which tend to come from a sense of giving, not taking. Insisting on fairness—call it justice—is a way we preserve ourselves and take care of our communities, our kind, and our world, thus enhancing our chances at life. It would help if we could lower our defenses, stop trying to conquer aspects of wildness which frighten us, and admit and follow our passion to care for nature and each other. If we want to be happy, we should learn to be generous. What would paradise on earth be like? Start with a process, I think, with everybody involved, taking part in the reimagining, thinking up the land of our hearts' desiring, how things could be if cherishing were our main concern. Think of it as a story which can be lived, a sensible plot which can be acted out.

On warm afternoons in Missoula, the autumn sky can be blue, white, and infinite in its distance from our concerns; the needles off the larch in the high country have gone golden, falling like glory on the logging roads; cottonwood along the rivers bloom yellow and huge against evergreen mountains, and in that little eternity, we're untouchable. We will never grow old. Connection to the natural world can sometimes make us comfortable enough to try thinking that way. Too much order and artificiality make us crazy. The feel of mud where the leeches breed as it oozes around my ankles and the osprey fishing with their killing clarity of purpose—all the stink and predatory swiftness of things are part of what I understand as most valuable, thus sacred. Seacoasts can be heart stopping, a meld of aspects both actual and imagined, where we are drawn to believe that actuality does not proceed in haphazard ways, that our stories are not meaningless.

We're programmed by evolution to be both selfish and generous. But we're also gifted with language, with the ability to think and make moral decisions. We can decide to be as generous, as giving as we possibly can in our society, in our relationship to nature, in our relationship to other creatures—all those kinds of things.

* * *

Opening doors, undercutting received opinions, letting in air, sticking pins into sacred balloons, being irreverent, refusing to go on being somebody else's baby—these are all life-affirming actions. The Hopi and the Zuni and other pueblo Indians know this and include mudhead mockery, tricksters, and chaos in their sacred ceremonies.

Thinking accurately, thus surviving, depends on our ability to recognize what's really going on instead of what's supposed to be going on and, on that basis, to rethink our most basic relationships to one another and where we live. Stories and the arts help us see, as Coleridge said, by disassociating the sensibilities, fracturing the ordinary. Chemicals, alcohol, and other drugs often figure in shamanistic traditions, but, as we so sadly know, they can also lead to disassociations which take us beyond uselessness into the tragically dysfunctional.

In *Rabelais and His World*, Mikhail Bakhtin, the Russian sociopolitical theorist, said that carnivals celebrated temporary liberation from the prevailing truth and established order. They marked the suspension of all hierarchical ranks, privileges, norms, and prohibitions. Pleasure seeking, upsetting apple carts, recognitions and reversals, casting off our official personas, game faces which feel like sanctioned straightjackets may all be related activities. Carnivals, Bakhtin wrote, are feasts of becoming, change, and renewal. We break patterns to free ourselves, move on. Most of us, when we feel secure, enjoy liberation from repetition of established order. We embrace psychic and social change and renewal. During medieval carnivals, Bakhtin continued, all were considered equal. People were, so to speak, reborn into new, purely human relationships.[1] The arts of carnival can be considered techniques for bloodless uprisings. Carnivals are political events. We can take off and put on masks, real or metaphorical, trying to sense what it would be like if we were someone else. Permissiveness is all. We celebrate otherness and bring down the elegant or mighty through mockery and satire.

And what are parties—the good ones—except for private carnivals? Travel can be a form of carnival. We go out, we travel, with the deliberate intention of reseeing, rethinking. We want to fracture ritual, a version of carnival, the fleshly feast, the party. We consider most useful those stories that are reaffirming, while simultaneously fracturing. They remind us of who and what we are: an evolving creature who's profoundly dependent on the goodwill of others; they remind us to stay alert because our relationships, even if only with ourselves, must be constantly, all and every day, reinvented. So many stories, parties, ceremonies laced with humor, parody, humiliations, triumphs, profanations, mudhead clowning, crowning and uncrowning—all helping us see and evolve.

Early in the seventh century B.C., clowns wandered the marketplaces of Greece, lampooning soldiers and slaves, senators, even idiots and gods. Political and social satire evolved into dramatic comedy and occasionally profound art as in Aristophanes. The fool, the jester in medieval courts, said the unsayable, scattered anarchy, and allowed nobility and kings to laugh at and see through their otherwise untouchable personas. The fool is essential in *King Lear*, and Falstaff is an emblematic figure we recognize in taverns today. In the tenth century, the Romany came to Europe from their Asian homelands, bringing their way of telling fortunes with taro decks featuring one unnumbered card: the fool. They became known as Gypsies and were popular entertainers in the marketplaces and courts all over Europe. Street comedy in Italy evolved into the commedia del l'arte with its stock figures: the Harlequin and Patchwork and Pierrot with the elegant white face. In America, commedia became vaudeville, the popular public entertainment of the late-nineteenth century, formative in the evolution of early jazz and at the core of classical film comedies. We recognize Harlequin and his straight man, white-faced Pierrot, in Abbott and Costello and the Marx Brothers and the Three Stooges, in Lucy and Desi; we see the fool tripping along innocently in Charlie Chaplin and Jerry Lewis; thwarting the trickster in Crazy Kat and Tom and Jerry and Roadrunner cartoons.

Thinking transgressively is clearly an ancient and ongoing cross-cultural necessity. Fools, tricksters, jugglers, Gypsies, mimes, contemporary mudheads and their flute-playing, humpback predecessors, the kokopelli, and the surreal, half-animal figures painted on to Mimbres bowls—all of them sacred while at play. Their wit fragments the ordinary. Maybe we could use a few ironic, mouthy mudheads wandering around the halls of the U.S. Congress. Think of the Beetles and Dylan and hard-time rock and roll and Thomas Jefferson who said, "I hold that a little rebellion now and then is a good thing and is necessary in the political world as storms in the physical."[2]

Seeking homelands, we come and go, always hoping to nest in one. We need and yearn to believe, yet to survive, we need to be deflated and driven to start over continually y reexamining what we believe. Humor is a door to insight and a survival skill. It's said that language is the singular human discovery, but maybe not. Maybe laughter is.

"Now the Sun Has Come to Earth"

Ken Brewer

From Ian Campbell's "The Sun Is Burning,"
sung by Kate Wolf (Gold in California)

1.

All summer we watch
the white-lined sphinx at dusk
gathering nectar in Bobbie's flowers.
Bergamot seems a favorite.

The caterpillar, though, eats
my evening primrose
and I'd be angry save
the metamorphosis.

On summer twilights
I've been known to pull a lawn chair
to a stand of evening primrose
and stare as the yellow blossoms un-

fold like small suns
bursting open in the dark.
I will also watch the sphinx
hover from flower to flower for hours.

2.

The first summer of the 21st century
we drive the 40 miles to Ogden
every day of May and June
so a human sun can burn

through the crosshairs of four tattoos
on Bobbie's body, small crosses
nearly invisible, unlike
the rose on her shoulder.

In the hospital waiting room,
each day I add some pieces
to a jigsaw puzzle, a half-formed
schooner on a half-formed sea.

3.

On a map I have, the radiation
fallout from the Nevada tests
stretch like black fingers across
the country west to east and beyond.

Utah is not visible on the map.
Nothing but black on the spot
where over a million people live,
the place of "the low use segment."

4.

I hover for weeks after, afraid
to touch her in our bedded nights,
afraid we will not survive
such fierce sun come to earth.

5.

But we do.

The Pleiades

Susan J. Tweit

Susan J. Tweit is the author of eight books about the West, including Seasons on the Pacific Coast *and the national award–winning children's book,* City Foxes. *Her essays, articles, and stories have been published in numerous publications, such as* Audubon, New Mexico Magazine, Bloomsbury Review, *and the* Denver Post. *Tweit studied vegetation ecology and journalism at the University of Wyoming and Colorado University from 1979–1983. She would like to thank the love of her life, her husband, Richard Cobe, and her family. This essay is excerpted from* Navigating by the Stars.

The Pleiades is a small, tight cluster of bright stars located in the constellation Taurus, which lies on the ecliptic between Gemini and Aries. High in the sky at night from October through March, this group is sometimes described as a swarm of twinkling flies on the celestial bull's shoulder, and sometimes as a miniature dipper, since its stars look like a squashed ladle. Its most common moniker, however, is the Seven Sisters.

In Greek Myth, the Pleiades were the seven beautiful daughters of Atlas and Pleione. These virgin consorts of Artemis appealed to the gods for help when the hunter Orion pursued them. Transformed into doves, the sisters flew into the sky to escape Orion's advances. There they remain, with Orion to the southeast, forever chasing them through the heavens.

The Pleiades is one of the first star-groups I learned to recognize in my childhood, along with Orion and the Big Dipper. My mother patiently showed us how to locate this cluster of stars: Beginning at Orion, draw an imaginary straight line from Bellatrix, the yellowish star marking Orion's left shoulder (the right-hand one when viewed from Earth) through Aldebaran, the bright orange star marking the eye of Taurus. From there, the line points directly at the small bunch of bright stars that is the Pleiades. When I look up at this star cluster, I am reminded of my grandmother Chris and her bevy of sisters.

Nearly every winter of my childhood, my parents packed us into the camper and set out for the long drive to visit Chris and my grandfather Olav, my dad's parents, at their retirement place on the Gulf Coast of Florida. On the way, we'd stop at parks and monuments, visiting Civil War battlefields and Indian mounds, antebellum mansions and cypress swamps, learning the stories of the landscape we passed through.

At my grandparents', we'd walk the boardwalk at a local state park, looking for birds; we'd putter out the canal in the boat with my granddad; we'd head to the beach to collect shells and swim. And whenever my brother and I came inside to rest, grandmother Chris told us stories.

She loved the sound of language, the ring and rhyme of it. She knew Robert Burns' poetry by heart, and could recite it in a Scottish burr, rolling her Rs and transforming her precise Vermont vowels into "bonny braw Scot." She recited nonsense rhymes just for the fun of them, and read from her favorite children's authors, including Robert Louis Stevenson and A. A. Milne. She sang songs about Bonnie Prince Charlie and Nessie, the monster of Loch Ness. She told tales of *selchies,* the magical water creatures that turn from seal in the ocean to human on land; of *kelpies,* Scottish water witches; and of lairds and their ladies, castles, dragons, and the clans with their plaids.

Once as I was helping her in the kitchen, she stopped what she was doing, took my chin in her slender, wrinkled fingers, and looked into my eyes. "You've got rings in your eyes," she said, her voice solemn. "That makes you a kelpie. Only kelpies have ringed eyes."

I must have seemed puzzled, because she pulled me into the bathroom. "Look into the mirror," she commanded.

I did, and saw the same old me: skinny, tousled blond hair, freckled face, two eyes of indistinct hue, neither the sky blue of my mom's nor the warm green of my dad's.

"What color are your eyes?" she demanded.

I peered at them, trying to decide. "Green?"

"Nay," she said, slipping into Scots, "they're ringed. See the starburst pattern next to your pupil? That's brown. Then right there," she said, pointing carefully with one manicured pinkie, "see how it changes to green? And the outside, the very edge is a distinct line of blue."

As she said it, I could see the rings of color in my eyes.

"You've kelpie eyes," she said. "That makes you special."

My gran was a tiny woman, just over five feet tall, slender, with fair skin, and a delicate bone structure. She was pretty and lively, with a mischievous smile, and she was loquacious, chipper and cheery as a robin singing on a spring morning, forever whistling an upbeat tune, reciting a rhyme, singing an old song, telling a story. Her clipped New England accent held traces of a Gaelic lilt, perhaps from her father, Robert G. Farquharson, a Scot who immigrated to the United States in the late 1800s and settled in northern Vermont. He was the son of a Highland laird, she always said; in America, he was a stonemason, cutting granite for gravestones and church walls. Chris was the middle sister of five girls born to his second wife, Christie Morrison.

Like music playing without pause, Chris's stories were a constant background to those early childhood visits. As I grew older, however, my grandmother's flow of tales diminished and finally ceased. Over the years, I forgot the sound of her storytelling voice.

Chris and Olav moved to Tucson in the mid-1980s to be near my parents. Within a few years, Alzheimer's Disease took my grandmother into another world: she no longer recognized her family, even my grandfather. I visited her whenever I came to Tucson, entering the locked wing in the nursing home where she lived and walking the long hall to her room. Chris sat strapped in her wheelchair, her once-ladylike, rigidly upright carriage sagging and hunched, her eyes fixed in the distance beyond my face.

There, lost in the mists of Alzheimer's, my grandmother began to tell stories again. She talked continuously, heedless of her audience, but I could not understand her mumbled flow of words. My father, who could decipher bits and pieces, said that she had returned to her childhood, and was telling tales of her four sisters, Jean, Dora, Marian, and Peg.

"She never told us those stories," I said, frustrated. I longed to know the world that had shaped my father's mother.

"I imagine it was a hard life," he said, "one she didn't want to re-live, much less re-tell."

Is that why she wove a world of myth and magic for us? I wondered. Why had she gone back to her childhood and her sisters now?

At the nursing home, I would reach for her delicate, blue-veined hand and squeeze it gently.

"Grandmother, it's me, Susan," I'd say.

No response, no flicker in her eyes, no change in the murmuring stream of words. She'd talk on, oblivious.

I'd listen intently, searching for a thread, a guide to help discern the pattern of the stories. I could pick out individual words, but I couldn't follow the whole. I could no more understand her than she could recognize me. I'd sit as long as I could, holding her limp hand, listening to her voice, and watching her sagging body. Then I'd flee the room, down the corridors, through the door that locked behind me, and into the car. I'd sob as my husband Richard drove away. Her stories were gone.

The stars that I know as the Pleiades figure in the lore of many cultures as either siblings or groups of friends. Australian aborigines say that this cluster of stars is a group of young women playing music for the constellation The Young Men (the three stars of Orion's belt). In Hindu skylore, the Pleiades are six nurses who cared for one of the sons of the god Shiva.

In a tale from the Monache Indians of California, the Pleiades are a group of wives who banded together and left their cruel husbands. In a story much like the Greek myth, the Luiseño Indians of southern California see the Pleiades as seven young sisters who climbed into the sky to escape the attentions of the trickster Coyote.

The Greeks say that the seven sisters shimmer because they weep in mourning for the loss of a missing star. This story may have its basis in fact: Pleione, the star named for the Pleiades' mother, is a variable called a shell star that rotates so quickly, about 100 times faster than our own sun, that it throws off shells of gas, causing its brightness to vary greatly over time. Currently, Pleione is barely visible to the naked eye, its brightness varying from magnitude 4.8 to 5.5. If Pleione was easily visible in past eras, it could be the "missing" Pleiad.

In 1990, Richard, my stepdaughter Molly, and I moved to southern New Mexico. About a year later, Chris died of pneumonia. We set out for Tucson on a hot September afternoon to attend her memorial service. Molly, who sometimes gets carsick, was in the front seat with the fresh air vents aimed at her face. As we climbed a pass in the jagged spine of a desert mountain range where New Mexico meets Arizona, the fiery orange ball of the sun sank below the horizon and the air began to cool.

"Do you mind if I practice?" Molly asked. "It takes my mind off my stomach."

"Of course not, Sweetie," I said.

She pulled her sheet music and flute case from her overstuffed knapsack, then got out her silver flute. After fitting the pieces together, she lifted the instrument to her lips and began to play, practicing the music she would perform at the memorial service. Dusk blurred the hard edges of the desert landscape as we drove on, the achingly sweet notes of Molly's flute pouring out the car windows.

After we returned, I began writing and taping a weekly commentary on desert nature for the local public radio station. One evening, I sat in the small recording studio as my producer re-played the voice tape for the 3.5-minute show. Tom listened carefully to the beginning of one segment, then stopped the tape and played it over, his eyebrows drawn together into a frown. "Listen to that," he said, slowing the tape, rewinding it, and playing it back again. "There! Do you hear it?"

"That clicking sound?" I asked.

"That's it! You're making odd mouth noises."

He stopped the tape, re-wound it, and played one short segment once more, head tilted in concentration. "Do you know what's happening there?" he asked.

"I have no idea," I said.

"It's weird. I've never heard mouth noises like that. It's like your tongue is clicking against the side of your mouth."

"Do you want me to record these again?"

Tom thought for a minute. "No," he said, "it's soft enough that it won't be noticeable when I add the music background."

"Let's change the position of the microphone next time you record," he continued. "And I want you to start doing voice exercises so that your voice is warmed up before you begin taping. On your way to the studio, sing out loud, opening your mouth really wide, like this," he said, demonstrating. "Then try reading a couple of sentences from your script before you start the tape."

I followed Tom's suggestions. Walking to the radio station, I sang at the top of my voice—after looking around to make sure no one could hear me. I opened my mouth wide, like a rattlesnake trying to swallow plump prey, stretching my face muscles and the hinges of my jaw. I read part of the script into the microphone to warm up before recording.

The odd clicking noises faded, but didn't go away. Tom fiddled with the angle of the microphone, changed the sound levels on the master tape. Each time I came in to record, he had another suggestion: "Take several deep breaths to relax before reading." "Try sipping water between takes." "Use plenty of lip balm so your lips don't dry out." Still, the mouth noises persisted in the background of my recordings, like ghosts clapping. Tom couldn't figure them out.

"I've asked around to other producers on the NPR net," he said one evening as we sat in the studio, "and no one's come across this problem before. You have a great radio voice except for those weird noises. I just don't get it."

That winter, I went in for a physical exam. The doctor asked about my work, my family, and my medical history. When I mentioned my diagnosis with an autoimmune disease twelve years before, she ordered a complete blood test.

One evening a few weeks later, I was at home, lying on the couch reading a novel. Richard sat nearby, preparing his lectures for the next day; Molly sprawled on the floor doing her homework. The phone rang. Richard answered it.

"It's the doctor," he said, handing me the telephone. I sat up and he put his arm around me.

"Susan? It's Denise," she said. "I got the blood test results. Your Anti-Nuclear Antibody test came back as a strong positive. That implies some kind of autoimmune disease. Sometimes stress can cause a false positive result," she continued, "so I think we should re-test in six months. But first I want you to come to my office so we can talk."

My vision grayed. The blood roared inside my head. I must have made some small sound of distress, because Richard's arm tightened around me. It seemed like a long time before I found my voice.

"Okay," I said into the phone, struggling to speak even that single word.

"This isn't anything unexpected given your history," she said. "And it isn't necessarily cause for alarm. Autoimmune diseases come and go, and sometimes people have positive ANA results without any illness at all. I want you to come in and talk with me."

I took a deep breath. "Okay," I said again.

I was just twenty-three years old when I was diagnosed with an illness in the group that includes multiple sclerosis, rheumatoid arthritis, and lupus. In these diseases, the immune system turns on the sufferer's own body, producing antibodies that destroy our connective tissue, the stuff that cushions joints and links muscle to bone, nerve fiber to muscle and cell to cell, allowing us to feel, to think, to walk, to talk, to make love. There is no cure for my illness; doctors don't even understand what causes it. When I was first diagnosed, I lived with a near-perpetual chill that turned my skin yellow and jaundiced-looking, my toes, lips, and fingertips numb. Most mornings, my joints ached fiercely and creaked audibly, snapping and popping like Rice Crispies in a bowl of milk. My hips were unreliable; I dropped things without knowing why. From time to time, my teeth shed small chips of enamel and my finger and toe joints swelled, flushing red and hot to the touch. I would wake at night, drenched with sweat, wracked by fevers and muscle pains. For the past few years, however, I had felt better. My Anti-Nuclear Antibody test several years before was borderline, and my previous doctor had suggested that perhaps I had banished the disease.

A few days later, I sat in my new doctor's office. We discussed the test results.

"The titer of 1 to 180 makes it a strong positive," she said, "and the pattern of the cells is speckled, which suggests either Mixed Connective Tissue Disease, Systemic Lupus Erythematosus, or Rheumatoid Arthritis."

"What does the titer mean?" I asked.

"It's how many times the blood sample has to be diluted before the antinuclear antibodies don't show up," she said. "A titer of 1 to 80 and above is considered positive."

"I've marked these sections in the *Handbook of Rheumatology* for you to read," she continued. "It looks to me like you fit the description of Mixed Connective Tissue Disease best. We know you don't have Rheumatoid Arthritis because your RA test is negative, and although you have joint pain and stiffness, there doesn't appear to be significant degradation."

She stopped to look over at me. "Are you okay?"

My mind was far away. I returned my attention to her slowly. "Yes," I said, "it's just hard to hear. I thought it was gone."

"I know," she said. "But you're a scientist. Knowing is better than not knowing."

"Nor does it look like you have Lupus," she went on, "since you don't test positive for the specific antibodies correlated with Lupus. These diseases are very difficult to diagnose, because they really aren't well understood. After you read what I've given you, we'll talk more." She stood up and gave me a hug. "Call me," she said before she went down the hall to her next patient.

At home, I struggled through the medical jargon in the rheumatology handbook. The section on Mixed Connective Tissue Disease sounded uncomfortably familiar. Since my previous doctor had suggested I'd banished my illness, I had convinced myself that I was fine. My symptoms hadn't vanished, however, I had simply stopped paying attention to them. Data don't go away just because you stop measuring them. I was not ready to recognize myself in the pages of a medical text. I wanted to quit reading, to close the book, to ignore its words. I didn't. I reminded myself that knowledge is important, and I read on.

Six months later, I went back for the re-test. The results were not good.

"Your Anti-Nuclear Antibody test yielded an even stronger positive reading, I'm afraid," said the doctor, looking at me over the top of her half-glasses. "This time the titer is 1 to 320. That means you're producing higher levels of the antibodies." "How are you feeling?" she asked. "I mean both physically and mentally."

I carefully enumerated the symptoms I wanted to forget: joint and muscle pain, especially in the mornings; the perpetual chill; frequent respiratory infections; unexplained fevers; fatigue. "I just hit a wall sometimes and have to rest," I said. "But I think I'm handling it okay."

"And your emotions?" she asked.

I shrugged. I didn't want to go there.

"Is there anything new I should know about?"

"Richard thinks I should ask you about the mouth noises."

She looked puzzled.

"If you listen carefully to my radio program," I explained, "you'll hear clicking and tapping noises in the background, as if my tongue is sticking to my mouth as I speak. The noises are driving my producer nuts, and Richard wonders if they are related to Mixed Connective Tissue Disease."

"Is your mouth dry?" she asked.

"Sometimes," I said, "especially when I'm nervous. Then my tongue feels clumsy."

"Do you have dry, scratchy eyes? Do you use eye drops frequently?"

"Yes to both," I said.

"What about vaginal moisture—do you have to use a lubricant?"

My cheeks flushed. "Not if we're patient."

She ran her fingers gently under my jaw, between my throat and my jawbone. "Does that hurt?"

"It's a little achy," I said.

"Your salivary glands are slightly swollen," she said. "You're showing the classic signs of Sjögren's Syndrome. People with Mixed Connective Tissue Disease often develop symptoms of Sjögren's. In fact, Mixed Connective Tissue Disease used to be called 'overlap syndrome' because its symptoms overlap those defined for Sjögren's, Lupus, and Rheumatoid Arthritis."

I remembered reading about Sjögren's, also called Sicca, or dry mouth syndrome. In this autoimmune disease, lymphocytes attack the body's moisture-producing glands. Symptoms include dry, gritty eyes and thick mucous, a sticky or tacky feeling in the mouth or tongue, swollen glands in the cheek or jaw, dry nasal membranes, vaginal dryness, and, in extreme cases, fatigue.

"The Sjögren's symptoms would explain the mouth noises," she said. "With insufficient saliva, your tongue would stick to the skin on the sides of your mouth, making small noises as you talk. It's probably worse when you're nervous or tense. If you can learn to relax when you tape your shows, that will help."

She looked at my file, paging back in the notes. "What about caffeine?" she asked. "Did you give up coffee after we talked about how it affects your illness"

"Mostly," I said. "Sometimes I drink a cup of decaf, but usually I stick to tea."

"I'd like you to give up all caffeine," she said. "New research suggests that caffeine may cause flares in autoimmune conditions. Quitting caffeine might help alleviate your Sjögren's."

"No caffeine at all?" I asked. "I gave up coffee, but I don't know if I could give up black tea. I need its kick."

"Drink herbal tea instead," she said firmly. "No caffeine."

"Okay," I sighed, "but it's hard to give up my little indulgences."

She looked at me over the top of her reading glasses. "If you want to stay healthy, find something else to indulge in," she said.

I shut up.

"Pay attention to the dryness," she continued, "and to your other symptoms. If anything becomes a problem, there are medications that might help. But with your sensitivity to drugs, they should be the choice of last resort."

She took off her glasses, rubbed her eyes, and then looked back at me. "I wish we knew more about this," she said. "Call me right away if you notice any changes. You should also have a complete blood test every year."

I nodded, suddenly too tired to speak.

"You have to make your health the top priority," she said. "Do whatever you need to take good care of yourself."

I couldn't think about my renewed illness. Instead, I threw myself into my writing. I had started a book on the desert, but I couldn't seem to find my voice. I read archeology, anthropology, and history. I waded through hydrology and water law. I burrowed into geology, botany, and zoology. I searched out journals of early explorers, pored over Spanish land grants, went to the county courthouse to examine old deeds. I found stories galore, but no matter what I wrote, the words came out stiff, the tales lifeless. My voice simply didn't sing.

In humans' long adolescence—the longest by far of any animals—we are taught a set of habits, beliefs, behaviors, prejudices, rituals, and likes and dislikes that constitute the culture of our families and communities. This characteristic collection of baggage is made up in part by what evolutionary biologist Richard Dawkins calls *memes,* the units of cultural transmission (as opposed to *genes,* the units of biological inheritance). "Just as genes propagate themselves in the gene pool by leaping from body to body . . ." writes naturalist Lyall Watson in *Dark Nature,* quoting Dawkins, "so memes propagate themselves in the meme pool by leaping from brain to brain."[1] Memes are bits of information that pass on culture: songs, advertisements, myths, family stories, slang, fashion, decorating styles. Memes are to cultural evolution what genes are to biological evolution; our combination of memes and genes makes each of us who we are.

Stories are one way we transmit memes. Whether purely imaginative or purely fact, stories pass on our cultural values, our spiritual beliefs, our knowledge. When my radio voice faltered and I found myself unable to write the stories of the desert, I turned to the voices of my past, those who passed on my memes. From my grandmother Chris comes my fascination with myth and magic, my love of the tone and meter of language. From my grandfather Olav, who immigrated to America from Norway in the 1920s with few words of English, yet excelled in solving the complex problems of industrial design, I learned to pick out the essence of complicated systems and to appreciate the elegance in simplicity. From my accountant grandfather Milner, I learned the importance of ideas and the delight of droll humor. He could unravel the brain-twisting abstractions of his favorite philosophers as easily as he could slip a sly joke past my grandmother.

The voice I heard most clearly, though, was that of my mother's grandfather, Dr. William Austin Cannon, who died when I was 16 months old. On a visit to Tucson not long after my Sjögren's symptoms were diagnosed, I accompanied my mom to a ceremony dedicating two historic houses, one built by Dr. William, as he is called in my family. I knew almost nothing about this ancestor; I read his brief biography on the program and pestered my mom with questions. In answer, she gave me several scholarly articles on his life. I learned with surprise that my great-granddad was one of the early practitioners in my specialty of ecology. The questions he asked in his work were very similar to those that intrigued me in my research three generations later. Much of his research was in arid climates, as mine was, but he spent his career studying plants of hot deserts around the world, while I focused on the cold desert of the sagebrush country of western North America.

He was born in Washington, Michigan, in 1870, and earned his master's degree in botany at Stanford University in 1900, the year of the new century. In 1902, he finished his Ph.D. at Columbia University. That same year, the Carnegie Institute asked him to serve as their first "resident investigator" for the soon-to-be-finished Desert Botanical Laboratory in Tucson, Arizona. Dr. William arrived in Tucson in September of 1903, charged with establishing the lab and beginning research on the surrounding desert. He stayed there until 1918, when he moved to another lab in Carmel, California, then taught at Stanford University until his death in 1958. Over his long career, he wrote 64 scientific works, including seven book-length monographs, on subjects ranging from the botanical features of the Algerian Sahara to the relationship between fog and the distribution of redwood trees. He was married four times—my great-grandmother was his second wife and the mother of his two children, including my grandfather Milner.

Dr. William's instructions in founding the Desert Botanical Laboratory were broad. He was to look into the "morphology, physiology, habit, and general life-history of the species indigenous to the desert of North America."[2] In his first year there, according to Janice Bowers in an article on his research in *Madroño,* my great-grandfather managed to investigate a dizzying number of questions, all the while supervising completion of the laboratory and hosting its first team of visiting researchers. He studied the anatomy of ocotillo and barrel cactus; measured the transpiration of nipple cactus, giant saguaro, creosote bush, brittle bush, and ocotillo; determined the water content of a barrel cactus; measured the diameter changes over time in barrel and saguaro cacti; and excavated root systems of a number of desert plants. He invented many of his own lab instruments and techniques. He also noted and described the multitude of Indian artifacts atop Tumamoc Hill, where the lab was located, recorded the daily changes in the desert weather, explored the "forests" of giant cactus around Tucson, and trekked to the San Francisco Peaks in northern Arizona. He was, in effect, hunting stories.

I know that wide-ranging curiosity, that need to understand why, the thrill of searching for answers. It's what got me into trouble in graduate school, where I could never focus on just one research question for long enough to finish any of the several degrees I began. Like Dr. William, I'm fascinated by the stories I see in the world around me. Unlike my great-grandfather, however, I'm impatient and too easily distracted to be a successful research scientist. I love to speculate, but I don't love the tedious-to-me work of gathering supporting details. I rush ahead, wanting to know what happens, how the story ends.

I am better at writing the tales of science than I am at practicing it. We write best about what we know, and having grown up with a research chemist father who did ornithology fieldwork and a librarian mother interested in natural history, a large part of what I know is field science. The memes of science—the tendency to ask structured questions, to observe, to seek answers—are part my legacy. I grew up with the language of science; I know its idioms and jargon. The culture of science shapes my voice.

As I searched for my writing voice, I worked to find quiet in my daily life so that I could hear it. Each weekday morning after Richard and Molly left the house, I made myself a cup of herb tea and sat down at my computer to write. For the first half-hour or so, I spilled whatever entered my mind, laying down words with no thought other than to get them out of my way. After that, my brain stilled, I settled in and did my best to ignore interruptions. In the silence, I began to notice noises I hadn't paid attention to before: the soft chatter of a black-chinned hummingbird as she sipped sugar water from the feeder outside my window, the swooshing waves of desert wind passing through the trees, the buzzing of digger bees quartering the ground for nest sites, the mutter of distant thunder. Where household and human noises were so often irritating, these noises from nature outside were soothing. In their rhythm, I could begin to hear my stories.

At the radio station, the mouth noises waxed and waned in my recordings. After one session, my producer commented that the past few times I'd recorded, the clicks and taps had been almost inaudible. "I think you're finally getting it," he said after we finished listening to the most recent batch of voice recordings. "I'm proud of you."

On my walk home, I scanned the sky for stars in between the streetlights and wondered what it was I had "gotten." I stopped in the cotton fields near our neighborhood and spotted the giant figure of Orion overhead. Off to the west was the V-shaped face of Taurus, and on the bull's shoulder, the bright cluster of the Pleiades. I counted the stars in that hazy grouping and thought of my grandmother Chris and her sisters, of the stories I would never know.

The Seven Sisters are part of a still-evolving star cluster born some 50 million years ago. The shimmering cloud of stellar dust and gas that surrounds the cluster has given birth to more than a hundred stars. The brightest of the Pleiades, those visible to the naked eye, including all seven sisters, are the youngest stars, each no more than a few million years old. As more stars form from the stellar cloud, the story of the Pleiades continues to evolve.

At home, I read back through my journal, scanning what I'd written on the days I'd recorded my radio show, searching for something to explain the pattern in the mouth noises. It wasn't hard to see: on fragmented days when I got caught up in unfocused busyness, I lost not only my writing voice, but also my speaking voice—I couldn't seem to quiet the clicks and taps of my tongue. When I'd achieved a quiet rhythm with the pulse of nature around me, I wrote well and the thrashing noises subsided. I needed the stillness. Without it, I lost my voice.

I talked to Richard about my need for quiet. My office was the former formal living room of our house and I had no doors to shut: two open archways kept it exposed to the rest of the house. I wanted doors, in particular, French doors with panes of glass to let in plenty of light while keeping out noise and distraction.

Richard demurred. "That'll be expensive," he said.

He was right, and once I would have bowed to that logic. But my new voice was no good girl. "I need those doors," I said. "It's part of taking care of myself, part of staying healthy."

Richard thought about it. "If doors are that important to you, we'll get you some."

A few months later, two pairs of French doors graced the entranceways to my office. Each door was constructed of tight-grained Douglas-fir, lighted by eight glass panes. Curving brass handles opened them to welcome visitors or shut them to preserve my quiet.

Quakers find their voices in silence. Believing that the voice of the divine can only be heard when we are still and quiet, Friends worship silently, listening attentively for that inner voice. Out of the silence comes speech as individual Friends rise and deliver insights yielded from their inner search. In Quaker jargon, those who speak in meeting for worship are "called to vocal ministry." Called, that is, by the spirit that lives within each of our hearts. In Quaker practice, silence speaks.

Quaker Elisabeth Salisbury describes the powerful urge to speak in British Yearly Meeting's *Quaker Faith and Practice*:

> My heart was pounding uncomfortably and I began to shiver. . . . Now I sat conscious only of this overpowering force which was pushing me to my feet until finally I had to give in to it.
>
> Afterwards I found it difficult to believe that I had spoken. . . . I had been driven by some inner prompting which, for want of a more precise

word, one might well call spirit; and yes, I had quaked, most fearfully, with something which was more than just the fear of making a fool of myself before family and friends.[3]

That quaking call to speak is what finally brought home my writing voice. The force that moves Friends to vocal ministry is similar, I think, to the prompting of the soul that stimulates any kind of creative work. A trembling within urges us until we cannot keep from speaking out: putting hands to keyboard, chisel to stone, paint to canvas.

For me, the call began with a chance sighting of a petroglyph of a long-clawed grizzly bear footprint etched on a ridge that rose out of the desert. Working in grizzly country years before, I had come to respect the big bears. Grizzlies do not adapt to human habitat, and in fact, tolerate our presence only if we remember our role in their ecosystems: we are prey. Understanding their essential wildness taught me to appreciate the wildness buried so deeply in myself—and in all of us.

I had never imagined grizzlies in the sun-baked desert, but the image would not be denied. I dug into the history of the big bears in the Southwest, and discovered that they had inhabited the region until the early decades of the twentieth century. The last grizzly in New Mexico had been killed in 1923; the final one in Arizona in 1935, they hung on in northern Chihuahua into the 1960s. As soon as their growling voices were stilled, however, their story was forgotten. Our perception of the desert is impoverished by the loss: we no longer think of "desert" and "grizzly" in the same sentence. I researched the people who had painstakingly chipped the outline of the grizzly paw into the rock and learned that they were gone too: their voices stilled by relocation and imported diseases after the Spaniards arrived in the 1600s. Their stories, and their connection to our own wildness, were lost as well.

"Story is the umbilical cord between the past and the future,"[4] says writer Terry Tempest Williams. Stories show us where we've been and where we can go. And no one story can give us the whole picture. We need every voice to speak truth from the silence. We need every story to guide our lives. When we lose stories, our understanding of the world is less rich, less true. Each voice lost, human or wild, erodes our knowledge of who we are.

Once, when I was researching a story on Indian treaty rights, I met a leader of the Nisqually tribe in Washington State. We talked about his tribe's fight for the right to fish for salmon in their traditional places, and about the role of salmon in their understanding of their environment. The fish, he said, stood for the health of the whole region, including human cultures. They told a story that people needed to hear.

"I speak for the salmon," he said. "He is out there swimming around and cannot come in here and talk to you. So I speak for the salmon—and people listen."

I come from the culture of science, from a discipline that studies the relationships and interconnections that make this earth a uniquely green and habitable place. The science of ecology listens to the voices that make up earth's ecosystems, giving words to those lives we otherwise would not know. Its stories are full of connection and creativity, elegance and endurance, necessity and innovation, birth and death—the stuff of life. They contain crucial instructions on how to be human. Those are the stories I want to tell.

The clicking and tapping of my tongue reminded me vividly that my own voice would someday be stilled, like that of the desert's grizzly bears and the petroglyph-carvers, like that of my grandmother Chris. In the meantime, from the quiet, I had stories to tell.

Scarlet Penstemon

Ken Brewer

—for Keith Wilson

Bees can't see red
but hummingbirds can
so the scarlet penstemon
curls its lower lip,
picks its lover as certain
as Cleopatra picked Caesar.

In the southern Utah summer,
in the late afternoon
of long shadows, shimmering,
the scarlet penstemon pouts,
and, oh, sweet Jesus, to be
a broad-tailed hummingbird then.

Poetry Reading at the Tanner Conference

Keith Wilson

Night

How still the Llano is in full moon.
Light is every thing here, a new world
come into focus, no movement at all.

The silver grass, pale hills at the edge
of the cap rocks. Down there, the Rio.
There, the Military Road where the Kid
still walks, moon glints for eyes, stalking
whatever memory he had that he holds dear.

The old men sit by the store and talk
and talk, maybe spitting to show they
still remember, have feeling, and are
not as dead as they are beginning to look.

Later they sleep, the Llano moon locked
outside, the curtains of their windows
hang magically, keep all loneliness out.

River Girl

—for my wife, Heloise

> *more precious is the touch*
> *of your mouth in the shadow*
> >   —Borges

and I remember the shade
of cottonwoods, the deepgreen solitude.
Cedar breaks, with wind.

How you never stood beside me
there, where shadows became dreams:
sunlight, a confusion, a breaking of mirrors.

Wherever we are now, in the turnings
of nightmare, our worlds speeding us on
to separate destinies (though together)

we still walk that whispering River back
to our young faces enshrouded by trees, and green.
I have always held your eyes.
You cannot have them back now.

Los Penitentes hermanos

de la luz,
Hermanos de sangre. Out of a New Mexican night a memory that
has haunted me all my life
                penitentes, marching
                singing, their torches
                high arc against
                the crest of the Hill

                Sensing my mother, her fear
                I holding her hand, 4, knowing
                nothing of the needs of men—

                backs raw from cactus whips
                yet singing of light, they were
                truly Brothers of the Light, brown men

                chanting

                —little Christs, singing
                to the agonies, o of the wounds
                of the dying Cristo who led them
                bearing their sins with his own

                it is His blood dripping
                from that sky 64 years ago
                that calls them forth singing now

                they, climbing the high Hill
                with Him, His neck bowed under
                His cross, they light His way

                torches, smoking and flaming
                above the tall grass, after all
                these years it is the
                darkness they left behind.

"Where There Is Water"*

Place is your honor
as it is your wisdom.
                    —Eudora Welty

But what could be made
of a place like this? I used
to ask. Such a small gash
on the face of spinning rock,
tiny to stars . . . .

a patch of green and brown
bright glint of the Pecos River
surrounded by sand and rock—
miles, miles of scrub brush.

How then does it hold me so
in my heart that I can go
away and yet hear clearly
the wind through the leaves
of its history so sharply
it slices the years away?

   *Indian meaning of "pecos"

River Scenes

—for Joe Somoza

All rivers are highways to the mind.
That this one, Pecos, place of water,
was dry most of the year was no obstacle
to the dreams it could hold, pathway
that leads from wherever one wishes
not to be. The crows, the rabbits
snakes and mockingbirds become audience
as the fantasies of boyhood play
in theaters of tree and brush, wind
tugging at the hair, eyes halfclosed.

ii

We are what we come to by the River.
I having known mostly deserts cling
to any memory of water: its glint
a beacon no green valleys can dim.
Always my eye goes straight to the water,
no matter where I am. It is one of the marks
of a desert person to be obsessed by water.

iii

In the silence that comes internally,
the rustling of other animals is distant
assurance, the light, shadow mingling
as worlds try to meet, hover on peripheries,
geographies of momentary agreement,

all holding to what seems safe, possible.
A watersnake raises his head, watches the shore.
Boy, he watches watersnake while crow, he
fixes them both with his glassy black eye
and who's to say who watches them all?

Cow Dogs

The ranches I knew as a boy....
It was the Depression then,
though as my father used to say,
"It's all we've ever known,
Depression, but we do all right."

Skinny steers and no market,
ranchers doing the hard work
because they've always done it,
waiting, nursing Durham butts,
cursing the lack of rain.

Even the dogs were thin
in those years. Dogs were part
of a ranch, guarding, yelping,
chasing chickens for sport
when nobody was looking, cocky

plumetailed dogs who looked like
four-legged cowpunchers, took
the same airs, the same lazy tensions
as they waited for action, any kind
of excitement. One old dog I remember

used to be able to throw a young calf
without hurting him much. In the evenings
the hands would gather and he would rise
slowly, carefully, walk to the corral
catch the calf running and throw him

neat as the devil into a cloud of early
evening dust. "It wasn't much," Old Jonesy
used to say, "but it sure as Hell
took your mind off your problems."

—Dust rising from the baked earth,
night settling on the silent ranch.

Village Ways

—are you now,
or have you ever been?
—from the old Loyalty Oath

In the hot sun of the Llano, the cool
shadows of arroyos, the question hangs
like that redtailed hawk or the buzzard,
his mottled neck stretching out towards the sun.

I choose to let my nature, the contradictions
stay where they are. . . .

        In an earlier, simpler time
most people thought they knew who they were.
Folks identified each other by their grandfathers,
and by whether a person had travelled and how far.

"Old Joe's mother went to St. Louis once."
"She did!" And one knew that Old Joe's mother
was just a mite questionable. Good people stayed
put and usually died within a hundred yards
at most of where they were born and God help
them, whatever they did, they tried to hide
in the darkness of nighttime village streets
or the guttering of a coaloil lamp

        the hump of covers, the
loneliness of men, women who slept alone and called out
to Baptist gods or, worst of all, kept their silences,
died without ever hearing or speaking a word of softness,
or known the tremor or love, peace of sin but
"By damnation," as Jim used to say, "every stemwinding
sonofabitch knew who his grandpappy was and just where
he'd lie his own bones down which is a hell of a lot
more than most of them city folks can say!"

Maybe. But for me, the darkness still swirls
with question. The villages are pretty much gone and
who's to tell the dark-eyed ones now where their past
lies or the meaning of the fearful song the wind sings?

The People from the Valley

—for Frank Waters
in affectionate and grateful memory

The farmers come, come
on down the Pecos Valley
in busted-bottom wagons

their children thin
blonde cornhusk hair
blowing

Sparrows watch dry ruts
for spilled kernels
the men, stiff, formal

black suits, white shirts,
the women searching for
other wagons, bright bonnets

Cottonwood leaves clash
green in Saturday's wind
as the quiet children sit

aware they
will be watched by
town boys in their victor's clothes
the dark eyes of townsmen

watching for any beauty
the land has missed, its
women, this land hungers

for women, and for farmers
who can write their own obituaries
in the lines of their hard hands.

River Bottom

where as boys we played in beds of quicksand,
teasing with it as it sucked our feet down, one boy
always standing clear to help as it slowly crept up
our ankles, to our knees, nearly to our hips.

Then the shouts of laughter as we'd fall forward,
float on the greyish water that rose through the sand,
wiggle our ways out. Jimmy (killed in WWII),
Tom (became a drunk), Juan (died in a barrio in
Albuquerque from knife wounds), me, still feeling
the suction of those sands

Tomasino

Who was a good man in some village
where I lived, sometime, who knew
the secret names of the hills, the valleys.

When he spoke of earth, it lighted
like the yes that he carried always
in his eyes, his hands outstretched

in welcome. A poor man. Tomasino,
who lived a frugal life on his farm
but his arms were strong, his face

even today, long after, is the flare
of a match struck to light a lantern,
or the race of brown water down

a furrow when the irrigation gate
is first opened among the spring flowers.
So do I remember him, standing in a field

saying "it will rain soon, the tomatoes
will grow and the winter will be late
this year, the birds will sing songs

and not eat tomatoes." Most of it
didn't happen but such was the faith
of Tomasino that I can see his eyes now.

The Grain of Sand

—for Jim Harris & Hawk

There he goes, old hawk, he touches
the thermal, rises, lifts himself to dot
sky bending in a semicircle of blue heat.

The grey shimmer of mirage standing unbroken
until the strike

      down he drops knocking
a buck rabbit off his feet, flurry of dust,

rises again, talons blooded,
crippled rabbit hiding in the sage and brush
for coyotes to find:

      desert, crawling under heat,
slick glass sand tumbles in little avalanches and
the tarantula flashes back, her catch firmly
in her hairy mandibles. The quick awkward gait
of the Giant Desert Scorpion. His more deadly
kin, the strawcolored Durango, all cocked, waiting

as this desert sun goes down, as blue, grey
and pink spread themselves to silence and I hear
tiny feet and scales flee the hunting night.

In the New Mexico Territory,
As Best I Understand,

The lights were softer, dangers
came more unannounced, more dashingly dressed.

There was a silence, surrounded by a violence,
potential, lethal, always from the shadows.

The distances between towns, the hard roads,
let the men, though they damned each other,

hardly ever meet, but then came the swift swift shots
of eyes, the clenched fists. . . .

It all began with men, and with women
edging, nudging them on. Perhaps the horses

were partly to blame, the killings sent the horses
wild, they danced on their whitestockinged feet

in their great eyes gunfire flashed and rolled.
Now we have all this. The gunfighters still hold

the cities and some of the towns. The horses are
mostly gone and it is the land that is dying.

My coyote friends and I sit separate in darkness
watching the winking lights. We remember.

Valley of the Rio Chama

—near Ghost Ranch, Rio Grande Institute

The River, small at Fall, drifts through cottonwoods,
greypinkblue hills, dropping slowly
down past Abiquiu, Española on its way to the sea

leaves, twigs, pieces of the mountain life upstream
carried along like picture postcards, or paintings

All this great flow, color, wind, light is center
that has to be something deeply anciently holy:

          the leaves are
masks, the twigs dancing legs and arms, held
spun to the beat of River and an earth swirling under
the weakening autumnal sun of harvest promise
before the high mountain winter comes with its own
icy mask
    Most of us here today are artists of some
sort, all caught embarrassed before this magnificence,
these glories of canyons, bluffs carved into standing
hooded figures, multicolored giant crayons the sun
has melted until they stand layer upon layer
in rich pastel, as if a prism had broken strewing
raw light into colors, freezing them there in sand
stone clay

    We walk away, murmur to each other of the
weather, our small arts, our tiny worlds of
imitation, longing that only we can inhabit.

My new friend, a painter, says, "I'm old enough to know
better than to try painting all that!" and shakes his head.
But colors are words the voices of rock and canyon speak.
How can they not be spoken? How can we not listen?

—seeing the stream, hearing the leaves golden and
brown in their own falling splendor, earth holding
all in Her cupped hands of rock and color and
light.

The Old Man at Evening

i

Which world should I speak of?
The one by the Pecos River, volumes of sound,
the wind through cedars, echoes of rabbits,
their dying cries, or the quick memories
of wolves?

I know with whatever sadness
the truth of lamplight in autumn,
the sandpaper brush of lips,
women that believe in some strength
held, secretly, against the darkness.

I know I have lived before.
It is etched in me, modes of responses,
awarenesses that some others have and I
love you, knowing we have touched before,
coupled, talked, our eyes not unremembered
as the centuries concealed our true faces
and we made love with our imaginings.

ii

I am he who calls
the night, yet I
forget the words

in the darkness
we are all afraid
lose touch, lost

I know whatever
I say gets swallowed
by something in the night

my love
the complicated stars
sometimes seem

to spell out your name
I do not know how
to answer them, hold

you close, my lips
trembling as I try
to speak the correct

charm, the final phrase
before their light
I speak this love for you

Spring

—for my compadre Rudy Anaya
Who grew up on the Pecos too

All night he could hear the noise.
In the morning, the plains lay
like pages of sunlight, no wind.
He hurried past the village,
through the Breaks, saw the crest
come down, heaving, adobe earth,
carrying uprooted trees, parts
of wooden houses from upstream.

The Rio Pecos had gone crazy again.
Rio Loco, the old man had called it once.
Quicksand in the Summer, floods in the Spring,
dry as hell in Winter. Rio Loco.
Ought to build a dam, the old man said.
Stop that crazy river in its tracks.
Now he could see what Old Tom meant.
A heavy snake gutting the Valley.

A young girl in a pinafore, pale
silk hair spun by him, her arms out
stretched, blue eyes open, was gone
before his muscles could even tense,
whirled away, turning and turning
into the dark water and he knew
through his trembling that this
was the first Spring he had ever known
with some kind of truth and backed up
quickly as the River ate the land
from under his feet, passed him by.

The Old Man & His Snake

The two lived there, almost together—
he in the shack, the snake below under
the warped floorboards in the cool darkness
cut by rays of light from the lamp above.

A thick Diamondback, nearly six feet long,
it moved out in moonlight to stalk rabbits
and rats. Out his window the old man pointed;
"There he goes, not enough to feed him around
here no more. Ain't had a rat or a mouse
in near two years. He's the reason, Old
Snake!"

  The two of them, growing older, keeping
careful distances from each other, geographies
of agreement (the old man stayed in at night,
the snake never went out in the day . . . .)

The old man pointed to his chamber pot. "Bought
that to keep from tangling with him. Can't use
the outhouse at night. Kill him? Why the hell
do that? He's got a right to live, ain't he?
Besides, I always know he's there, down under
the boards, hear him move every once in a while,
and there's worse critters than snakes
lots worse than snakes . . . ."

  —for Lem Lyons

Brother & Sister Dancing:
Cantina And the Mariachis Are Playing

Here we are
dancing out the wild songs, the heritage
our feet touch when our souls
dare not trespass.

The sharp note climbs, and high.

His trumpet catches in
smoky light, is an explosion against
his straining face, his great hat, the
racing gilded laces are real silver in the light

& all the while the dancers
whirl, mariachis sing
of revolution, love

Here is a center formed
by you and me, the others break
around us, strangers, agonies
of music snapping between
passing. . . .

   —for Marjorie Ann

The Voice of the Earth Is My Voice

—from a Navajo prayer

And we are the syllables on Her tongue,
Bright words held to the clear water, the soft
Marbled coloring of sandstone, framed in wind.

We are of the earth and should never bravely
Forget or fail to give thanks to the dust
That bore us here, speaking, the voice of whirlwind

Knows our names, holds us past the time we imagine.
In no way less than the earth, nor greater
Our eyes hold canyons, and willows, we last and last.

Desert Cenote*

There is sadness among the stones
today, the rabbits are silent.

No wind. The heat bears down.
It has not rained for one year.

We have faith out here, desert
people, we wait, knowing with sureness

the swift cross of clouds, the blessings
of moisture (to deprive a man is to give

charms to him). I love this dry land
am caught even by blowing sand, reaches

of hot winds. I am not the desert
but its name is not so far from mine.

*Spanish-Aztec for "water hole, oasis"

The Way Things Are Going

New Mexico will soon have passed away,
gasping like a minnow on a clay bottom of the Pecos.
I know, I feel the same. The air drifting up
from El Paso, down from Albuquerque, East from Tucson
West from Odessa is heavy, hangs like plastic rock
above us I know

       nothing but that beauty is the most
transitory while ugliness lasts and lasts. One comes
to hail the shining moment for what it is: one scale
of one tiny minnow flashing in the dying light, one face
—so loved—aging in this still brilliant, holy Sun.

     Horsehead Crossing
     South of Fort Sumner

The Arrival of My Mother

—New Mexico Territory, 1906

She got off, according to her diary,
dressed in a lovely beaded gown, fresh
from Washington with sixteen trunks of ballgowns
chemises, blouses (4 Middie), shoes and assorted
lingerie. She was at that time about 25, old
for an unmarried woman. Her stiff mother was at
her side, she also wildly overdressed for New Mexico
sun and wind.

What must she have thought, seeing my uncle standing
hat in hand in the dust of that lonely train station
cracked yellow paint, faded letters of welcome
for passengers who rarely come?

The buckboard was waiting and they rode out into
the darkness of evening toward the tent and the half
built frame homestead house, wind dying as the sun
sank birdcries stilled.

I see her now outshooting my father and me, laughing
at our pride and embarrassment. My sister, as good a
shot, waiting her turn. Or that picture of her
on horseback, in Eastern riding clothes beside the Pecos.
A picnic when I was small and how my father lifted me up
to her and she carefully walked the horse around rock
and sand.

I suppose she finally arrived in New Mexico
in the April of one year when my sister and I sat beside
a rented bed, each holding one of her hands and watched
her eyes go childlike, unmasked as a kachina
entering the final kiva of this Dance. The graceful
the slim laughing woman of my childhood. The old mother
heavy with years slipped away and the woods of New
England dimmed as these dry hills ripened and caught
her last breath, drums, drums should have sounded
for the arrival of my mother.

The Encircled Grove

I never understand anything until I have written about it.

—Horace Walpole

And written here is the ceremony of the land
itself, without commentary, other than what it,
this grove, places before the senses. In the deep cool
of glades, clumps of twisted salt cedar, snake
barked cottonwoods with trunks twice as thick
as a man, broad leaves pushing at the sunlight
that only glimmers down to the moist earth
with its beetles and ferns.

The grove is circular out of ancient incantation,
some enchantment older than Comanche spoke here,
formed this protected world and held it against
wind or geology. The high plain stops at the edge
of its greenness, swirls around it, continues
as far as the eye travels the spreading land
and domed blue hold it in their rushing powers.
Sky Father. Earth Mother. Here is the point
equidistant, focused, the navel that magic flows
through

       As I passed through
shaped, protected, set free by the Pecos River
and the wind from the quarrels of family, whispers
that held our old house fast. Grandmother's ghost
could never walk in the Bosque where silence became
a moistness, held your breath like another pair
of murmuring lips

    —for my brother, Simon Ortiz

Revista

Now in these years when looking back
becomes blurred, uncertain, the days
too much like the nights, faces,
always reminding of another, thus
dismissed in their own certainties
because of a chance resemblance
to someone long dead, or lost.

—bouys on a still sea. Gullcries
haunt my head and still I long
for the seafall that will announce
my coming home, my sailing in

—this windy mesa, no sea at all,
yet this waving grass, even the stubble
catches at my heart with the old
longing. How far is the home the heart
needs, how long the night's dawn
that awaits the coming of light.

Behind me, the moon rises.

Common Cause in Common Voice

Robert Michael Pyle

I would like to begin by expressing appreciation to the funders and organizers of the Tanner Symposium for bringing us all here together to make common cause in common voice.

For there are consequences when our language, and experience, are neither common nor consistent. And there are forces against the free exchange of accurate information and artistic impression because these lead to truth, which can foil the intentions of powerful interests. Hartmut Grassl showed clearly and powerfully how unorganized and underfunded scientists, an indifferent public, a body politic preoccupied with crises of their own making, and lobbyists who actively fund disinformation all work together to permit dangerous trends to go on mostly unchallenged. And through his own limpid language and solid science, he showed how serious may be the consequences of failing to find a common understanding of human impact on climate change, species, soils, and toxics. For where, Grassl asks, are the butterflies? The wings of the butterflies? And how will we know where their flapping may affect the T-junction choices to come, if we cannot talk?

In contrast, Annick Smith shared with us the potential good that can result when we do talk; when those who care pursue a common theme with mutually supportive rhetoric and lyric. She took us down rivers on the land and rivers in our minds as we considered words flowing like water, connecting our stories with everyone else's stories, as in the collections of writings published in passionate defense of the red-rock desert, the Arctic plain, the Blackfoot watershed. Still to come: Rick Bass's Yaak-lovers' anthology. Maybe, after one of the most protracted writer's martyrdoms to activism, Montana's roadless Yaak will finally receive protection through these testimonies. If we can't all organize or even stand meetings, Smith promises, at least we can tell our tales, and who knows? It might do the trick.

In her poem "Geocentric," Pattiann Rogers uses language we know and recoil from to deliver a delicious and delirious valentine to the earth. Common words, unexpected outcomes. To me what the term *common language* means is the concurrent flow of words and ideas, creating those confluences about which Smith writes. It's like a synapse that flashes ON, a pheromone that strikes home and makes all the bells go off at once. Common language does not mean concordance, but it suggests the possibility of concordance. When we speak without shared values, experience, assumptions, or desire, the synapses are duds. Yet it is hard to imagine two humans with no contact points between them. The job, then, is to find the way through the scrim of intellectual gauze and emotional swaddling that prevents communication.

We found such a passage by considering the premise of Ted Kerasote, who asked us to imagine for the moment that the issue of guns in society might be set aside in favor of the huge voting bloc that this polarizing issue denies to conservation. That's a big "if"—but the rewards could be even bigger. Through the story of a grieving wapiti mother, Ted built a parable that could make an animal rightist pause to listen to a hunter. It is just that pause to listen that we seek.

We heard it again in the paean paid to wild animals by Dan Flores. We had a bouquet of responses and questions, not all of them posies; but the linkage of minds wrought by story and the interplay of respective, respectful knowledge and opinion let us talk about it. If we weren't all convinced, we all thought, and listened, and watched as the world became more complex, more potent with possibility. When Flores spoke of "tangible, touchable rock, grass, and flesh," we knew we were on solid ground in a place we all recognized. Now, tell me about it, we said. Tell me more.

Connections where we have made separations. The connections are there if we are willing to find them: they lie between Grassl's Mongolian goats and Kerasote's Sierran sheep, all of them together qualifying as Muir's mountain maggots and hoofed locusts. The connection was there even between John Muir and Gifford Pinchot until Pinchot left the gate open, allowing the sheep into the national forests. Intersection may be found, too, between Grassl's particulate aerosols and Craig Stanford's great but diminishing apes through the sad agency of wildfire in Indonesia; and they exist as well between Jennifer Price's L.A. River and Kent Ryden's Tuttle Road road trip, both of them proving beyond a doubt that nature is the whole show: the urban, the wild, the urban wild; the human, the more than human. A permeable membrane indeed! And as for the human and the human-plus, Charles Darwin said that the point of separation between man and not-man has no fixed place and is, in any case, "a matter of very little importance."[1] Thoreau said, "We are conscious of an animal in us."[2] Stanford proved both of these statements to be true and also pointed out the irony of looking for life in all the wrong places, like Mars, when our own life sources, the great apes, are dying right here at home.

The degrees of separation are far fewer than six. Are there any two experiences that cannot connect if only we choose the honest words, the right stories, for the bonding agent?

Our job as researchers is to ask the questions, find out the facts and laws, and communicate them, which should lead to common language and action. But as Grassl reminded us (and we do need reminding again and again about our national embarrassments), the action can be painfully— perhaps disastrously—slow. Nor is there any way out. We have that on the authority of no less than Bishop Carolyn Tanner Irish, who said (and I fully agree), "Well, the environment: it's just about everything, isn't it?"[3]

As if in reply, Kent Ryden said, "Nature is more than a stage set: landscape is a cooperation between nature and culture, and we ignore either at peril to both."

Jenny Price joined in, "The idea of nature has a powerful sidekick—the natural."

"Yet to many," said Ryden, "we seem to be living more and more in a postnatural world."

"Maybe so," replied Bishop Irish. "But we are subjects, objects, and agents within this world. We weep in the presence of wonder, and wonder has consequences: we judge for the dolphins; we act on our moral sensibilities as we become aware. We are response-able so we can be responsible."

"Right," said Ryden, "and just wait. Agency *will* reassert itself."

To even now wonder so that we have the chance to weep and act, we learned over and over that we must *go out*. We swapped yarns of the virtual, sneaking in to steal the real from our experience, or extinguish it altogether, in company with all the forces that erase the beloved features of the land. Some of us parlayed in a workshop over the countervailing forces, the good ones that are working to keep the real alive and to take the young out of doors: places like the Teton Science School and Journey School, the North Cascades Institute, the Orion Institutes, and our own wonderful Stokes Nature Center, just up Logan Canyon. These programs seek to bring people, places, knowledge, and experience together to benefit us all.

And some of us actually went outdoors, thanks to naturalist extraordinaire Susan Tweit. We heard the bunchgrass greening, smelled the towhee calling, and watched north-slope snow sublimate in the sun. Twelve glossy ibises sickled overhead toward the Bear River marshes; a redtail rose and swooped and fell and rose with heavy prey a'talon, made an exchange with its mate, and flew up to the nest in a cottonwood as deer stotted below. We realized again that getting out is what it's all about.

Back inside, we heard about flagship species and Bubba Thoreaus, how learning to use nature well will save our souls, and that our mountains are not just an elaborate hoax. Surely a common language must be based on the utterances of lips run by the engine of minds that are both free and open, and voices that are willing to speak with honesty and compassion.

We discovered a duet of natural habitats for all these traits in the humane and wise offerings of Ellen Meloy and Bill Kittredge. Meloy defined the wild more in her person than in all her elegant words—the wild lies beneath her feet, which are bare. Many people may be tortoises on their backs, but not this wise woman, this exhibitionist hermit, who knows the "raw instinct, the uncooked act of creativity," great squalls of the heart, the notion of expansion.

And as for Bill Kittredge, what can you say about him, but that he goes out, away to the world with hope? Well, as he battles the bastard unfairness of things, reawakening love in the shifting presence of the ten thousand things, he reminds us that we understand place in terms of stories, where we seek the right way to live and maybe find out what we're up to. And he loves a good party: he urges us on toward bloodless uprisings, to play among Bob Dylan and Thomas Jefferson and the other good mudheads in revolution and reexamination of the carnival of life.

But surely it is the poets who finally lead us into the territory of the common, uncommon tongue. Ken Brewer said of words, "Ah, my friends, again you have fooled me!" We beg to differ. Singing the poems of dogs and dust mites, happy slugs and tarantula hawks making love to flowers, the joy of failed divorce, the joy of surviving the sun come to earth, the joy of loons and sweet, sweet clarinets. Just one more word, he offered—"to the moon."

"The moon—there's the moon," wrote Keith Wilson. "The Llano moon locked outside." Wilson too croons to dogs, and crows, and snakes—"there's worse critters than snakes, you know." The presence of the backyard. What can be made of a place like this, he asks; and then makes something of it. The lines in hard hands that throw the stick to wherever, where Old Red lives always. The suction of the sands, the hot air between us and the echoes of rabbits. Wilson told us, and it is true: "We are of the earth—we are the syllables on her tongue." We have only to open our mouths to sing.

As a Navajo wrangler once told me, we've got to take our imaginations out of our back pockets. As we know in our hearts, we must get out. A dear friend, Mía Monroe, manager of Muir Woods and other National Park Service treasures nearby, e-mailed me this today, and it gladdened my heart:

> Image of Mía-as-modern-manager: my cell phone only works in a few spots, and wouldn't you know, those "touch-bases-with-staff" spots just happen to be where a covey of quail do their stretches in the A.M. AND, moving on and later in [the] day ... pipevine swallowtails float downslope in midday, AND, final check-in before they go home ... the great horned owlets get their evening meal in the P.M.

Surely this is how it should be: our busy-ness secondary to life itself.

Finally, I wish to share the thoughts of two old sages whose words still ring true. The first is Herman Melville. In the voice of Ishmael and in words all writers will recognize, he moaned, "This book is but a draught—nay, the draught of a draught! Ah, time, cash, patience, and strength!" And yet he later prayed, "Hold me, keep me, bind me, all ye Influences!"[4] Could we ask for any more in our search for the wily words of common thought?

And the second is the great Costa Rican naturalist Alexander Skutch, whose ethic should underlie all environmental writing and education: "Those who care greatly because they appreciate greatly have no more sacred obligation than to do everything in their power to preserve the kind of world that will nourish appreciative minds for countless generations. Appreciative, cherishing minds are the world's best hope."[5]

Notes

Introduction—Paul Crumbley and Melody Graulich

1. Aldo Leopold, *A Sand County Almanac: Wild Essays on Conservation from Round River* (1949; reprint, New York: Ballantine Books, 1970), 262.
2. Ibid., 189.
3. Ibid., 262.
4. Barry Lopez, "Children in the Woods," in *Crossing Open Ground* (New York: Vintage Books, 1989), 149.
5. Chris Cokinos, "Vision Statement," *Isotope* 1, no.1 (spring/summer 2003): inside front cover.
6. E. O. Wilson, *Consilience: The Unity of Knowledge* (New York: Vintage Books, 1998), 230.
7. Ibid.
8. Ibid., 292.

Who Lost the Limberlost? Education in a Mis-Placed Age—Robert Michael Pyle

1. Robert Michael Pyle, "The Rise and Fall of Natural History," *Orion* (Autumn 2001).
2. Anna Botsford Comstock, *Handbook of Nature Study* (1911 Ithaca, New York: Comstock Publishing Co., 1947).
3. Clifton Hodge, *Nature-Study and Life* (Boston: Ginn and Company, 1902).
4. Comstock. *Handbook of Nature Study.*
5. David James Duncan, Lecture delivered to Utah Academy of Science, Utah State University, Logan. March 2002.
6. Robert Michael Pyle, *Walking the High Ridge: Life as Field Trip* (Minneapolis: Milkweed Editions, 2000).
7. Comstock, *Handbook of Nature Study.*
8. Sallie Tisdale, *Stepping Westward* (New York: Henry Holt and Co. 1991).
9. Robert Michael Pyle, *The Thunder Tree: Lesson from an Urban Wildland* (Boston: Houghton Mifflin Co., 1993).
10. Gary Paul Nabhan, *The Desert Smells Like Rain* (Berkeley: North Point Press, 1982).
11. Christopher Smith, "Fond or Otherwise, Worldwide Images of Utah May Be Fleeting," *Salt Lake Tribune*, 2002.
12. William Arkin, "Pentagon Revamps Nuke Use," *Los Angeles Times*, 2002.
13. Henry David Thoreau, *Walking* (*Atlantic Monthly*, Autumn 1862; Boston: Beacon Press, 2000).

14. Pattiann Rogers, "The Family Is All There Is," in *Firekeeper* (Minneapolis: Milkweed Editions, 1994).

15. Kim Stafford, *Having Everything Right* (Lewiston, Idaho: Confluence Press, 1986).

16. Vladimir Nabokov, "Audubon's Butterflies, Moths, and Other Studies," *The New York Times Book Review*, December 28, 1952, Reprinted in *Strong Opinions* (New York: Vintage Books, 1990).

17. Vladimir Nabokov, *Speak Memory: An Autobiography Revisited* (New York: G. P. Putnam's Sons, 1966).

18. Kittredge, William, *Hole in the Sky: A Memoir* (New York: Alfred A Knopf, 1992).

Cousins: What the Great Apes Tell Us about Human Origins—Craig B. Stanford

1. Jane Goodall, *The Chimpanzees of Gombe: Patterns of Behavior* (Cambridge: Harvard University Press, 1986); Geza Teleki, *The Predatory Behavior of Wild Chimpanzees* (Lewisburg, Pa.: Bucknell University Press, 1973).

2. S. Uehara, T. Nishida, M. Hamai, T. Hasegawa, H. Hayaki, M. Huffman, K. Kawanaka, S. Kobayoshi, J. Mitani, Y. Takahata, H. Takasaki, and T. Tsukahara, "Characteristics of Predation by the Chimpanzees in the Mahale Mountains National Park, Tanzania," in *Human Origins*, vol. 1 of *Topics in Primatology*, ed. T. Nishida, W. C. McGrew, P. Marler, M. Pickford, and F. B. M. deWaal (Tokyo: University of Tokyo Press, 1992), 143–58.

3. C. Boesch and H. Boesch, "Hunting Behavior of Wild Chimpanzees in the Taï National Park," *American Journal of Physical Anthropology* 78 (1989): 547–73.

4. Richard W. Wrangham, "Behavioural Ecology of Chimpanzees in Gombe National Park, Tanzania" (Ph.D. diss., Cambridge University, 1975).

5. Goodall, *Chimpanzees of Gombe.*

6. Richard W. Wrangham and E. van Zinnicq Bergmann-Riss, "Rates of Predation on Mammals by Gombe Chimpanzees, 1972–1975," *Primates* 31 (1990): 157–70.

7. Craig B. Stanford, J. Wallis, H. Matama, and Jane Goodall, "Patterns of Predation by Chimpanzees on Red Colobus Monkeys in Gombe National Park, Tanzania, 1982–1991," *American Journal of Physical Anthropology* 94 (1994): 213–28.

8. Ibid., Craig B. Stanford, J. Wallis, E. Mpongo, and Jane Goodall, "Hunting Decisions in Wild Chimpanzees," *Behaviour* 131 (1994): 1–20.

9. S. L. Washburn and J. B. Lancaster, "The Evolution of Hunting," in *Man the Hunter*, ed. R. Lee and I. DeVore (Chicago: Aldine, 1968): 293–303.

10. Boesch, "Hunting Behavior of Wild Chimpanzees"; Stanford and others, "Patterns of Predation."

11. C. Boesch, "Hunting Strategies of Gombe and Taï Chimpanzees," in *Chimpanzee Cultures*, ed. W. C. McGrew, F. B. M. de Waal, R. W. Wrangham, and P. Heltne (Cambridge: Harvard University Press, in press).

12. Stanford and others, "Patterns of Predation"; Stanford and others, "Hunting Decisions in Wild Chimpanzees."
13. Wrangham, "Behavioural Ecology of Chimpanzees."
14. J. D. Speth, "Early Hominid Hunting and Scavenging: The Role of Meat as an Energy Source," *Journal of Human Evolution* 18 (1989): 329–43.
15. Stanford and others, "Patterns of Predation"; Stanford and others, "Hunting Decisions in Wild Chimpanzees."
16. Goodall, *Chimpanzees of Gombe.*
17. Stanford and others, "Patterns of Predation"; Stanford and others, "Hunting Decisions in Wild Chimpanzees."
18. Stanford and others, "Patterns of Predation"; Stanford and others, "Hunting Decisions in Wild Chimpanzees."
19. Teleki, *The Predatory Behavior of Wild Chimpanzees.*
20. A. Kortlandt, "New Perspectives on Ape and Human Evolution, in *Stichting Voor Psychobiologie* (Amsterdam: publisher is missing, 1972).
21. Wrangham, "Behavioural Ecology of Chimpanzees."
22. Ibid.
23. William C. McGrew, *Chimpanzee Material Culture* (Cambridge: Cambridge University Press, 1992).
24. Stanford and others, "Patterns of Predation."
25. Ibid., Stanford and others, "Hunting Decisions in Wild Chimpanzees."
26. Ibid.
27. H. T. Bunn and E. M. Kroll, "Systematic Butchery by Plio/Pleistocene Hominids at Olduvai Gorge, Tanzania," *Current Anthropology* 27 (1986): 431–52.
28. R. J. Blumenschine, "Characteristics of an Early Hominid Scavenging Niche," *Current Anthropology* 28 (1987): 383–407.
29. C. W. Marean, "Sabertooth Cats and Their Relevance for Early Hominid Diet and Evolution," *Journal of Human Evolution* 18 (1989): 559–82.
30. Speth, "Early Hominid Hunting."

The Unexpected Environmentalist: Building a Centrist Coalition—Ted Kerasote

1. Gifford Pinchot, *Breaking New Ground* (New York: Harcourt, Brace and Company, 1947) 100.
2. John Muir, "The American Forests," *The Atlantic Monthly,* August 1897, 147.
3. Ibid., 145.
4. Ibid., 146.
5. John Muir, "The National Parks and Forest Reservations," *Harper's Weekly,* 5 June 1897, 566.
6. Ibid.
7. John Muir, *Our National Parks* (Boston and New York: Houghton Mifflin Company, 1917), 16.
8. Linnie Marsh Wolfe, *Son of the Wilderness, The Life of John Muir* (New York: Alfred A. Knopf, 1946), 275–76.

9. Pinchot, *Breaking New Ground,* 179.
10. Ibid., 180.
11. Ibid., 31.
12. John Muir, "The Wild Parks and Forest Reservations of the West," *The Atlantic Monthly,* January 1898, 15.
13. Henry Beston, *The Outermost House* (New York: Ballantine Books, 1971), 20.
14. Aldo Leopold, *A Sand County Almanac: Wild Essays on Conservation from Round River* (New York: Oxford University Press, 1975), 204.
15. Personal communications from the conservation organizations cited in the text.
16. These figures come from Rocky Mountain Elk Foundation, National Wild Turkey Federation, Foundation for North American Wild Sheep, and Buckmaster's American? Deer Foundation.
17. Tim Richardson, personal communication, March 31, 2002.
18. Daniel R. Faber and Deborah McCarthy, *Green of Another Color: Building Effective Partnerships between Foundations and the Environmental Justice Movement, A Report by the Philanthropy and Environmental Justice Research Project, Northeastern University,* 10 April 2001, available online at http://www.casdn.neu.edu/~socant/Another%20Color%20Final%20Report.pdf
19. Environmental Protection Agency's Environmental Justice Web page, available online at http://www.epa.gov/swerosps/ej/
20. Faber and McCarthy, *Green of Another Color,* 1, 3.
21. Gretchen C. Daily, "Introduction: What are Ecosystem Services?" in *Nature's Services: Societal Dependence on Natural Ecosystems,* ed. Gretchen C. Daily (Washington, D.C.: Island Press, 1997), 3–4.
22. Michael Pollan, "Power Steer," *The New York Times Magazine,* 31 March 2002, 71.
23. Ted Kerasote, "A Killing at Dawn," *Audubon,* March–April 2000, 41.

Tuttle Road: Landscape as Environmental Text—Kent C. Ryden

1. Robert Finch, *The Primal Place* (New York: Norton, 1983), 8.
2. Ibid., 9–10.

Begin with a River—Annick Smith

1. Richard Hugo, "Plans for Altering the River," in *Making Certain it Goes on: The Collected Poems of Richard Hugo* (New York: Norton, 1984), 256–57.
2. John Keeble, "Junk: The Entropy of Imagination." *Arctic Refuge: A Circle of Testimony,* edited by Hank Lentfer and Carolyn Servid (Minneapolis, Minn.: Milkweed Editions, 2001), 59–60.
3. Debra Earling, "River Home," *The River We Carry with Us* (Missoula, Mont.: Clark City Press, 2002), 205.
4. Ibid, 206.

5. Ian Frazier, "A View of the Clark Ford," in *The River We Carry with Us* (Missoula, Mont.: Clark City Press, 2002), 127.

6. Annick Smith, *Homestead* (Milkweed: Minneapolis Minn. 1995), 102–3.

7. Greg Keeler, "Your Waking Thoughts of Quack," *Headwaters: Montana Writers on Water and Wilderness* (Missoula, Mont.: Hellgate Writers, 1996), 54.

The Natural West—Dan Flores

1. Ralph Waldo Emerson, "On Nature," *Essay by Ralph Waldo Emerson,* edited by Irwin Edman (1926; reprint, New York: Harper and Row, 1988), 200.

2. Herman Hesse, *Steppenwolf,* translated by Basil Creighton (London: Allen Lane, 1974), 3.

3. Henry David Thoreau, *The Heart of Thoreau's Journals,* edited by Odell Shepard (Boston and New York: Houghton-Mifflin, 1906), entry for 23 March, 1856.

4. E.O. Wilson, *Biophilia: The Human Bond With Other Species* (Cambridge: Harvard University Press, 1984).

5. John James Audubon, "Missouri River Journals," in *Audubon and His Journals,* edited by Maria Audubon (New York: Charles Scribner's sons, 1897), 2 vols. 1:24–67

6. Quoted in Jane Tompkins, *West of Everything: The Inner Life of Westerns* (New York: Oxford University Press, 1992), 166.

Separation Anxiety: The Perilous Alienation of Humans from the Wild—Ellen Meloy

1. Eudora Welty, "Place in Fiction," in *The Eye of the Story* (New York: Vintage Books 1979).

2. Toni Morrison, "Strangers," in *The Norton Reader,* eleventh ed., ed. Linda H. Peterson and John C. Brereton, (New York: Norton, 2003).

Going South—William Kittredge

1. Mikhail Bakhtin, *Rabelais and His World,* trans. Helene Iswolsky (Bloomington: Indiana University Press, 1984).

2. Thomas Jefferson, Letter to James Madison, January 30, 1787, in *The Portable Thomas Jefferson,* ed. Merrill D. Peterson. (New York: Penguin Books, 1975), 415.

The Pleiades—Susan Tweit

1. Richard Dawkins, quoted in Lyall Watson, *Dark Nature: A Natural History of Evil* (New York: Harper Collins, 1995), 212–13.

2. Janice Bowers, "William A. Cannon: The Sonoran Desert's First Resident Ecologist," *Madroño,* Vol. 37, no. 1 (1990): 6-27.

3. Elisabeth Salisbury, *Quaker Faith and Patience* (Worwick, England: Yearly

Meeting of the Religious Society of Friends [Quakers] in Briain, 1994), 2.58.

4. Terry Tempest Williams, Talk at "Writing and the Natural World," Ranchos De Taos, NM, 1994.

Common Cause in Common Voice—Robert Michael Pyle

1. Charles Darwin, *The Decent of Man and Selection in Relation to Sex* (London: John Murray, 1871).

2. Henry David Thoreau, *Walden* (Boston: Ticknor & Fields, 1854; reprinted ed., Boston: Beacon Press, 1997).

3. The quotations and paraphrases here in are of remarks made at the symposium in delivered papers and related discussions. They may differ from or not appear in the texts published in this book.

4. Herman Melville, *Moby Dick* (1851; reprinted ed., New York: Crown Publisher, 1987).

5. Alexander Skutch, *Life Ascending* (Austin: University of Texas Press, 1985).